SECURE
ELECTRONIC VOTING

Advances in Information Security

Sushil Jajodia
Consulting editor
Center for Secure Information Systems
George Mason University
Fairfax, VA 22030-4444
email: jajodia@gmu.edu

The goals of Kluwer International Series on ADVANCES IN INFORMATION SECURITY are, one, to establish the state of the art of, and set the course for future research in information security and, two, to serve as a central reference source for advanced and timely topics in information security research and development. The scope of this series includes all aspects of computer and network security and related areas such as fault tolerance and software assurance.

ADVANCES IN INFORMATION SECURITY aims to publish thorough and cohesive overviews of specific topics in information security, as well as works that are larger in scope or that contain more detailed background information than can be accommodated in shorter survey articles. The series also serves as a forum for topics that may not have reached a level of maturity to warrant a comprehensive textbook treatment.

Researchers as well as developers are encouraged to contact Professor Sushil Jajodia with ideas for books under this series.

Additional titles in the series:

APPLICATIONS OF DATA MINING IN COMPUTER SECURITY, edited by Daniel Barbará, Sushil Jajodia; ISBN: 1-4020-7054-3
MOBILE COMPUTATION WITH FUNCTIONS by Zeliha Dilsun Kırlı, ISBN: 1-4020-7024-1
TRUSTED RECOVERY AND DEFENSIVE INFORMATION WARFARE by Peng Liu and Sushil Jajodia, ISBN: 0-7923-7572-6
RECENT ADVANCES IN RSA CRYPTOGRAPHY by Stefan Katzenbeisser, ISBN: 0-7923-7438-X
E-COMMERCE SECURITY AND PRIVACY by Anup K. Ghosh, ISBN: 0-7923-7399-5
INFORMATION HIDING: Steganography and Watermarking-Attacks and Countermeasures by Neil F. Johnson, Zoran Duric, and Sushil Jajodia, ISBN: 0-7923-7204-2

Additional information about this series can be obtained from
www.wkap.nl/series.htm/ADIS.

SECURE
ELECTRONIC VOTING

edited by

Dimitris A. Gritzalis
Athens University of Economics and Business, Greece

KLUWER ACADEMIC PUBLISHERS
Boston / Dordrecht / London

Distributors for North, Central and South America:
Kluwer Academic Publishers
101 Philip Drive
Assinippi Park
Norwell, Massachusetts 02061 USA
Telephone (781) 871-6600
Fax (781) 681-9045
E-Mail: kluwer@wkap.com

Distributors for all other countries:
Kluwer Academic Publishers Group
Post Office Box 322
3300 AH Dordrecht, THE NETHERLANDS
Telephone 31 78 6576 000
Fax 31 78 6576 254
E-Mail: services@wkap.nl

   Electronic Services < http://www.wkap.nl >

Library of Congress Cataloging-in-Publication Data

A C.I.P. Catalogue record for this book is available
from the Library of Congress.

Gritzalis, Dimitris A.
SECURE ELECTRONIC VOTING
ISBN: 1-4020-7301-1

Printed on acid-free paper.

Printed in Great Britain by IBT Global, London

Contents

Contributing Authors

(in alphabetical order)

Danilo Bruschi is an Associate Professor of Computer Science with the Dept. of Information Science of the University of Milan. His research interests focus on computer and network security, operating systems, computer networks, and distributed systems. He is the Scientific Director of the *True-Vote* project (realization of a polling system for Internet), which is sponsored by the IST Programme of the European Union.

Mike Burmester is a Professor of Computer Science at Florida State University. Earlier, he was at Royal Holloway, London University. He got his BSc from University of Athens, and PhD from Rome University. His interests include privacy, anonymity, network security and watermarking.

Lorrie Faith Cranor is a Principal Technical Staff Member in the Secure Systems Research Department at AT&T Labs-Research. She has been studying electronic voting systems since 1994. In 2000 she served on the Executive Committee of a United States National Science Foundation sponsored Internet voting taskforce.

David Chaum received a PhD from the University of California at Berkeley. He taught, led a crypto research group, and founded DigiCash. He is widely recognized as the inventor of electronic cash; he was also the first to show how network voting could be private and secure. In 2000 he began developing new innovations for automated elections.

Ivan Damgård holds a PhD in Computer Science (1988). He has held a post-doctoral position at the Dept. of Computer Science of Aarhus University, where he currently is an Associate Professor, heading the Department's Research Group on Cryptography. He is a co-founder/co-owner of Cryptomathic A/S, and the author of about 100 research papers.

Ed Gerck holds a PhD in Physics from Ludwig-Maximilians University and Max-Planck Institute for Quantum Optics, Munich. He is the CEO of Safevote, Inc. His work in Internet security, cryptography, and voting received press coverage from New York Times, Le Monde, O'Globo, Forbes, Wired, CNN, CBS, Business Week, and USA Today.

Dimitris Gritzalis holds a PhD in Informatics (1994). He is an Assistant Professor of I&CT Security, with the Dept. of Informatics of the Athens University of Economics and Business, where he leads the Infosec Research Group. He is an Associate Data Protection Commissioner of Greece, and a Managing Board Member of the *e-vote* project of the European Commission.

Jens Groth holds an MSc in Mathematics from the University of Aarhus (2001). Currently he is working at Cryptomathic A/S and pursuing a PhD in Cryptography at BRICS, Dept. of Computer Science, University of Aarhus. His research interests include zero-knowledge proofs and electronic voting.

Spyros Ikonomopoulos holds an MSc in Information Systems from the Athens University of Economics and Business. He is a PhD candidate with the Dept. of Information and Communication Systems Engineering of the University of the Aegean. His research interests include software design patterns and software agents.

Douglas Jones received a PhD in Computer Science from the University of Illinois at Urbana (1980). Currently, he is an Associate Professor of Computer Science at the University of Iowa, and serves as Chair of the Iowa Board of Examiners for Voting Machines and Electronic Voting Systems.

Maria Karyda holds an MSc in Information Systems from the Athens University of Economics and Business, where she is a PhD candidate and a member of the Infosec Research Group. Her research interests focus on information systems security policies and management.

Sokratis Katsikas is a Professor of Informatics with the Dept. of Information and Communication Systems Engineering, and the Vice-Rector of the University of the Aegean. He is the Scientific Director of the *e-vote* project (an Internet-based electronic voting system), which is sponsored by the IST Programme of the European Commission.

Aggelos Kiayias holds a PhD and a MA in Computer Science from the City University of New York. His main research area is cryptography and computer security. Dr. Kiayias is a graduate of the Dept. of Mathematics of the University of Athens and a Fulbright Fellow.

Raphaël Kies is a PhD candidate with the Dept. of Political Sciences at the European University Institute, Italy. He graduated in Political Science and is currently working in the field of e-democracy and the public sphere.

Costas Lambrinoudakis holds a PhD in Computer Science from the University of London. He is a Lecturer with the Dept. of Information and Communication Systems Engineering of the University of the Aegean. He is the Technical Director of the *e-vote* project (an Internet-based electronic voting system), which is sponsored by the European Commission. His research interests include secure systems, smart cards, and risk assessment methods.

Emmanouil Magkos is a PhD student with the Dept. of Informatics of Piraeus University, where from he got his BSc on Informatics. His research interests include cryptography and techniques for securing electronic voting, auctions, key escrow, and copyright protection.

Fernando Mendez is a PhD candidate with the Dept. of Political Sciences at the European University Institute, Italy. He holds an MSc in European Politics from the London School of Economics and is conducting research on the United States and the European Union Internet policies.

Rebecca Mercuri holds a PhD from the University of Pennsylvania. She is an Assistant Professor with the Computer Science faculty at Bryn Mawr College. Her research efforts are focused on interactive, real-time systems and digital multimedia. She is the author of a computer security column for *Communications of the ACM*. Her website can be viewed at: http://www.notablesoftware.com/evote.html

Lilian Mitrou holds a PhD in Data Protection from Goethe University of Frankfurt (1992). She is an Assistant Professor of Law with the Dept. of Information and Communication Systems Engineering of the University of the Aegean. She is, also, the Head of the Organization and Administration Directorate of the Office of the Prime Minister of Greece, and an Associate Data Protection Commissioner of Greece.

Peter Neumann holds PhD degrees from Harvard and Darmstadt Universities. He is a Fellow and Principal Scientist at SRI International's Computer Science Laboratory, where he conducts research on computer systems and networks, security, reliability, survivability, safety, and risks-related issues. His book, *Computer-Related Risks*, is in its fifth printing by Addison-Wesley. His website can be viewed at: http://www.csl.sri.com/neumann

Rene Peralta holds a PhD in Computer Science from the University of California at Berkeley. He also studied Economics and Mathematics. He has worked at institutions including the Catholic University of Chile, University of Wisconsin, Amsterdam's Mathematics Center, and Japan's Advanced Institute of Science and Technology. Currently, he is with the Dept of Computer Science of Yale University.

Giusi Poletti holds a PhD in Computer Science (2001). She is a Research Associate with the Dept. of Computer Science of the University of Milan. Her research interests include system security and - in particular - online voting protocols.

Gerald Quirchmayr holds a PhD in Computer Science and Law from Johannes Kepler University. He is a Professor with the Institute for Computer Science and Business Informatics of the University of Vienna. On 1995 he received the IFIP Silver Core Award. His research interests focus on information systems (formal representations of decision-making, security aspects, legal issues).

Emilia Rosti holds a PhD in Computer Science (1993). She is an Associate Professor at the Dept. of Computer Science of the University of Milan, where she teaches operating systems. Her research interests include computer and network security, and computer system performance evaluation.

Gorm Salomonsen holds a PhD in Mathematics (1996). He has held post-doctoral positions at the University of Bonn and at the University of Aarhus. On 1999 he joined Cryptomathic A/S, where he has been working with PKI, electronic voting and other topics.

Roy Saltman, MS, MPA, has worked in the field of election policy and technology for over 25 years. He has served as a consultant to international organizations and vendors of election equipment and software. He is well known for his reports published by the National Institute of Standards and Technology (NIST).

Alexander Trechsel is a graduate in Political Sciences of the University of Geneva, where he took his PhD in 1999. He is the Vice-Director of the Research and Documentation Centre on Direct Democracy (c2d) at the University of Geneva, where he also teaches. His research interests focus on direct democracy and e-democracy.

Vassilis Tsoumas holds an MSc in Information Systems from the Athens University of Economics and Business, where he is a PhD candidate and a member of the Infosec Research Group. His research interests include voting systems, network security, and risk assessment methods.

Moti Yung is the Chief Scientist of CertCo and a visiting faculty at Columbia University. Previously, he was with IBM Research where he received IBM's outstanding innovation award. He is an Editor of the *Journal of Cryptology* and of the *International Journal for Information Security*.

Preface

Elections, referenda and polls are critical processes and tools for the appropriate operation of a modern democracy. Not only do they provide the means for the transfer of power from the citizens to their representatives, but they also support citizen's trust and confidence in government and democracy, provided they are functioning as required and designed.

Although election systems were usually the focus of attention of mainly the politicians and the election officials, the case of Florida (US Presidential election 2000) attracted international attention, especially on how elections are administered. Since then, the capabilities and the limitations of electronic voting systems have come to the center of attention. Electronic election systems are, nowadays and in several countries, under intense scrutiny by policy makers, social scientists, computer and network engineers, and activist groups. The issues are whether more reliable, user-friendly and less costly voting systems should be developed, what are the essential legal and constitutional requirements that should be met and how these systems would stimulate citizen participation in the elections. The discussions on these issues have not reached an end; instead, a long lasting and interesting debate is still ongoing.

Citizen's participation is a major aspect of a democratic system. Nowadays the number of citizens who participate in the elections decreases every year. Because of this, among other reasons lately, there has been a growing interest in online voting or voting over the Internet (electronic voting). Electronic voting is seen as a means to make voting more convenient to the average citizen, thus increasing participation. In the beginning, electronic voting was considered as a simple extension of Internet applications from commerce to government. This approach is, however, incorrect, since election systems must meet certain high standards with regards to security, privacy, etc. Thus, electronic voting is far more challenging, in terms of requirements, than most e-commerce applications. On the other hand, although the democratic process requires and warrants a high level of security, the implemented security measures should not be cumbersome to the voters, otherwise participation may be discouraged.

Recent reports (e.g. CalTech-MIT Report, California Internet Voting Task Force, IPI National Workshop on Internet Voting, European Union IST Projects, etc.) describe the capabilities of e-voting systems, and at the same time identify their limitations, the risks and vulnerabilities they are exposed to, as well as the social concerns such systems give birth to. For example, the possibility of malicious software attacks against computers used for electronic voting cannot be ignored. Such an attack could result in a denial of service, in the submission of software-altered ballots, etc. Some reports argue that despite these challenges, it is technologically feasible to build an electronic voting system that is at least as secure from vote tampering as the current absentee ballot schemes. In any case, most experts in the field agree that an appropriate balance between security, accessibility and ease-of-use must be achieved before an electronic voting system is deployed.

According to recent reports, e-voting systems can be generically grouped into three general categories: Poll, Info-kiosk, and Remote. The means used for their grouping is the location where the ballot is cast. The location leads to the identification of the social concerns and the risks and vulnerabilities, which are associated with each group. Poll voting (e-polling) seems to be more convenient and efficient than traditional voting systems, because the voters can cast their ballots from any location, and the tallying process is fast and valid. Provided that the election officials can control the voting platform and the physical environment, effective management of the inherent security risks seems feasible. In Info-kiosk schemes (i-voting), voting machines are located away from traditional polling places. The i-voting platform and physical installation should be under the control of election officials and should also be appropriately monitored in order to meet security and privacy requirements and to prevent intervention (e.g. coercion). I-voting computers are exposed to more risks than poll systems are.

It is arguable whether all risks and vulnerabilities can be faced with through existing or emerging security technologies. Remote Internet voting (r-voting) provides the voters with convenience and ease-of-access, by enabling them to cast ballots from any Internet accessible location. R-voting offers significant benefits but it also poses substantial security risks and other social concerns. Without official control of the r-voting platform and the physical environment, there are several known ways for one to intervene and alter the election results. Current and emerging technologies seem, for the time being, inadequate to address the inherent risks.

This volume addresses the capabilities and limitations and the trends and perspectives of e-voting technologies, with a particular emphasis on security and privacy issues. It also discusses the feasibility of the different forms of electronic voting, from both the technical and social science perspectives. Finally, it discusses whether electronic voting is to be viable in the foreseeable future, and - if yes - under what conditions.

The volume is divided into three parts. The first part introduces the reader to the current electronic voting scene. The second part refers to the trends and perspectives in this field, worldwide. Finally, the third part provides the reader with state-of-the-art research results, focusing on the capabilities and limitations of the existing and emerging electronic voting technologies.

Part I addresses the current status in the electronic voting arena. It includes four papers, and its aim is twofold; first, to provide the reader with an extensive introduction to the emerging electronic voting scene; second, to describe the generic requirements for the electronic voting systems. *Jones* provides an evaluation of the existing voting technologies, considering them as part of a larger social and legal system. *Cranor* discusses the search of the perfect voting technology. After a thorough analysis, she argues that there might be partial answers to this problem but an appropriate solution is still pending. *Mercuri and Neumann*, after referring to the risks that pertain to system design, misuse, and sociological factors, describe the difficulties in validating fully computerized election equipment, and express their concerns for Internet-based systems. *Mitrou, Gritzalis, Katsikas and Quirchmayr* review the legal and constitutional needs, and identify and describe the reflecting technical requirements that a voting system should comply with.

Part II refers to the trends and perspectives in the electronic voting world. It includes three papers, which address existing and emerging methodologies for the development of secure electronic voting systems. *Burmester and Magkos* overview the main electronic voting schemes, assess their security and practicality, analyze the security risks and discuss methods to minimize them. *Damgård, Groth and Salomonsen* describe the theory and discuss various issues regarding the security of an online voting scheme, based on homomorphic encryption. *Lambrinoudakis, Gritzalis, Tsoumas, Karyda and Ikonomopoulos*, after presenting the security requirements and the system-wide properties that an electronic voting system is expected to fulfill, provide an overview of the existing voting protocols and a brief analysis of their characteristics.

Part III includes seven papers; it addresses electronic voting systems capabilities and limitations, and provides the reader with a series of answers on how to cope with the issues appearing during the development of secure electronic voting systems. *Saltman* discusses the auditability and voter confidence issues in direct-recording voting systems. *Kiayias and Yung* present a robust verifiable non-interactive zero-sharing voting utility, which enables a set of voters to protect the privacy of their votes, even in settings where all authorities may be dishonest and try to violate a voter's privacy. *Peralta* provides the readers with arguments for and against deploying electronic voting technology; he concludes that a multidisciplinary effort is essential to build, deploy, and evaluate the new technology. *Gerck* describes the Distributed Voting System, an Internet voting system using mesh networks to implement a protocol offering privacy, security and auditing, with receipt-freeness and universal verifiability. *Treschel, Mendez and Kies* describe and discuss - from a social scientist's point of view - the Canton of Geneva (Switzerland) pilot project on remote voting via the Internet. Digital divide, desirability and user friendliness are issues, which are discussed and comment upon. *Bruschi, Poletti and Rosti* describe how a Public Key Infrastructure may be used in electronic voting, with an eye towards performance issues and in particular in the case of disaster recovery. The book concludes with a paper authored by *Chaum*, which focuses on untraceable electronic mail, return addresses, and digital pseudonyms; the paper appeared for the first time (in *Com. of the ACM*) more than 20 years ago and it is considered a breakthrough in the field.

In summary, the volume provides researchers, legal experts, public policy makers, and practitioners with an in-depth review on secure electronic voting trends and perspectives, capabilities and limitations. In particular, practitioners, researchers, and legal experts can benefit from the data protection and privacy papers, in addition to the state-of-the-art research results, which are also described and commented upon. Public policy makers, election organizers and social scientists can gain insight from the analysis of the socio-technical context of the electronic voting systems and technologies.

Several distinguished experts in the field of IT security or electronic voting accepted my invitation and prepared valuable contributions. Kluwer Academic Publishers accepted my proposal and gave me the opportunity to serve as the editor of this volume. S. Lagerstrom-Fife - my publishing editor - was always ready to help, when I needed her advice and guidance. S. Jajodia, the Consulting Editor of the *Advances in Information Security Series*, offered me his generous encouragement and continuous support. My wife and our daughters provided me with their strongest support and understanding - as always. Thank you all, folks!

Dimitris A. Gritzalis (dgrit@aueb.gr)
Dept. of Informatics
Athens University of Economics and Business
Athens, Greece

Part I

SETTING THE SCENE

Chapter 1

THE EVALUATION OF VOTING TECHNOLOGY

Douglas W. Jones

Dept. of Computer Science, University of Iowa, USA
jones@cs.iowa.edu

Abstract: The voting technologies in common use today each have distinct strengths and weaknesses. These technologies cannot be evaluated in isolation, but must be evaluated as parts of a larger social and legal system, as demonstrated by a discussion of the problems with the voting technologies in wide use today, the Australian ballot, including punched card and optical mark-sense ballots, and direct recording voting machines, including mechanical lever machines. Alternate models for canvassing and remote voting further complicate the evaluation.

Key words: History; Australian ballot; Human factors; Canvassing; Remote Voting.

1.   INTRODUCTION

We are in the midst of a revolution in the way we vote. This revolution began in the 1960's with the introduction of punched-card ballots, continued with the introduction of optical mark-sense ballots and direct-recording electronic voting machines in the 1970's, and it continues as we begin tentative experiments with Internet voting. As a result, a jurisdiction interested in upgrading its voting technology today faces more choices than ever before.

It is important to emphasize that voting technology cannot be evaluated in isolation. Each voting technology is used in the context of a larger system, whether the voting technology rests on hand-counted paper ballots or on modern electronics. Some components of this larger system may be mechanical or electronic, but the system also includes the laws, administrative rules, and manual procedures surrounding the voting technology.

Thus, whenever votes are counted by hand, we must examine the laws and administrative rules governing the count, and when there are mechanical processes, we must ask how the mechanisms are prepared, maintained and inspected. When computer systems are involved, we must ask how the computers are programmed and what assurances we have that the intended programs are also the ones used to administer the election.

The suggestion that an honest electoral system must be based on trust is a dangerous one. If we extend our trust to any individual or organization, crooks intent on subverting the electoral system will certainly find a way to suborn that individual or organization. Therefore, we must design our electoral systems under the assumption that every participant is a partisan of some candidate and not fully trustworthy.

2.   A BRIEF SURVEY OF VOTING TECHNOLOGIES

There are five broad classes of voting technology in use today, hand counted paper ballots, lever voting machines, punched card ballots, optical mark-sense ballots, and direct-recording electronic voting machines. Each of these has its strong points, and each has significant weaknesses. It is important to recognize that none of these technologies is ancient. Prior to 1858, paper ballots were provided by voters or by political parties, and in many jurisdictions, voting was by voice.

In the US, it was not until 1888 that modern voting systems came into use. Reform was driven by two factors: First, election fraud was widespread and not at all secret [1]. Second, the institution of the general election, with several tens of offices on the ballot made it difficult and expensive to tally votes from unstructured ballots [2]. It is therefore quite correct to view today's revolution in voting technology as the second revolution, while viewing the changes of the 19th century as the first revolution.

2.1 The Australian Paper Ballot

The Australian Secret Ballot, first used in that country in 1858, is the form of paper ballot most widely used today. Unlike earlier paper ballots, Australian ballots are printed at government expense, with qualifying candidates and parties listed on the face of the ballot. The use of pre-printed candidate names in a fixed order within each jurisdiction greatly simplifies hand counting, and the use of uniformly printed ballots makes it far more difficult to stuff the ballot box.

An election conducted using the Australian ballot is only trustworthy if every ballot is strictly accounted for. Every ballot distributed to voters must be accounted for, and no blank ballots must escape the control of the election officials. Because we expect each official to have partisan interests, ballots must never be handled by one official without close supervision by someone representing an opposing political party. Because of this, the partisan affiliations of each election official must be declared in advance. This scheme works best in a pure two-party system because systems with more parties are frequently dominated by coalition politics, and the constant shifting of coalition structures can make it difficult to ensure that those monitoring any part of the process oppose those who they are monitoring.

The single greatest weakness in the Australian ballot lies in how the votes are counted. As with all other ballot handling, tally teams must include representatives of opposing parties, and if the team members use different criteria for accepting a mark on a ballot as a vote, the count may be biased. If one party can control the makeup of the tally teams, for example, by ensuring that the representatives of the opposing party are relatively naive, they can bias the counting in their favor. This is most effective if the rules for what constitutes a legal mark on the ballot are complex but objective, allowing large numbers of marks that express the clear intent of the voter, marks acceptable to a naive counter, to be disqualified by the more experienced tally-team member. By 1910, this weakness was well understood, and it was not uncommon for 5% to 40% of the ballots to be discounted in the tally of any particular race [3].

It was only after the intensive scrutiny of the 2000 presidential election in Florida that a related problem with all forms of the Australian Ballot came to be widely recognized. Poor ballot design can mislead voters into casting invalid votes. Bad layout of the races in an election, poorly worded instructions and poor illustrations of the acceptable form of marking on the ballot are all commonplace in today's ballots. These human factors problems are found in all forms of the Australian ballot.

2.2 Lever Voting Machines

Mechanical lever voting machines were first used in 1892 in New York, and by the 1930's, all of the larger urban centers in the United States had moved to this technology. The primary motivation for the introduction of this technology appears to have been twofold: first, that they are not subject to bias in counting, and second, because they offered instant election results even when several tens of offices appeared on the ballot with as many as ten competing parties.

From the start, lever voting machines were seen as automated versions of the Australian ballot, where the automation specifically addressed the principal weaknesses of the manual system. Indeed, with lever machines, votes are counted as the voter leaves the voting machine, so the entire totals for each precinct can be obtained within minutes of closing the polls, and counting is objective. These benefits were so persuasive that by the mid 20th century, as a result, the phrase to pull the lever had become synonymous with to vote.

Lever voting machines suffer from many weaknesses [4]. These fall into two broad categories: First, they maintain no backup record of the votes cast. The totals for each candidate are maintained on a mechanical register that can be likened to an automotive odometer mechanism. If this fails or if there is tampering, there is no way to recover the votes. With paper ballots, it is possible to conduct a recount, but the most that can be done with lever machines is to check that the counts on the odometer wheels were correctly transcribed.

Second, lever machines are very complex. A machine designed to accommodate 20 partisan races with 10 parties and able to accumulate 999 votes for any particular candidate will have 20 times 10 times 3 or 600 odometer wheels in its mechanism and 400 carry propagation wheels. In theory, these thousands of moving parts should be tested prior to each election, but this is rarely done, and when it is done, it is typically done by unsupervised technicians. Thus, we must trust the technicians, and audits of lever machines show that around one in three lever voting machines contain at least one defective counter [5].

2.3   Punched Card Voting

The Votomatic system of voting on punched cards was first used in Georgia in 1964, using IBM's Portapunch punch mechanism. By 1972, this new voting system was used by 10% of the voters in the United States [6], and by 1998, roughly 1 in 3 voters in the United States used this system [7]. The Votomatic ballot is a form of Australian ballot designed to be tallied using standard punched-card data processing equipment, and with a mechanical aid, the Votomatic or Portapunch machine, used to ensure that votes are cast in a uniform manner. It should be noted that a competing punched card voting system, the DataVote system, overcomes some of the problems with the Votomatic system, but it has never been widely used.

The Votomatic punched card system has several major problems: The first arises because of the way the cards are punched. Each potential voting position on the ballot is pre-scored, and votes are cast by punching the chad out of the pre-scored position, making a hole. Unfortunately, the Votomatic punch mechanism does not guarantee a clean punch, and there is no intuitive basis on which to judge the dimpled, punctured or dangling chad resulting from mispunches. In the 2000 general election in Palm Beach County, Florida, 6,358 of 433,043 presidential votes, or 1.5% of the total, were dimpled or otherwise mispunched, with dimpling rates for three of the minor candidates in this 10-way race of over 50% [8]. Furthermore, handling can both dislodge bits of chad, press loose chad back into holes other than the holes from which it was punched.

Another second major problem with punched card ballots is that there is nothing intuitive about the interpretation of holes in the card, so even the best of rules for interpreting pinholes, dangling or dimpled chad all appear to be both arbitrary and arcane. We need such rules both for audits of the correct functioning of the machinery and for recounts of contested elections.

The format of punched card ballots, based on standard tabulating machine cards that are about 83x187 mm (3 1/4 by 7 3/8 in) severely limits what may be printed on the face of the ballot. The standard 228 positions Votomatic ballot has only 68 mm^2 (0.1 in^2) per voting position, ignoring the space occupied by margins. This is just enough space for a 3-digit position number. Therefore, the candidate names must be printed on multiple pages attached to the face of the Votomatic machine. As a result, any race involving over 18 to 20 candidate names must be split across multiple ballot pages. The now infamous butterfly ballot used in Palm Beach County in the election of 2000 was a direct consequence of this limitation.

As a consequence of the separation of the lack of space on the ballot face for candidate names, there is no easy way for the voter to determine whether the holes punched were the holes actually intended. While the ballot is in the Votomatic machine, the holes are clearly labeled with candidate names, but the ballot itself is hidden inside the mechanism. Once punched and removed from the machine, the holes are anonymous, identified only by numbers. While it is possible, with the aid of an appropriate key, for a voter to decode these numbers and verify the correctness of the ballot, this is far more difficult than verifying the correctness of a pencil mark on an Australian ballot.

Finally, machine counting of punched card ballots does not require the use of computers; it can be done with classical electromechanical card sorters. In the 1960's, this was probably common, but doing so requires multiple passes through the sorter, and with each pass, there is an increased risk that the outcome will be changed by the accidental dislodging or replacement of bits of chad. To avoid this, most use of punched-card ballots since the early 1970's has relied on computerized ballot counting, where the entire set of ballots are read on one pass through the card reader, and the votes are tallied by software. This raises the final problem: How do we know that this software is trustworthy?

2.4   Optical Mark-Sense Voting

The optical mark-sense scanner was developed in the 1950's to automate the grading of the ACT college entrance exam, and Westinghouse Learning Systems, the licensee of this technology, began exploring its application to elections in the 1970's. By 1998, optical mark-sense ballots were being used by close to 1 in 4 voters in the United States [8]. To the voter, optical mark-sense ballots appear very similar to the classical Australian ballot, except for index marks in the margins used by the ballot scanner to locate voting targets, and except for the instructions for marking the targets themselves. The latter usually state something like: "To vote for a candidate, completely darken the oval by the candidate's name. Use only number-two soft lead pencil or black ink."

Optical mark-sense tabulators have evolved considerably from the 1950's to the present. The first generation of tabulators used in voting applications used infrared light and were not able to reliably count marks made with anything but graphite or carbon-black based inks or marks that filled less than the entire voting target. In contrast, most of the current generation of mark-sense tabulators use visible light and generously accept single lines, check marks or X marks in or near the voting target [9].

Optical mark-sense ballots are voted without the use of special fixtures, using commonplace pencils and pens. As a result, voters can easily interpret the marks on their own ballots, and a hand recount does not require arcane knowledge of such things as dimpled chad. Unfortunately, mark-sense ballot tabulators judge ballots using mechanical criteria that differ significantly from the intuitive criteria people use. Identical same ballots may be read differently by different machines, because they use different sensing technologies. Typically, marks made exactly as prescribed will be reliably detected on all machines able to read a particular ballot, but marks that deviate from the prescription may be read differently.

An evaluation of the accuracy of mark-sense ballot tabulators without reference to human factors issues is almost meaningless. Typical standards for the combined hardware and software of mark-sense ballot tabulators call for an accuracy of one part in 10^7 [10]. Unfortunately, these standards only apply to votes cast using exactly the marking required by the manufacturer, while empirical data from audits of the 2000 general election in Florida show that over 1 voter in 2000 who voted on optical mark-sense voting systems used the wrong type of marking implement, or voted using the wrong type of mark (either a circle around the voting target, or an X or check in the target) [11]. In the face of this high error rate due to human factors problems, the standards for hardware and software error rates are entirely irrelevant!

Optical mark-sense ballots can be quite large. Fidlar Doubleday, for example, offers a ballot scanner that can accommodate 11 by 17 in ballots (approximately A3). Such a ballot can easily give a full-face display of an entire election, that is, display all of the candidates and offices in a large general election on a single side. Most optical mark-sense ballots are smaller, requiring two-sided printing. Despite these large expanses of paper, many jurisdictions have successfully adopted ballot formats that use paper very ineffectively. In Florida during the 2000 general election, for example, 12 of 36 counties using optical mark-sense ballots managed to split the 11-way presidential race across two columns, leading large numbers of voters. In these counties, over 1 in 20 voters were misled into overvotes, voting for multiple candidates when only one was allowed, whereas in counties where this mistake was not made, fewer than 1 in 100 voters overvoted.

All optical mark-sense ballot tabulators are computer based, so as with punched-card tabulating systems, we must ask whether the software is trustworthy. Because both punched cards and mark-sense ballots are physical objects that can be hand counted, they provide the necessary physical evidence required for a recount in the event that an error is suspected in the tabulating software. On the other hand, as with classical Australian ballots, anyone who has access to the ballots may easily tamper with them, so physical security of the ballots must be carefully maintained.

2.5 Direct Recording Electronic Voting

Direct-recording electronic voting systems were introduced by Shoup and Microvote (the latter in 1986). These early machines emulated the look and feel of classical lever voting machines, to the extent that unfolding the machine created a complete voting booth. Essentially, these machines emulated the look and feel of lever voting machines, while replacing the levers and electromechanical counters of the originals with push buttons and microprocessor software. The second generation of direct recording electronic voting machines, introduced in the 1990's, uses flat panel displays, frequently with touch-screen input.

The phrase direct-recording electronic properly suggests that we could call conventional lever voting machines direct-recording mechanical voting machines. In both classes of machines, we rely on the mechanism of the voting machines to record the vote, and there is no independent physical record of the votes cast. Thus, just as we must trust the technicians who maintain the lever machines, we must trust the programmers who develop software for the electronic voting machines.

With the old mechanical machines, the only record of the votes was the reading on the odometer mechanism behind each lever. For over a decade, all direct-recording electronic machines have been required to contain redundant storage [12], but this redundant storage is not an independent record of the votes, because it is created by the same software that created the original record. As a result, recounts are of limited use with these machines; in contrast, with computer-tabulated punched-card or mark-sense ballots, a hand recount is reasonable way to check the correctness of the software.

Because direct recording electronic voting machines are the youngest class of voting system, their human interface designs are the most fluid. There are a number of unresolved issues; one of the first to be noticed involved how the voter goes about logically depositing a voted ballot in the electronic ballot box. On mechanical lever voting machines, the commit operation involved pulling a large lever that both opened the curtain to allowing exit from the machine and incremented the registers inside the machine to count the votes for the selected candidates. This was an excellent example of good design. On direct-recording electronic voting machines, in contrast, there have been two common human factors errors: First, the pushbutton used to commit the vote has been too inviting, so that the voter is tempted to push it as soon as one ballot selection has been made. In this case, a largely blank ballot is tabulated and the voter is locked out of making further selections. The most obvious way of avoiding this is to give the voter a second chance, asking did you really mean you are finished voting? Unfortunately, by the time this message is displayed, many voters will have already turned away and left the machine, leaving their partially voted ballot displayed on the screen open to the next voter.

The original Shoup direct-recording voting machine displayed a full-face ballot in almost exactly the layout that was used on lever voting machines, all of which offered a full-face display. This is not the case with any of the other direct-recording voting machines, all of which force the division of the ballot into sections, only one of which is visible at a time. The constraints of the touch-screen based machines are nowhere near as severe as the constraints imposed by the Votomatic ballot format, but the problem of navigating through a multi-screen ballots are poorly addressed on many of these machines, and many developers have not grappled with the style of ballot common in some municipal elections where there may be hundreds of candidates on the ballot in a single race.

3.   ALTERNATIVE CANVASSING MODELS

The canvass of an election involves the consolidation of the vote totals from many precincts in order to compute the vote totals for each candidate for each office. There are two primary models for canvassing that differ significantly in where the votes are counted, precinct count and central count.

3.1   Precinct Count

In a precinct-count system, all votes cast in a particular precinct are counted at that precinct, and the precinct totals are then delivered from the precinct polling place to the central election offices. Classical Australian ballots can be hand counted by the local election officials in a precinct-count system, and all of the mechanical lever voting machines are precinct count systems.

In any precinct-count system, vote counting is decentralized and therefore, strict supervision is difficult. Provisions allowing independent observers at each precinct are essential, and a culture of volunteerism is required in order to assure that there will be a sufficient number of observers available to properly monitor the count. The other major problem is accurate transmission of election totals from the precinct to the central election office. One classical way of doing this is to post a publicly verified copy of the results at the precinct and then require that the totals received by the election headquarters be published, so that all living in the precinct have the opportunity to verify the transmission. In this context, it should be noted that a hand-carried tally sheet is just as much an example of data transmission as the use of electronic means!

Precinct-count Votomatic systems are available from Election Systems and Software, and have been used in Chicago for several years. Precinct-count optical mark-sense systems have been available for decades from several manufacturers. All of these systems offer a local check, at the precinct, of the readability of the ballot marked or punched by the voter; typically, if an error is detected, the ballot can be returned and the voter offered a chance to correct it. How this ability is administered varies significantly between jurisdictions and can have a significant impact on the outcome of an election! In Manatee County Florida, during the 2000 general election, this feature was disabled, allowing over 1 in 100 voters to cast overvotes. In counties using the same system and with comparable ballot layouts, but where overvote detection was enabled, the rate of overvotes was below 1 in 300 [11].

Direct recording electronic voting systems have been configured as precinct-count systems, and if there is any doubt about the reliability or security of the transmission from the polling place to the election headquarters, such a configuration allows posting precinct election totals locally in order to allow public verification of the transmission. Overvotes are not a problem with direct-recording voting systems; interlocks to prevent overvoting have been available on lever voting machines for many decades, and all direct-recording electronic voting machines allow such interlocks.

If physical ballots or even electronic ballot images are available in a precinct-count system, they should be retained in secure storage in order to allow the count for each precinct to be reconstructed or checked. This retention is a matter of insurance, so they need not be transported or transmitted immediately, so long as secure storage is available.

3.2   Central Count

In a central-count system, all ballots voted in each precinct are transmitted to a central location for counting. With such a system, secure and rapid ballot transmission is essential, but once ballots are received at the counting center, security and proper oversight are easily arranged. Central counting is commonly used with classical, punched-card and optical mark-sense Australian ballots. As a result, most of us are familiar with the problems of ballot box theft and tampering; these are classical examples of the problems with ballot transmission in central-count systems.

In general, central-count systems based on punched-card or optical mark-sense ballot counting cannot offer the voter an opportunity to correct errors such as overvotes. If we want to allow the voters protection comparable to what precinct-count ballot tabulators allow, then the central tabulators must sort out each overvoted ballot for hand examination and possible correction. In jurisdictions that allow voting by mail, there are usually procedures in place for correcting ballots damaged by postal accidents; these procedures and the safeguards surrounding them are appropriate models for the processing needed here [9].

New direct-recording electronic voting systems usually function as central count systems, retaining redundant electronic images of all ballots cast on each machine, and including provisions to automatically consolidate the ballots collected by each machines at a precinct for either a precinct count or for transmission to a central counting center. This means that the machines include provisions for local communication within the precinct as well as remote communication from the precinct to a counting center.

It is worth noting that in-precinct communication and remote communication between direct-recording electronic voting systems need not involve the same technology. For local communication within a precinct, for example, the Election Systems and Software iVotronic system uses hand-carried data cartridges while the Fidlar Doubleday EV 2000 uses Ethernet. For communication between the polling place and the counting center, both offer similar ranges of options, including printouts of the precinct vote totals and modem transmission of ballot images.

4. REMOTE VOTING

Remote voting, where voters are not constrained to vote at designated precinct polling places on election day, is largely a matter of law, but it relies on many enabling technologies. Remote voting on election day is sometimes described as the vote anywhere model. In this model, voters may use any polling place; this model was almost universally eliminated by mid-century because of its high susceptibility to fraud, but the combination of smart cards, biometrics and highly available on-line voting systems may allow such systems to re-emerge. The arguments of the California Internet Voting Task Force against Internet voting on election day apply to most versions of the vote anywhere model, so there is good reason to be skeptical about such systems [13].

Remote voting before election day is called early voting. This can be done at satellite polling places, locations that are run like a precinct polling place, with supervision, ballot boxes and similar protections, or it can be done using absentee voting, in which case, the voter never has direct contact with any election officials. Traditionally, absentee voters request a ballot by mail, vote from wherever they happen to be, and mail their ballots back to the offices of their home jurisdiction prior to election day.

A conventional precinct typically requires, at most, one or two ballot styles, but across an entire jurisdiction, there may be many different styles. In Johnson County Iowa, for example, with a population of around 100,000, a typical general election involves around 70 distinct ballot styles, depending on the offices up for election and how their districts overlay the different precincts of the county. Laws allowing any form of remote voting usually require the ability to deliver the correct ballot for the voter's home precinct, no matter where the voter votes. Stocking huge numbers of ballot styles at regular or satellite polling places is impractical, and accidental mailing of the wrong ballot to absentee voters is quite likely in a vote by mail system where many ballot formats are in use. As a result, advocates of remote voting strongly favor either direct-recording electronic voting systems that can present many different ballot formats, or optical mark-sense systems that support ballot printing on demand using inexpensive computer printers.

If ballots from early voting are counted before the polls close on election day, there is a risk that the election process will be biased by the release of preliminary results. Therefore, it is common to require that all early voting ballots be held uncounted and under seal until election day. This leads to a central count model for early voting, and it limits the technologies that may be used. Even when direct recording voting technology is used at regular polling sites, remote voting is frequently conducted on mark-sense or punched-card ballots, and the protection against overvotes offered by precinct-count machines are generally unavailable.

In principle, a precinct-count ballot tabulator could be programmed for use in satellite polling places by having it check for blank ballots and overvotes without accumulating any totals; unfortunately, today's machines do not allow for this. In contrast, many direct-recording electronic voting machines apply interlocks that prevent overvotes and blank ballots while the voter is present, and then they save the ballot image internally for later counting when the polls close. Thus, these systems offer the potential to serve in satellite polling places.

The single largest problem with absentee voting, historically, has been the opportunities it provides for vote fraud. There are many stories of family members voting the absentee ballots of other family members, and one of the most effective ways for crooks to buy votes is to buy blank absentee ballots from voters.

The best-known defense against such fraud involves a form of provisional voting in which a voter may cancel any previously voted ballot by depositing a new ballot. This requires that each ballot be tied to the voter who deposited it until the time comes to count the votes. Elections of corporate boards in the United States are routinely done this way, but these are not subject to the requirement of a secret ballot. If we wish to allow this while preserving the anonymity of the voter, we must seal each ballot in an envelope with the voter's identity and time stamp on the outside. At the time of the vote count, all envelopes deposited by a given voter must be gathered; and only the envelope with the latest time stamp should be opened for counting while all others remain forever sealed. The ballot itself should not be inspected until its connection to the envelope has been forgotten. This procedure is not legal in most jurisdictions, but in electronic form, using encryption instead of envelopes, it is very appealing.

The usual conception of Internet voting, that where a voter may vote from any computer connected to the network, can be classified as absentee direct-recording electronic voting. Such Internet voting therefore poses all of the problems of absentee voting combined with all of the problems of direct-recording electronic voting. In addition, such Internet voting requires that the voting software run on a machine and possibly an operating system and web browser that is outside the control of the election jurisdiction. This is an extremely difficult problem [14].

In contrast, use of the Internet for voting from polling places poses few special problems, and in fact, many currently available direct-recording electronic voting machines and precinct-count ballot tabulators offer Internet -based options for transmission of ballot images or precinct totals to the election headquarters. In this context, the security required for use of the

Internet is not significantly different from that required for transmission over the public telephone network, or transmission by radio, and fallback communication paths based on other communications media (including hand carried results, in the extreme case) are easily arranged.

5. EVALUATION

The number of different criteria against which a voting system must be tested is large, but they fall into several categories. The first should be quite obvious: Does the voting system meet the legal constraints of the jurisdiction? Here, issues of privacy and secret ballots arise, but most of the constraints are more mundane, governing such things basic rules as how many offices, parties and candidates the machine accommodates, how the votes are counted, what audit information must be preserved.

The second major question is how do voters react to the system. Controlled experiments with large numbers of voters are generally impractical, but in many cases, small inexpensive tests are straightforward. It only takes a few hours in a busy downtown area or shopping mall to allow perhaps a hundred random potential voters to test a voting system, observing the voter responses to the instructions, ballot layout and user interface.

The third major question is, who must we trust, and how is the system constructed and administered in order to ensure that they are trustworthy. Programmers, technicians, and election officials should all face this question. Open source software, oversight and audit trails for all maintenance activity, and monitoring by opposing parties are non-technical means of ensuring trust. Cryptography, electronic signatures, modularization and redundancy are technical means, but it must be emphasized that the mere use of such mechanisms guarantees nothing.

Finally, in today's marketplace with rapidly changing technology, it is important to ask about compatibility. Can the new voting technology be integrated into the larger system, or does it require complete replacement of the entire system. Vendors encourage complete replacement by use of incompatible proprietary data formats, and as a result, upgrades to voting systems today are generally extremely expensive. Open standards for electronic ballot formatting, transmission and storage offer a tremendous potential that has yet to be effectively exploited in the marketplace.

REFERENCES

[1]   Miller, W. R. Harrison County Methods: Election Fraud in Late 19th Century Texas. *Locus: Regional and Local History 7*, 2 (Spring 1995) 111-128; http://history.smsu.edu /wrmiller/Populism/texts/Harrison_county_methods.htm

[2]   See, for example, the collection of 19th century ballots on the web at http://www.cs. uiowa.edu/~jones/voting/pictures/

[3]   Voting Machines, *Encyclopaedia Britannica*, 11th Edition, 1910.

[4]   Saltman, R. Section 3.3 of *Accuracy, Integrity, and Security in Computerized Vote-Tallying*. National Bureau of Standards Special Publication 500-158, August 1988; http://www.itl.nist.gov/lab/specpubs/500-158.htm

[5]   Saltman, R. Oral testimony before e the Committee on Science, House of Representatives, 107th Congress, Washington DC, May 22, 2001. USGPO Serial No. 107-20.

[6]   Saltman, R. Section 3.4 of *Accuracy, Integrity, and Security in Computerized Vote-Tallying*.

[7]   Fischer, E.A. Table 1 of *Voting Technologies in the United States: Overview and Issues for Congress*. Congressional Research Service RL30773, March 2001; http://www. cnie.org/NLE/CRSreports/Risk/rsk-55.cfm

[8]   Jones, D.W. *Chad - From Waste Product to Headline*, January 2002; http://www.cs. uiowa.edu/~jones/cards/chad.html

[9]   Jones, D.W. *Counting Mark-Sense Ballots - Relating Technology, the Law and Common Sense*, January 2002; http://www.cs.uiowa.edu/~jones/voting/optical/

[10] Section 3.2 of *Performance and Test Standards for Punchcard, Marksense and Direct Recording Electronic Voting Systems*, Federal Election Commission, US Government Printing Office, January 1990; Section 3.2.1 of the April 2002 retains the 1 in 10^7 requirement with some elaboration; http://www.fec.gov/pages/vssfinal/ vss.html

[11] This data is a composite of data gleaned from the *Miami-Herald Knight-Ridder USA-Today* audit of ballots from the 2000 general election in Florida, combined with the official election returns from the Division of Elections of the Florida Dept. of State.

[12] Section 2.3.2 of *Performance and Test Standards for Punchcard, Marksense and Direct Recording Electronic Voting Systems*, January 1990.

[13] *Final Report of the California Internet Voting Task Force*, California Secretary of State, January 2000, on the net at: http://www.ss.ca.gov/executive/ivote/

[14] Jones, D.W. Trustworthy Systems on Untrusted Machines, presented at the Georgia Tech Workshop on the Future of Voting Technology in a Networked Environment, Atlanta, June 4-5, 2002; on the web at: http://www.cs.uiowa.edu/~jones/voting/atlanta/

Chapter 2

IN SEARCH OF THE PERFECT VOTING TECHNOLOGY: NO EASY ANSWERS

Lorrie Faith Cranor

AT&T Labs-Research, USA
lorrie@research.att.com

Abstract   As the world watched the electoral drama unfold in Florida at the end of 2000, my phone started ringing off the hook. I spoke with reporters, state officials, and colleagues and friends. And even while the actual outcome of the Presidential election remained unknown, it became clear that throughout the US people were soon going to be taking a hard look at their voting equipment and procedures, and trying to figure out how to improve them. After they finished debating the events in Florida, what everyone really wanted to know was what new technology their state could buy that would ensure that in future elections all votes would be fairly counted. But, I am afraid, there are no easy answers.

1.   MY PERSONAL EXPERIENCE

I began studying electronic voting when I was a graduate student in 1994. After I berated an undergraduate for deploying a poorly implemented electronic voting system on the engineering school servers and advertising it as a way to provide confidential feedback about courses and professors, my advisor challenged me to design a better system - one that really would provide for secret balloting and prevent people from stuffing the ballot box. After several days of library research I returned to my advisor to report that this appeared to be a completely solved problem.

I had found several papers in the theoretical computer science literature that described secure and private secret balloting schemes. These papers seemed to take into account most of the important issues I could think of, and the schemes they described sounded like they would work. But I could not find any evidence that the authors had actually implemented any of these schemes. So, I spent the next year learning more about the cryptographic protocols behind these schemes and implementing a working prototype of an electronic voting system called 'Sensus', which allowed voters to cast secure and private ballots over the Internet [1]. This would eventually become my Master's degree project. Sensus was based on a previously published algorithm that used a cryptographic technique called a blind signature to maintain ballot secrecy, while simultaneously ensuring that each eligible voter could vote only once [2]. Essentially, voters prepared their ballots using a computer program that encrypted them and created a unique digital fingerprint of each ballot. The program then multiplied the numbers in the fingerprint by a random factor and sent the result, along with the voter's digital signature, to a computer run by the election authority called a validator. The validator checked the voter's digital signature and made sure the voter was eligible to vote and had not yet voted. The validator then digitally signed the randomised fingerprint and returned it to the voter. The voter's computer then divided out the random factor, resulting in a ballot fingerprint signed by the validator. However, since the validator signed the version of the fingerprint that was multiplied by the random factor, the validator had no way of knowing what the original fingerprint looked like, or which voter it was associated with. The voter's computer then sent the signed fingerprint and the corresponding encrypted ballot to another computer called the tallier. The tallier used the signed fingerprint to verify that the ballot was certified by the validator, and provided an acknowledgement to the voter that the ballot was acceptable. The voter then sent the tallier the key necessary to decrypt the ballot for tallying. Variations on this scheme have since been implemented as part of a number of other student projects, including an ongoing project at MIT [3]. Other researchers have also proposed more sophisticated schemes that allow election observers to cryptographically "prove" that all the votes in an election have been tallied correctly [4,5].

I continued studying both traditional and electronic voting as part of my dissertation work, and created an electronic voting resources web page to share the information I had gathered with anyone else who was interested. This web page was soon indexed by all the major search engines and became the first stop for anyone looking for electronic voting information. By the time I graduated and started working at AT&T Labs-Research in 1996, I was receiving electronic voting inquiries on a regular basis from the press, researchers, and government officials.

In 1997, I was approached by the Centre for Information Law and Policy at the Villanova University School of Law to help design the technical aspects of an electronic voting system trial for Costa Rica. I enlisted my colleagues in the secure systems research department at AT&T, and together we began analysing the requirements and outlining a system design. Many of the requirements were conveyed to me through an interpreter during an all-day meeting at the office of the electoral tribunal in San Jose, Costa Rica. What the tribunal had in mind was to use the personal computers recently purchased for the country's elementary schools as voting terminals at each polling place. By connecting the computers via the Internet, they hoped to enable a centralized system for checking voter registration that would allow voters to vote at any polling place - not just their assigned precinct. The computers would also have to be capable of fetching the appropriate ballot for each voter (determined by where he or she lived), and for transmitting the ballots for central tallying. The motivations behind this project seemed to be to demonstrate the technological sophistication of the Costa Rican people and to save the government money. It seems that the government spends a lot of money each election day bussing people around the country so they can get to their home precinct (people in Costa Rica do not update their voter registration when they move within the country). By allowing people to vote at any precinct, they hoped to save money.

My colleagues and I soon realized that this was going to be a difficult problem to solve. While the tribunal wanted to use the PCs already in the schools, it was apparent that a large percentage of the population was not computer literate and would be unable to use a standard PC equipped with mouse and keyboard without substantial training. No budget was available for purchasing touch screens, so we searched computer stores and electronics catalogues for an alternative solution. Light pens seemed to offer a potential solution, as they could be added to a standard PC at a fraction of the cost of a touch screen monitor and required little training to use.

The US crypto export rules in effect at the time proved to be another obstacle, as it soon became clear that we would be unable to export cryptographic software developed in the US to Costa Rica. And even if we could use the best cryptography, it was questionable as to whether most voters would trust a system based on mathematical functions that they could not understand. We eventually decided to forego the cryptographic protocols for ensuring secret ballots, and instead rely on a physical separation between the voter authentication computers and the voting terminals. Because this system was designed to use at a polling place, poll workers could operate the authentication computers and, upon authenticating a voter, could unlock a voting terminal, allowing that voter to cast one vote. This solution would not work if voters were to cast their votes from home or from unattended voting kiosks, but it seemed workable for a system designed for use at staffed polling places. Ultimately, the Costa Rican government got cold feet and decided to cancel the electronic voting trial, so our design was never completed or tested. A few months later we were approached to work on another electronic voting project, this time by the state of Florida. We had one meeting with the Florida officials before their project was put on hold indefinitely after evidence of widespread absentee ballot fraud was discovered in Miami. At the time that we worked on these projects, our group was aware of the awesome responsibility associated with designing voting technology, but this really hit home two-and-a-half years later as we discussed the 2000 Presidential election in Florida. "They could have been using our system," said one of my colleagues over lunch one day. And we all laughed uncomfortably, relieved that they were not.

2.   VOTING TECHNOLOGY

2.1   Mechanical lever voting machines

Mechanical lever voting machines have been in use in parts of the United States since 1892. Voters pull levers that correspond with the candidates and issues they wish to vote for. When a lever is pulled it causes a counter wheel to rotate. At the end of an election, officials open up the back of each machine to read the counter wheels and determine how many votes were cast for each candidate. By the 60's, these machines were used by about half the voters in the US. These machines were appealing because they allowed election results to be determined quickly, and because they were able to thwart the voting fraud schemes that had become widespread using paper ballots.

One of the main disadvantages of lever machines is there is no ability to audit them and to "recount" individual ballots. If the machine malfunctions and a counter wheel fails to turn, no record exists from which a proper tally can be determined. Sometimes levers are mislabeled (either accidentally or deliberately). Lever machines are also difficult to test exhaustively, as a person has to manually enter large numbers of votes into each machine that is to be tested. These machines have also been known to cause confusion when recording and tallying write-in ballots. Because of their size and weight, these machines are expensive to store and transport. Lever machines were used by 15% of counties in the US for the 2000 Presidential election. However, because they are no longer manufactured, it is becoming difficult to obtain spare parts for them. Indeed, during the 2000 Presidential election, New York City voters reported that levers were broken off of some machines, making it impossible for them to vote for some local offices.

2.2 Punch card voting systems

The State of Florida had been using punch card voting machines for about 20 years prior to the 2000 election. These machines had been purchased to replace the lever machines they were using at the time. Interestingly, it's been reported that the mechanical machines were sold to the State of New Jersey, which was still using them in some counties during the 2000 election (I used them the first three years I lived in New Jersey - I found them pretty easy to use, except for the fact that at 5-foot-2 I had trouble reaching the top row of levers). The Florida punch card machines are manufactured by a company called Election Resources Corporation and known as Votomatic machines. The cards used by these machines are printed with rows of marks where holes can be punched. The names of the candidates are not printed on the cards themselves, but rather on a ballot holder device that looks something like a book with cardboard pages. When the card is properly inserted into the ballot holder, one column of holes is visible through the "spine" of the book. Each hole lines up with the name of a candidate printed on the book's pages. Election officials try to print candidate names only on the left side of each two-page spread, so that the holes are to the right of the candidates' names. But sometimes they end up with ballot layouts that use both the left and right sides of the page. Having used this system - butterfly ballots and all - when I lived in St. Louis, I can assure anyone who insists that the system shouldn't be that difficult to figure out, that indeed it is. Especially when two page "butterfly" layouts are used, the system can be quite confusing even to someone with 20-20 vision and good hand-eye coordination. Press quoted one of the inventors of the Votomatic system as saying that he had never intended it to be used with a butterfly layout.

And, it turns out that the 2000 Presidential election was not the first time that there were law suits over Votomatic ballot confusion. In 1987 it was found that ballots cast in predominantly black wards in the city of St. Louis were more than three times as likely to be improperly punched - and therefore not counted - as those cast in predominantly white wards. A federal judge subsequently ruled that the punch card system used in St. Louis "denies blacks an equal opportunity with whites to participate in the political process." The judge ordered the city to increase voter education in black wards and count improperly marked ballots by hand.

Another kind of punch card ballot system called Datavote reduces voter confusion about which hole to punch by printing the candidate names directly on the ballot. However, Datavote systems can cause problems and added expense because most elections require voters to use multiple ballot cards. In precincts where these systems are used, under votes are common when voters forget to vote in the races listed on the back of the punch cards, or neglect to vote all of the punch cards they are given. Sometimes Datavote systems also have a high rate of over votes for reasons that are not entirely clear. Datavote cards are voted using a special mechanical hole punch device that cleanly removes the chad from each hole a voter punches.

Besides the difficulty in understanding and marking punch card ballots, these ballots have also been known for a long time to be difficult to tally accurately. Votomatic systems suffer from the frequent occurrence of hanging, swinging, pregnant, and dimpled chad. These terms have now become household words in the US and the butts of many jokes. But in early November 2000, most Americans had never heard these terms. The word chad first came to my attention when I read R. Saltman's 1988 National Bureau of Standards report "Accuracy, Integrity and Security in Computerized Vote-Tallying" while working on my dissertation [6]. Saltman described a large number of problems with punch card ballots, and highlighted the chad problem in particular. Despite these warnings, punch card systems were used in 20% of US counties for the 2000 Presidential election. One of the issues that Saltman discussed was that most punch card systems in use in the US use pre-scored cards, in which the spots where holes can be punched are perforated. It is these perforations that lead to many of the chad problems. Saltman suggested that punch card systems would be more accurate if they used cards without perforations and required voters to use a spring-loaded stylus to punch their cards. Over a decade later this suggestion does not appear to have been widely adopted. Many of the problems with partially punched cards in Florida would probably have been avoided if pre-scored cards had not been used. But I have been unable to find recent statistics on the extent to which non-scored cards are used and their impact on the percentage of uncounted ballots. It does appear that the problems associated with Datavote cards (which are non-scored except when used for absentee ballots) are not related to chads, providing evidence that scoring is a factor.

A November 1988 New Yorker article by R. Dugger also contained a scathing analysis of the use of punch card ballots as well as other computerised voting systems [7]. Dugger described the St. Louis case as well as a number of other computer-related vote counting problems and dubbed "the inexact science of divining what the voter intended in the case of a mere indentation or whether the card reader counted a hole that was partly or wholly blocked by a hanging "chad" as "chadology."

2.3   Optical-scan voting systems

One popular alternative to punch card systems are optical-scan systems, used in 40% of counties in the US. These systems are similar to the systems used to administer college entrance exams and other standardized tests. Voters use a pen or pencil to fill in an oval or connect dots on a paper ballot. A machine scans these ballots to count the votes. Both punch card and optical-scan systems suffer from the problem that voters may improperly mark their ballots, causing the ballot-counting computer to count them incorrectly or not at all. And both kinds of ballots can be tampered with during the counting process. Both kinds of ballots might also be tampered with during the ballot printing (and in the case of punch cards, scoring) process. However, in many precincts where optical-scan ballots are used, a scanner is available in each precinct so that voters can feed their ballots into the scanner themselves and check to see if it is accepted by the machine. If the machine reports that the ballot is mismarked, the voter can correct the problem and submit it again. In precincts where such a scanner is available, the percentage of uncounted ballots is often reduced by roughly a factor of five (when no scanner is available, optical-scan and punch card ballots result in similar percentages of uncounted ballots). Similar improvements might be possible if punch card readers were available at precincts as well.

2.4 Direct recording electronic systems

In the aftermath of the 2000 Presidential election, people are calling for a voting system in which every vote cast will be counted. They want systems in which it is not possible for a voter to mark a ballot in such a way that it will not be counted. And they want systems that will allow for accurate recounts without the risk of ballot tampering or the need to argue about what constitutes a vote. Vendors of computerized voting systems, often referred to as direct recording electronic (DRE) systems, claim to have an answer. A computerized voting machine that allows voters to register their votes using a touch screen, ATM-machine like terminal, or a panel with buttons and lights, could ensure that voters do not unintentionally vote for too many or too few candidates. Indeed, in the 9% of counties in the US where these machines are already in use, the feedback from voters is generally positive. Voters typically find the machines easy to use, and like the fact that the machines warn them if they fail to vote for a particular office and do not permit overvotes. I have used these machines in New Jersey and found them quite simple to use, although a carelessly designed ballot could probably render even a DRE machine difficult to use and confusing to voters.

While DRE machines may be easy to use, produce unambiguous results, and do not involve paper ballots that might be tampered with, they are not without problems. DRE machines must be trusted to accurately record each vote as the voter entered it. If the machines do not record a vote accurately, or fail to record it at all, there is no record to go back to for a recount (as with lever machines). It has been argued that recounting paper ballots (punch card, optical-scan, etc.) is imperfect because of the risk of tampering or even accidental damage. However, when the recount is necessary due to computer failures during the first count - especially when those failures were not malicious - it appears to be quite useful to have the paper ballots available to recount. Indeed, there have been many documented cases of ballot counting machines that were accidentally programmed incorrectly or had the wrong software installed. Upon investigation - usually triggered by unexpected or bizarre election results - the problems were discovered and corrected and the ballots recounted. In fact, during the November 2000 US Presidential election a computer glitch was discovered in Roosevelt County, New Mexico that caused 533 absentee ballots not to be counted properly. These ballots had been voted "straight party" by the voters, but the computer had not been programmed to allocate these votes to the all of the corresponding party's candidates. Because optical-scan ballots were used, the software was fixed and two days after the election all of the ballots were rescanned. Without physical ballots to rescan, it might not have been possible to correct this problem.

DRE proponents argue that a properly designed and tested DRE machine should not suffer from programming errors, accidental or malicious, and should include internal audit logs that should make it possible to recover from accidental errors. Whether this is really true in practice remains a debatable question. While experts agree that a malicious programmer could write computer code that alters votes and even alters the audit logs to match, they disagree on whether such tampering would be detectable. Carnegie Mellon University Professor and experienced voting machine tester M. Shamos has gone so far as to challenge skeptics to tamper with a DRE system of his choosing, and see if he can detect the tampering. So far nobody has taken him up on his challenge.

I tend to think that with sufficient review and oversight, we should be able to deploy DRE machines that have a very low risk of failure (through either accidental error or fraud). I do not think we can build a perfect machine, but we should be able to build a machine with risks lower than the risks associated with a paper ballot system. I do not know enough about existing DRE systems to know whether any of them are good enough today, but have heard about enough problems to be suspicious. In the November 2000 election, a Sequoia Pacific DRE machine in New Jersey apparently failed to record about 50 votes (this was determined after observing that in one local race, none of the second-listed running mates received any votes on one voting machine, while they received approximately the same number of votes as the first-listed running mates on all the other machines). A spokesman for Sequoia Pacific told a reporter that the machine had not actually lost any votes because the "votes were never cast." But to the voters, it apparently looked like their votes had been cast. Such failures cannot be corrected after the fact in a DRE system, and are clearly problematic.

Another problem with DRE machines is the amount of time each machine is monopolized by a single voter. When paper ballots are used, it is inexpensive to provide enough private booths and equipment (Votomatic devices, pens, etc.) to keep voter lines to a minimum. Even if these ballots are to be scanned in each precinct, the amount of time it takes a computer to scan each ballot is much less than the time it takes a voter to mark it. But when DRE machines are used, each voter must have exclusive access to a terminal for the entire time it takes to mark the ballot. Election officials with experience using DRE machines report that generally about 30 voters per hour can use a single DRE machine (this is probably similar to the number of voters that can use a lever machine in an hour.) Thus, it takes a large number of machines to serve the voters in each county. The machines are expensive, and each must be configured and tested before every election.

Some vendors are promoting computerized systems that use off-the-shelf PCs as a much less expensive alternative to traditional DRE systems. Besides the significant cost advantage, some vendors claim that there is less of a risk of hardware tampering on such machines since they are not being manufactured for the express purpose of voting. However, because these computers are manufactured as general-purpose computers, there are more areas where things may go wrong and a lot more places where malicious code may be hidden. Conducting an election using a general-purpose operating system opens the voting computers up to a wide range of vulnerabilities.

2.5   Hand-counted paper ballots

The apparent lack of a perfect voting technology has lead many people to suggest that we just go back to the old hand-counted paper ballots used in the past in the US, and still used throughout most of the world. A well-designed paper ballot would probably use a separate ballot paper for each race, and include large boxes for voters to use to mark their preferences. In most countries where this system is used, ballots can be tallied very quickly - sometimes in a matter of hours - using government employees or citizen panels. But in most of these countries voters are asked to vote in only a few races - often only one race. With the large number of races and other ballot questions on US ballots, a hand counted paper ballot system would be more cumbersome. As suggested by computer-related risks expert P. Neumann, it might be practical if used for Presidential voting only, and not for other races. Even if a paper ballot system was practical, problems would remain. Voters could still accidentally skip over ballot questions or vote for too many candidates on a ballot. And paper ballots can be tampered with during transport and counting, and are subject to a range of voting fraud schemes that involve vote buying and ballot box stuffing. This option should be considered along with other possible options, but it does not appear to offer a perfect solution either.

3. INTERNET VOTING: DON'T TRY THIS AT HOME

Perhaps the questions I heard most frequently following the 2000 election were questions about Internet voting. As the popularity of online shopping and banking increase, so does voter interest in the possibility of voting from home or work over the Internet. The first governmental election to be conducted over the Internet in the US was the 1996 Reform Party Presidential primary, in which Internet voting was offered, along with vote-by-mail and vote-by-phone, as an option to party members who did not attend the party convention. In 2000 the Arizona Democratic Party offered Internet voting as an option in their Presidential primary. And Internet voting was used in the 2000 Alaska Republican Presidential straw poll as well as in a number of non-binding shadow elections. In the November 2000 Presidential election, a few hundred over seas military personal were given the opportunity to cast their absentee ballots via the Internet.

Most of the Internet voting trials went reasonably well. But given the small scale of the trials and the limited stakes involved, that is not a surprise. The Arizona election, the only large-scale binding governmental election to be conducted via the Internet in the US, did not experience any catastrophic failures, but did suffer from a number of relatively minor problems that would probably have been much more serious if they had occurred in an election in which the outcome was more contentious (one of the Democratic Presidential candidates withdrew during the voting period, leaving only one significant candidate on the ballot). The problems included incompatibilities between the software on some Macintosh computers and the voting system software, errors in voter registration logs that were being used to authenticate online voters, insufficient telephone help support, and a user interface that turned out to be inaccessible to blind voters. Later in the year, a large non-governmental online election to elect members of The Internet Corporation for Assigned Names and Numbers (ICANN) board suffered from voter registration problems as well as overloaded servers that caused many voters to be turned away from the voting web site.

The problems that have actually occurred in online elections to date are relatively minor compared with the types of problems that experts fear might occur if Internet voting was used in contentious governmental elections. At an NSF sponsored e-voting workshop in October 2000, security experts discussed a wide range of problems. Most significant were probably the vulnerabilities of the personal computer platform and the vulnerabilities of the Internet infrastructure itself. Individuals don't currently have the ability to shield their personal computers from viruses and trojan horses that might manifest themselves on election day. Furthermore, the ability to prevent denial of service attacks against voting servers or voters' Internet connections is limited. Hackers could design attacks to take out large portions of the Internet, or focus on neighbourhoods known to support a particular party [8].

The conclusions reached by workshop participants about the security risks of remote Internet voting were similar to the conclusions reached by the California Internet Voting Task Force in January 2000. The taskforce also outline security concerns, and suggested that if Internet voting was to be pursued, it should be introduced in several stages, beginning with Internet voting terminals in neighbourhood polling places. This first phase would not really offer any advantage to voters, but it would provide a more controlled environment in which to gain experience with Internet voting.

People often ask me why the security risks associated with Internet voting are different from the risks associated with online banking. Some have even suggested that Automatic Teller Machines be employed for voting, in addition to their primary banking functions. Voting is very different from banking applications for a number of reasons. One of the most important differences has to do with auditing and secret ballot requirements. When you do a financial transaction, generally you get a receipt. And periodically your bank sends you a statement that summarizes all of your transactions for the past month or quarter. You can compare this summary with the receipts you received for each transaction, and determine whether your bank made any errors. Furthermore, every financial transaction is recorded in great detail, along with information about who was involved in the transaction. But in secret ballot elections voters do not get receipts (if they did they could sell their votes or be coerced to vote in a particular way). And audit trails are specifically designed not to reveal the voter associated with each ballot. Also, while financial transactions occur every day of the year, perhaps peaking during certain parts of the business week, major elections occur on just one day. Even if we extended the voting period to several days or even a few weeks when introducing online elections, there will still be a relatively small window of opportunity that will be the focal point for those wishing to disrupt the election.

One of the primary motivations that has been given for remote Internet voting is the possibility of increased voter turnout. The idea of voting at home in ones pyjamas seems to be appealing to many. However, little evidence exists to suggest that the availability of remote Internet voting would succeed in bringing substantial increases in voter turnout. And any increase in turnout is likely to impact some voter groups more than others (in particular the people who have Internet connected computers in their homes). Thus, Internet voting could serve to widen the gap that already exists in the way different socio-economic groups are represented at the polls. Voting reforms such as extending the hours in which polling places are open, making it easier to obtain absentee ballots, and simplifying the voter registration process, have all been introduced with the hope of increasing voter turnout. But these reforms generally result in little if any increases in turnout. The reforms are none-the-less popular because they make it more convenient for those who would vote anyway to vote. And any increases in turnout tend to be among the groups that are already well represented at the polls. Before introducing Internet voting with the primary motivation of increasing voter turnout, it would be good to have convincing evidence that such an effect is likely.

Internet voting may be a good solution for non-governmental elections, especially for organizations that already have experience with vote-by-mail balloting. These elections generally are less interesting targets for hackers, involve smaller numbers of voters, and sometimes have less stringent secret ballot requirements than governmental elections. Internet voting has been used successfully in shareholder proxy balloting for several years. Many professional organizations are finding Internet voting to be a cost effective alternative to vote-by-mail.

4.   IS THE WILL OF THE PEOPLE COUNTABLE?

Many US citizens have begun to wonder whether it is even possible to determine the "will of the people" when an election is as close as the 2000 Presidential election outcome was. In Florida, it appears that the final difference in the tallies for the two top Presidential candidates was smaller than the statistical errors known to be associated with the voting equipment used. Since the error rates for each kind of voting equipment differ, and different voting equipment is used throughout the US (and equipment type even varies from county to county within most states), different error rates will be associated with each precinct. Statistically, in most cases we can expect candidates to be impacted by undercounts according to the proportion of votes they receive in each precinct. Thus, a candidate who does well in a given precinct is likely to lose more votes in that precinct to equipment error than one who does poorly. If it so happens that a given candidate tends to have more supporters in precincts that use equipment with higher error rates, and fewer supporters in precincts that use equipment with lower error rates, that candidate may be at a disadvantage in a close election simply due to the way voting equipment happens to be distributed in the state. Of course there are many other factors that may influence the outcome of a close election as well. But in the 2000 Presidential election, which appears to have been essentially a tie, the outcome may have been partially determined based on the distribution of voting equipment in the State of Florida.

Recognizing that computerized vote counting systems are often unreliable when the vote tallies for two candidates are within 1%, some states automatically recount ballots for races that are that close. With better technology, we may be able to reduce the statistical error associated with vote counting, but it seems unlikely that we will be able to eliminate it entirely unless we are able to develop an entirely electronic system (even for absentee ballots) that we have complete confidence in and which everyone agrees has zero error associated with it.

When an election outcome appears to be within the area of statistical uncertainty of the system, perhaps we would be best off declaring the election a tie. In many states, when two candidates get exactly the same number of votes the election is resolved through a game of chance. In some places, if no candidate gets a clear majority, the election is repeated until one candidate gets a majority. George Washington University Prof. D. Anderson proposed in a *Washington Post* opt-ed piece that close elections be held again. This idea is controversial, but probably worth further discussion. A new election or even a random outcome may ultimately be more satisfying than knowing that election results were probably determined by the idiosyncrasies of computerized vote counting machines and their distribution in particular precincts.

5.   THE BOTTOM LINE

Assuming we can find a better voting technology, how much would it cost? Cost estimates vary widely. DRE machines cost approximately $5,000 per unit. A system that uses off-the-shelf personal computers might be able to reduce that cost by as much as a factor of 10. Refinements on existing systems - such as putting scanners in every precinct that uses punch card or optical-scan ballots - might be substantially cheaper. Quotes in the media indicate that most states looking into replacing their voting equipment are assuming that they will have to spend up to 10^8. Replacing voting machines will cost a lot; most of that money will have to come out of state budget.

As I said from the beginning, there are no easy answers. It is my hope that states will proceed cautiously in adopting new voting technologies first establishing detailed requirements and certification criteria, and rigorously evaluating each candidate technology to see whether it meets the criteria.

The Federal government should assist in establishing requirements, but ultimately technology selection decisions are still probably best done at the state
and county level, where most election-related decisions are made in the US.
Technological systems must have the ability to provide audit trails that will
be able to demonstrate that votes have not been lost or miscounted. Their
inner workings and complete computer code must be available for the
scrutiny of experts (either under a non-disclosure agreement or as part of an
open source release). They must be tested for usability using actual ballot
questions prior to every election. And while we are investing in new voting
equipment, we should also make sure our new equipment is adaptable so that
we can provide secret balloting for the visually impaired and other disabled
individuals (perhaps by providing special devices for use by those people).
We should not rush to embrace new technology, such as Internet voting
systems, until we have evaluated it sufficiently and determined that it meets
our requirements. The technology development and evaluation necessary to
satisfy all these goals will be expensive. But by spending the money up
front, we are more likely to avoid costly law suits and maintain public confidence in our electoral process, something that is difficult to put a price on.

REFERENCES

[1]   Cranor, L., Cytron, R. Sensus: A Security-Conscious Electronic Polling System for the
      Internet. *Proc. of the Hawai`i International Conference on System Sciences,* January
      1997, Hawai, USA; http://lorrie.cranor.org/pubs/hicss/

[2]   Fujioka, A., Okamoto, T., Ohta, K. A practical secret voting scheme for large-scale ele-
      ctions. In *Advances in Cryptology - AUSCRYPT '92,* J. Seberry, Y. Zheng (Eds.), LNCS
      718, Springer-Verlag 1993, pp. 244-251.

[3]   Herschberg, M. *Secure Electronic Voting Over the World Wide Web.* MIT Masters
      Thesis, 1997; http://www.toc.lcs.mit.edu/~cis/voting/herschberg-thesis/index.html

[4]   Benaloh, J., Tuinstra, D. Receipt-Free Secret-Ballot Elections. *Proc. of the 26th ACM
      Symposium on Theory of Computing,* Canada, May 1994, pp. 544-553. http://doi.acm.
      org/10. 1145/195058.195407

[5]   Schoenmakers, B. A Simple Publicly Verifiable Secret Sharing Scheme and its Applica-
      tion to Electronic Voting. In *Proc. of PKC2000,* LNCS 1751, Springer-Verlag 2000, pp.
      293-305; http://www.win.tue.nl/~berry/papers/ crypto99.ps.gz

[6]   Saltman, R. *Accuracy, Integrity, and Security in Computerized Vote-Tallying. National
      Bureau of Standards,* 1988. http://www.itl.nist.gov/lab/specpubs/500-158.htm

[7]   Dugger R. Annals of Democracy: Counting votes. *New Yorker,* 64(38):40-108, Novem-
      ber 1988.

[8]   Rubin, A. *Security Considerations for Remote Electronic Voting,* 29th Research Confe-
      rence on Communication, Information and Internet Policy (TPRC2001), October 2001;
      http:// www.avirubin.com/e-voting.security.html

Chapter 3

VERIFICATION FOR ELECTRONIC BALLOTING SYSTEMS

Rebecca T. Mercuri[1], Peter G. Neumann[2]

[1] *Bryn Mawr College, Bryn Mawr, Pennsylvania, USA*
  mercuri@acm.org

[2] *Computer Science Laboratory, SRI International, Menlo Park, California, USA*
  neumann@csl.sri.com

Abstract: Electronic balloting systems are subject to a wide range of vulnerabilities that result in an inability to assure correctness in vote recording and tabulation. Risks that pertain to system design, misuse, and sociological factors are discussed in detail. Some standards that could assist in the design and testing of voting systems are cited. The difficulties in performing validation of fully computerized election equipment are described, with even greater concerns for Internet-based systems. A method whereby physical verifiability can be added to increase assurances of correctness is detailed.

Key words: Electronic Voting, Elections, Balloting, Computer Security, Computer System Standards, Cryptography, System Verification, Risks, Internet.

1.   INTRODUCTION

The use of computerized voting equipment has steadily increased world-wide in recent years. This move was accelerated by the events in Florida surrounding the November 2000 U.S. Presidential election, which caused government officials to consider the replacement of older voting systems (especially those using punch-cards) because of concerns for accuracy and fears of litigation. As well, communities using mechanical lever machines, many of which were first deployed for use four or more decades ago, have found these systems becoming difficult to repair and impossible to replace, since no new ones are being manufactured. The general perception regarding electronic voting is that it will be more user-friendly, cost-effective and reliable, tabulation will have better accuracy and speed, and voter turnout will improve. So far, though, the new equipment has not lived up to many of its vendors' promises and purchasers' expectations, in part due to secure design and ballot verification issues. Furthermore, existing fully electronic systems have a serious drawback that is discussed here at length: there is absolutely no assurance that votes cast are correctly recorded and counted.

Election systems may be used whenever votes are taken, such as for shareholders' meetings, election of officers in schools, clubs, societies and associations, award nominations, opinion surveys, and so on. These may have different requirements for security and auditability depending on their application. This chapter, though, will focus on the verification of voting systems that play a critical role in elective democratic governments. In this arena, it is imperative that citizens be able to accurately register their opinions by selecting representatives for public office who are viewed as capable of reflecting the views of the majority while serving their consti-tuents. Since this process is inherently adversarial, some controls (called "checks and balances") are typically established in order to better assure fair and correct results.

Beyond these checks and balances, most elective democracies also embody certain fundamental beliefs that are translated into election laws. These include such concepts as: "one person, one vote," "every vote must count," ballot casting performed in private, vote selling being illegal, and in-dependent election recounts made possible. Since these laws may differ sub-stantially between and within countries, election equipment is challenged to provide appropriate controls in multiply variant implementations. These issues have a serious impact on the effective construction and validation of electronic voting systems, since some of the constraints imposed turn out to be mutually incompatible.

2.   VULNERABILITIES

Inherent in the nature of electronic balloting systems (indeed, in all computers) are "gaps" that can intentionally or accidentally be used subver-sively. These gaps fall into three categories as follows:

1. **The technological gap** is that disparity between the expectations for the hardware and software, and what performance is capable of being delivered.
2. **The sociotechnical gap** involves the difference between social policies (laws, codes of ethics) and computer policies (procedures, function-ality).

3. **The social gap** focuses on the possibility of misuse, due to the gap between social policies and human behaviour.

The ramifications of each of these vulnerabilities for voting systems will be explored in the following subsections of this chapter.

2.1   System Design Criteria

Various technologies can be used in the construction of electronic voting equipment. Those that are paper-based, such as the punch card and mark-sense (optically scanned) systems, may only rely on computers for the tallying functions. Fully computerized voting systems typically use processors for all aspects of the election, including: ballot preparation, vote casting and recording, tabulation, and result reporting. Hybrid systems may involve non-computerized components, such as ballot-faces that are prepared by traditional printing. The fully computerized systems are of two formats - Direct Recording Electronic (DRE), where a voting kiosk (similar to an automatic bank teller machine) is provided at designated polling places, or networked systems that are used remotely, possibly via Internet/Web access.

Design considerations should focus on the elimination or mitigation of technological gaps. Generic criteria for the electronic aspects of election systems are suggested here as follows:

*   **System integrity.** The computer systems (both hardware and software) must be tamperproof. Ideally, system changes must be prohibited throughout the active stages of the election process. That is, once certified, the code, initial parameters, and configuration information must remain static. No run-time self-modifying software can be permitted. End-to-end configuration control is essential. Above all, vote counting must produce reproducibly correct results.
*   **Data integrity and reliability.** All data involved in entering and tabulating votes must be unalterable. Votes must be recorded correctly.
*   **Voter anonymity and data confidentiality.** The vote counts must be protected from external reading during the voting process. Any association between recorded votes and the identity of the voter must be completely unknown within the voting systems.
*   **Operator authentication.** All people authorized to administer an election must gain access with nontrivial authentication mechanisms. Fixed passwords are generally not adequate. There must be no trap-doors (such as reset buttons active during the election) that could be used for operational subversions.
*   **System accountability.** All internal operations must be monitored, without violating voter confidentiality. Monitoring must include votes

recorded and votes tabulated, and all system programming and administrative operations such as pre- and post-election testing. Any attempted and successful changes to configuration status (especially those in violation of the static system integrity requirement) must be noted. Monitoring must be non-bypassable, i.e. it must be impossible to turn off or circumvent. Monitoring and analysis of audit trails must themselves be non-tamperable. All operator authentication operations must be logged. Logs must be published after the election along with the vote results.

- **System disclosability.** The system software, hardware, microcode, and any custom circuitry must be open for random inspection at any time. Vendors should use copyright and patent rather than trade secret protection for their products so that full examination is possible.

- **System availability.** The system must be protected against both accidental and malicious denials of service, and must be available for use whenever it is expected to be operational.

- **System reliability.** System development should attempt to minimize the likelihood of accidental system bugs and malicious code. Backup mechanisms must be provided for critical data.

- **Interface usability.** Systems must be amenable to easy use by local election officials, and must not necessitate on-line control by external personnel (such as vendor-supplied operators). The interface to the system should be overly cautious in defending against accidental and intentional misuse.

- **Documentation and assurance.** The design, implementation, development practice, operational procedures, and testing procedures must all be unambiguously and consistently documented. Documentation must describe what assurance measures have been applied to each of those system aspects.

The above set of skeletal criteria is by no means complete. There are many other important attributes that election-computing systems need to satisfy operationally. For example, Saltman [1] notes that voting systems must conform with whatever election laws may be applicable, the systems must not be shared with other applications running concurrently, ballot images must be retained in case of challenges, pre- and post-election testing must take place, warning messages must occur during elections whenever appropriate, would-be voters must be properly authorized, disabled voters must have equal access, it must be possible to conduct recounts manually, and adequate training procedures must exist.

2.2 Misuse

Neumann and Parker [2] have defined a set of classes of computer misuse techniques. These are possible because of the socio-technical gap between what the computer can provide in terms of self-protection, and what actions are possible through malicious intent. The misuse categories applied to electronic balloting are as follows:

- **External misuse.** This involves the observation or theft of information relating to the voting system and may occur by rummaging through discarded printouts, monitoring systems via their RF emission patterns, or visually obtaining a password (by watching the keystrokes of an operator). These actions are generally passive, but the information obtained may later be useful in a more overt system misuse or attack.

- **Hardware misuse.** Passive actions could include the placement of a data collection device within the voting system, or obtaining a discarded ballot-recording device for the purpose of reverse engineering. Active misuse includes theft of systems or components, intentional physical damage (dropping, slashing of ballot-faces, cutting wires, insertion of glue in keys or switches, dousing with liquids, etc.), modifications (such as by adding Trojan horse devices), power supply tampering, and interference (magnetic, electrical, etc.).

- **Masquerading.** Consists of deliberate impersonation in order to obtain information or gain access to the system. Individuals might pose as service personnel or authorized operators before, during, or after an election. In this way they can collect passwords, tamper with hardware and software, or directly manipulate the programming and tabulation processes. Vendors and election boards may also employ double agents for other vendors or persons with hidden agendas.

- **Subsequent misuses.** These may be set up through the use of software Trojan horses that are time-triggered (so that they do not appear in pre- and post-election testing), or input-triggered (through the appearance of a particular data, command, or ballot casting sequence). Code for such misuse can be written to "self-destruct" following execution so that it does not appear in later system audits. Source code escrows can be rendered useless by involving the compilation or assembly process in performing the actual Trojan horse insertion.[3]

- **Bypass of controls.** Controls established within the system for security and auditability may be bypassed both intentionally and accidentally. Exploitation of design flaws in multi-user systems, by using installed trapdoor programs, may enable unauthorized access to election software and data by individuals logged in through separate accounts. Password attacks can be used to obtain system administrator status, from which audit trails can be turned off or modified to remove traces of system penetration.

- **Misuse of authority.** This can occur within the system by legitimate system administrators as well as those who are masquerading as such. Some of the misuses that could occur include: alteration of data, false data entry, and denial of service.
- **Passive misuse of resources.** This can include browsing of data, global searching for patterns, and access to groups of files that can be used collectively in a more powerful way than when used separately. Information gathered in this manner can generate statistics that could be used in subsequent attacks on the same system, or on others in remote locations. Direct access to vote totals, population statistics, and registration information can be applied in order to shift tallies in swing precincts in subtle ways that would be hard to detect. System-specific information, such as ballot storage programming or vote tabulation procedures, can be transmitted to other municipalities that have similar equipment installations, for use in large-scale election subversion.
- **Lack of timely intervention.** When this occurs in the event of a detected or potential problem, it can be viewed as a form of misuse. Actions can include inappropriate disposal or handling of election and computer media, non-reporting of an observed system attack, or other breaches of policy and procedure. Here a "cover-up" to save face in light of a system breach or malfunction can be considered to be an improper system use.
- **Uses leading to other criminal acts.** If the misuse of the system causes individuals to be illegitimately elected who have the intention of performing illegal activities involving misuse of power (such as inappropriate bidding for contracts, misuse of funds, or nepotism in hiring), there may be additional criminal consequences for the perpetrators.

It has been asserted that collusion would be necessary in order to tamper with an electronic balloting system. The above list of points of attack demonstrates that this is untrue. A single individual can perform system invasion, and since audit controls for access and use are often minimal or nonexistent, this can be done in a straightforward manner, even with only limited technical skills or knowledge. Such attacks may be motivated by politics, monetary rewards, power, foreign agencies, and terrorism, to name but a few reasons.

2.3 Sociology

Sociological aspects play a large role in election outcomes. The belief that one's vote actually "counts" is a major factor in the turnout on Election Day. For example, members of minority groups must feel that they can play a role in decision-making or they will not bother to participate. Some of the sociological issues that produce gaps in electronic balloting systems are as follows:

- **Personnel integrity.** People involved in developing, operating, selling, and administering electronic balloting systems must be of unquestioned integrity. For example, convicted felons, and members of organizations with large government contract interests, should be suspect. Election equipment companies based in foreign countries (to those where their machines are sold) may have questionable loyalties.
- **Usability.** Voting systems are required to serve a broad population in terms of age, physical abilities, education, and so on. Accepted methodologies for determining usability must be rigorously applied to system and ballot-face designs.
- **Fairness.** Care must be taken to ensure that ballot presentation does not favour some candidates over others. These influences may be subtle but can be revealed through appropriate pre-election testing.
- **Techno-disenfranchisement.** Voters must not be inadvertently excluded or restrained from full use of the voting system, because they are illiterate or inexperienced with the technology. Alternative balloting styles should be available for those who are unable to use the equipment.

3. STANDARDS

Standards for the construction and examination of voting systems have, until fairly recently, been primarily ad hoc. This section describes some of the documents that are available for standards use.

In the United States, the Federal Election Commission formulated a suggested standard for election equipment in 1990, but they lacked enforcement authority. The standard, criticized by some as favouring manufacturing interests, was only accepted by 2/3 of the States. In 2002, the FEC released a new standard [4], which is noticeably weak in the areas of secure system design and usability. Since this one is intended as a working document, it is hoped that future revisions will offer improved stringencies. In the absence of a required voting system standard from the U.S. Federal government, for now, its States and the municipalities within them must legislate their own policies in this regard. Similar situations can be found in other democratic countries.

The United Nations Department of Economic and Social Affairs, in conjunction with the International Foundation for Election Systems, and the International Institute for Democracy and Electoral Assistance, conducted a project on the Administration and Cost of Elections (ACE). The ACE Project resulted in a set of suggested guidelines for the design and management of electoral systems and procedures [5]. Although non-binding, the information presents a useful framework for consideration.

The Institute of Electrical and Electronics Engineers (IEEE) is presently developing an evaluation standard for election voting systems. The purpose of their project (P1583) is to "provide technical specifications for electronic, mechanical, and human factors that can be used by manufacturers of voting machines or by those purchasing such machines. The tests and criteria developed will assure equipment: accessibility, accuracy, confidentiality, reliability, security, and usability"[6]. Their detailed report is non-binding but could eventually be incorporated into election system legislation.

The accepted international standard for information security evaluation is the Common Criteria (CC) [7]. The goal of the CC is to provide security assurances via anticipation and elimination of vulnerabilities in the requirements, construction, and operation of information technology products through testing, design review, and implementation. Although use of the CC is currently mandated in the United States for government computational systems (typically military-related) that process sensitive information, and it has been voluntarily applied in other settings (such as health care), it is not yet required for use with electronic balloting equipment. In the U.S., oversight of CC product certification is provided by the National Institute of Standards and Technologies (NIST). Off-the-shelf products (such as microprocessors, operating systems and compilers) that are used in the creation of voting systems are often exempt from testing, but as they present a serious security loophole, only those that have received certification under the NIST program should be accepted. Another standard for computer security (though considerably less well-formulated than the CC) is the International Information Security Foundation's Generally-Accepted System Security Principles (GASSP) [8].

Both the CC and GASSP have great relevance to the design, procurement, evaluation, and testing of voting systems, and their use should be strongly encouraged. Both black-box (functionality) and white-box (code and circuitry) testing should be standard requirements for all voting systems, and the full scope and results of such tests must be available to the public for examination. Additionally, configuration control and management must be applied in order to assure that the products being used are the same as those that were examined. Strict security practices must be provided and applied in order to insure integrity throughout the lifetime of the systems.

4. SYSTEM VALIDATION

No matter how well-designed a voting system and its testing, certification and control processes may be, it is still theoretically impossible to demonstrate that intentional tampering, equipment malfunction, or erroneous programming has not affected the election data or results. This strong statement has its basis in computer science theory, since program provability is well understood to be NP-complete. The ramification of this for voting systems means that no implementation in hardware and/or software can be fully validated for correctness.

As bad as that sounds, in reality, the situation is much worse, since every voting system can only be as strong as its weakest components. Take, for example, any Internet-based balloting product - because of its connectivity, it is globally accessible for transmission and reception of data to/from any and all other Internet connected devices. Internet security features are large-ly add-ons (authentication, firewalls, encryption) and problems are numerous (denial-of-service attacks, spoofing, monitoring). Hence, interface to the Internet itself is a major breach of security practices, in that wide attack opportunities are provided that are not possible with stand-alone DRE kiosks, or closed-network systems. The Internet includes systems that are not subject to local laws, and whose operators cannot necessarily be expect-ed to comply with voting regulations. Off-site balloting introduces additional sociological problems involving voter identification, vote-selling, and coercion.

Some election violations have already occurred - an April 2002 hacker attack on Paris-based Vivendi Universal resulted in a large number of share-holder ballots being lost; and back in August 2000 a website named vote-auction.com breached New York State election laws by offering a forum where votes could be bought and sold. Despite what may be stated by vendors and researchers, there is no amount of data encryption or algorithmic processing that can secure Internet-based balloting systems.

Beyond this, any electronic voting system (networked or not) has the burden of assuring that each ballot is not traceable back to the voter (after the point of voter verification), and that it is transmitted intact through all levels of data collection and processing. The system must be capable of proving that it has:
- collected the ballot information as the voter intended,
- recorded it correctly (without voter identification information),

- transmitted it intact to the tabulation units, and
- produced a summary report that accurately reflects the contents of each of the ballots.

The requirement that this be done anonymously effectively precludes the use of any form of computerized security auditing, since these would involve time-based logs of all interactions with the system that could trace back to individual voter transactions. Hence, end-to-end internal validation of any fully computerized balloting system is not possible. There are schemes, though, that allow voter-verification of ballots, and these (described in the next section) can provide enhanced validation of election results.

5.   PHYSICALLY VERIFIABLE BALLOTS

Presently, fully computerized voting systems have been configured such that they rely on hidden, and often proprietary, self-auditing procedures. During an election, the system monitors itself for integrity and may even initiate a "shut-down" or "warning" mode if a problem is detected. At the end of the balloting session the recorded votes are tabulated internally, by the computer, and results are reported. Election officials play only a supervisory role, since they cannot actually observe the internal functioning of the machine on its ballot data (even if it were possible to do so, this has been precluded by trade secret and warranty protection clauses in some vendor purchasing agreements). Problems with this scheme are manifold. If the system is defective, it cannot be relied upon to provide warnings of erroneous operations. Malicious attacks may result in the appearance of integrity, such that pre- and post-testing data indicates correctness, for an otherwise corrupted device. Also, each of the many data transmission points can be compromised in such way that the totals look consistent, but are actually incorrect.

Basically, the voter needs to be able to independently verify that their ballot was entered properly into the system. A simple solution (described by Mercuri [9]) involves the addition of a printing device to each balloting kiosk. The voter makes selections on the computer system and then these are displayed on its screen and also printed. The voter confirms that the printout concurs with their choices (if not, an election worker is notified in order to initiate a corrective process) and then deposits the printout into a sealed ballot box. At the end of the election session, electronic tallies produced by the machine provide unofficial results, and are subsequently confirmed by the paper counts. If these totals differ, the printouts are used to produce the final result. Since the printed versions were prepared by a computer, in a human-readable format, they can be optically scanned or hand-tabulated.

These can also be retained for recount purposes if an election is contested. Independent agencies can later verify the paper ballots using their own scanning equipment, thus providing another independent check (note that this method can not eliminate the numerous sociological issues with on-line /Internet voting systems, so it is only applicable to precinct-based elections).

This physically verified voting method could be enhanced through the use of cryptographically encoded digital signatures for authentication of the paper ballots. It should be mentioned here that reliance on cryptography without paper recounting is insufficient for validation since cryptosystems, like the computers on which they reside, are also subject to various forms of attack. It is the fact that the voter has the opportunity to independently verify that their ballot was recorded as intended that provides the essential "checks and balances" for the electronic voting system.

Chaum has developed a variation of the physically verified balloting method that is of particular interest because it provides an additional way for the voter to later validate that their ballot was actually a part of the vote tally, without revealing the vote contents. This scheme requires considerable mathematics, but it yields a high assurance of correctness.

6.   CONCLUSION

Electronic balloting systems are similar to other secure computing applications in terms of the types of risks that must be mitigated. Even the best-planned systems, though, are still vulnerable, as Schneier wrote: "*...I have made a living as a cryptography consultant, designing and analysing security systems. To my initial surprise, I found that the weak points had nothing to do with the mathematics. They were in the hardware, the software, the networks, and the people. Beautiful pieces of mathematics were made irrelevant through bad programming, a lousy operating system, or someone's bad password choice*" [10].

Beyond these problems, voting implementations present additional difficult challenges for computer system design, because of the legal and sociological factors that must also be considered. Certain of these issues may always persist, so products should be augmented, as necessary, with non-computational solutions, like physical verifiability, for validation assurance.

REFERENCES

[1]   Saltman R., *Accuracy, Integrity, and Security in Computerized Vote-Tallying*, U.S. Dept. of Commerce, National Bureau of Standards, Special Publication 500-158, August 1988; http://www.nist.gov/itl/lab/specpubs/500-158.htm

[2]   Neumann P., Parker D., A Summary of Computer Misuse Techniques, *Proc. of the 12th National Computer Security Conference*, October 1989; http://www.csl.sri.com/ neumann/cs93. html

[3]   Thompson K., Reflections on Trusting Trust, *Com. of the ACM*, Vol. 27, No. 8, August 1984; http//www.acm.org/classics/sep95

[4]   Federal Election Commission, *Voting System Standards*, 2002; http://www.fec. gov/*****

[5]   IFES, UN-DESA, IDEA, *Administration and Cost of Elections Project*, 1998-2000; http://www.aceproject.org

[6]   IEEE, *Voting Equipment Standards*, Project 1583, June 19, 2002; http://grouper.ieee. org/groups/scc38/1583

[7]   Common Criteria Implementation Board, *Common Criteria for Information Security Evaluation*, ISO IS 15408, 1999; http://csrc.nist.gov/cc

[8]   International Information Security Foundation, *Generally-Accepted System Security Principles*, June 1997; http://web.mit.edu/security/www/GASSP/gassp021.html

[9]   Mercuri R., Physical Verifiability of Computer Systems, *Proc. of the 5th International Virus and Security Conference*, March 1992; http://www.notablesoftware.com/evote. html

[10] Schneier B., *Secrets and Lies: Digital Security in a Networked World*, John Wiley & Sons, 2000.

Chapter 4

ELECTRONIC VOTING: CONSTITUTIONAL AND LEGAL REQUIREMENTS, AND THEIR TECHNICAL IMPLICATIONS

Lilian Mitrou[1], Dimitris Gritzalis[2], Sokratis Katsikas[1], Gerald Quirchmayr[3,4]

[1] *Dept. of Information and Communication Systems Engineering, Univ. of the Aegean, Greece*
l.mitrou@primeminister.gr, ska@aegean.gr

[2] *Dept. of Informatics, Athens University of Economics and Business, Greece*
dgrit@aueb.gr

[3] *Institute for Computer Science and Business Informatics, University of Vienna, Austria*
Gerald.Quirchmayr@univie.ac.at

[4] *School of Computer and Information Science, University of South Australia, Australia*
Gerald.Quirchmayr@UniSA.edu.au

Abstract: This paper provides a systematic overview of the major constitutional and legal aspects of e-voting, together with their technical implications. All democracy-oriented legal and constitutional requirements of an Internet-based voting system are identified. Such a voting system has to comply with these, in order to encourage and promote the participation of citizens, without violating any of their fundamental rights (privacy, anonymity, equality, etc.).

Key words: E-voting, Legal Requirements, Digital Divide, Security, Privacy, Anonymity.

Acknowledgments: This work has been supported, in part, by the IST/*e-vote* project (*An Internet-based elctronic voting system*) of the European Commission.

1. E-VOTING: SUPPORTING PARTICIPATION

The diffusion of new information and communication technologies into every aspect of live and the dramatic impact of the Internet has led to visions, discussions and projects on e-democracy on a worldwide scale. Some (early) enthusiasts believed (and still do) that networks could some day replace representative democracy, enabling everyone to participate to the democratic process [26]. Over the last years there has been strong interest in online voting as a way to make voting more convenient and attractive, with the intention of coping with (to some extent) the problem of increasing abstention rates and raising low voter turnout, especially among younger people, foreign residents, business and holiday travelers, handicapped and elderly [6,18]. In order to maintain a central position in social processes and to adapt to the rapidly changing structures of communication in the information society, governments have to offer new ways and possibilities of participation and services through networks. These discussions and plans reflect the tendency towards the establishment of a modern formation of public and private life, where people substitute physical participation (to events) with using communication means [4,39]. Exercising political rights gradually loses its social and democratic nature in favor of an individualistic perception of life, which is a common characteristic of the overall social phenomenon [2]. However, democracy is not simply a matter of convenience: As e-voting is not merely a logical extension of everyday transactions and Internet applications in commerce and government [8,18], but a way to exercise a political right, deeply embedded in democratic traditions and constitutions, its introduction and acceptability depends upon its ability to respect, safeguard and promote the principles pertaining to this, most decisive, component of democracy.

The new culture introduced by information and communication technologies cannot and should not ignore the principles and values of democracy. Preconditions for this are transparency and confidence that democratic principles are respected [10]. The introduction of an e-voting system conforms to this demand if it respects fundamental democratic principles and citizen rights, and fulfills the requirements arising from these principles and rights. It is commonly accepted that parliamentary elections have to be free, equal and secret [6,12,13,15,16]. Furthermore, the principles of universal and direct suffrage belong to the European electoral heritage. The principles of freedom and secrecy, as well as the reference to fair elections are enshrined, explicitly or implicitly in a number of international instruments like the Additional Protocol to the European Convention on Human Rights or the International Covenant on Civil and Political Rights [41]. At the same time, the election procedure has to be transparent and subject to public control and scrutiny. Moreover, a democratic e-voting system should ensure integrity, availability, reliability and accountability.

Any attempt to introduce e-voting, i.e. a voting process, which enables voters to cast a secure and secret ballot over the Internet or an Intranet [23, 39], will have to address a series of complex constitutional and legal issues. Our paper refers to these democracy-oriented legal and constitutional requirements, which every electronic voting system has to comply with. Our

assertion is, that these requirements (should) cover every election or decision
-making process that takes place through voting, if - in view of the nature or/
and extent of these "private" elections - they could influence public discour-
ses and processes [23]. In light of their high significance, the emphasis of our
contribution is put on public elections.

2. E-VOTING AND DIGITAL DIVIDE: ACCESS AS A DEMOCRATIC PREREQUISITE

Increasing turnout could stand as a democratic goal by itself, a goal that
is being promoted through the introduction of e-voting procedures. However,
any concerns or recommendations related to electronic voting must be considered in the context of an agenda for making democracy more accessible and
meaningful [39]. The introduction of such a system conforms to democratic
requirements, if it is designed to encourage citizen participation in a quantitative (more voters) and a qualitative (more informed voters) way [15].

Differential access to online technology would be a serious issue and is a
primary concern. The experience gained in several countries leads to the conclusion that any election system can result in unequal access to the electoral
process. There are certain (categories/groups of) voters, who by having an
access advantage to technology, will be (unfairly?) advantaged by the implementation of remote online voting capabilities. The problem becomes more
complicated, taking into account that secure online voting would require not
just Internet access, but also additional security means to be available to the
voter, such as, for example, a digital certificate [21]. Offering new forms and
possibilities of participation, based on Information and Communication
Technologies (ICT), could lead to the exclusion of ICT illiterate voters from
the electoral body and consequently from the political process.

From this perspective the digital divide and access disparity constitute a
critical shortcoming for the feasibility and constitutionality of e-voting procedures. The digital divide can lead to inequalities and (indirect) discrimination: The introduction of e-voting could widen the access (as well as the participation) gap, as there is no prior guarantee that no population group will be
excluded from the democratic decision making process [4,24]. Undoubtedly,
the possibility of a citizen to vote at home is a "privilege", which could be
counter-balanced by the legitimate purpose, i.e. by increasing citizen participation and, consequently, the enlargement of the base of democracy. Therefore, in view of the access disparity and of the relevant risks, an e-voting
procedure could be introduced only as an alternative, supplementary capability. However, differential access is an essential problem, not only in terms of

equality of the voters. It also impinges upon the principle of fair elections and to the functioning of democracy: accessibility and usability of voting technology could be regarded as a critical factor, influencing the outcome of elections. One of the dangers is that e-voting could easily be used to manipulate election outcomes by structuring access to favor those who are the most Internet-connected [27,34], thus granting the more advantaged groups of society potentially greater influence over the election outcome.

In view of the current technological and societal trends, the right to "access to vote" must be extended to an interest in equal access [34]. Overcoming the digital divide by general access of the electorate to Internet polling stations or at public access points (kiosks) could be proposed as a solution, although "walking to the e-center to cast an electronic ballot hardly seems like much of a technological leap". Electronic voting will become democratically acceptable only when the majority of the eligible voters have easy access to the Internet [26]. An adequate non-discriminating procedure should be offered to the voters, in order to enable them to efficiently exercise their voting rights without any obstructions. From this perspective, the notion of universal access is not only critically important for ensuring social acceptability of ICT technologies and of the emerging Information Society [37]; it eventually becomes a constitutionally indispensable requirement [5].

Another dimension of accessibility concerns the voter capacity to use the technology to vote. Willingness to make use of and benefit from new voting possibilities is intrinsically linked with the experience of using the technology interactively [22]. The recent case of the State of Florida indicates that even low complexity in technology may result in very serious consequences for the legitimacy of the elections. Equal accessibility, as a precondition of democratic participation, means that the e-voting system to be introduced should not be complicated, i.e. it must not be "a test of computer literacy" [7]. On the contrary, it should be user-friendly and independent of the voter's education, age, and physical condition [15].

3. UNIVERSAL AND EQUAL E-VOTING (RIGHTS)

3.1 E-voting as an exceptional option

The kind, as well as the accessibility of the voting procedure affects the principles of universal and equal suffrage, which are among the cornerstones of democratic elections. According to the constitutional requirement of universal suffrage, every eligible voter can participate in the election process and nobody can be - directly or indirectly - excluded or discriminated. The principle of equality further requires that all participants, be they candidates or voters, should have equal chances and (voting) rights. The principle of universal suffrage primarily requires that every voter has the right to participate in an election process, while voting possibilities and technologies should be accessible by every voter. In this perspective, the supplementary and alternative nature of e-voting, as well as the necessity for publicly available and appropriate infrastructure respond to a constitutional requirement, embedded in many constitutional texts.

As e-voting improves the generality of election procedures by providing an additional option for exercising political rights [38], it prima facie raises no specific problems in relation to the principle of universal suffrage. A preliminary and essential question is whether the participation in an election through e-voting should be subject to the proof of special reasons. Do we have to distinguish e-voting, as a form of absentee voting, based on need and absentee voting based on demand? In most countries where postal voting, as a form of absentee/remote voting, has been established, only specific categories of individuals are allowed to exercise this option. According to the Dutch law, only voters who reside outside the Netherlands, or live outside the country because of their professional or other types of activities, or because of their (marital or not) partners or their closest relatives (parents), are allowed to vote by mail. As to the voting procedures, postal voting is allowed in Germany only if the eligible voter applies for this option on important grounds (infirmity, illness, absence, etc.), which prevent him/her from voting in his/her electoral district during voting day/hours.

Offering the option of remote voting for voters who are obstructed for some specific reason is undoubtedly in conformity with the principles of equality and universal suffrage, since it is justified by a difference of situation. The Federal Constitutional Court in Germany accepted the constitutionality of postal voting, when considering the balance between the improvement and broadening of generality, on one hand, and the risk of loss of freedom and secrecy of election - which is related to postal voting - on the other [33]. Some argue that there is no constitutional requirement to provide absentee voting and especially e-voting on demand [17]. Adopting an e-voting capability as an exceptional one (i.e. on the ground of the proof of a special condition, which prevents the eligible voter from physically casting his/her vote), is - from the legal point of view - a legally and constitutionally "safe" choice, well founded on the historical and legal basis that voting in a physical voting station is and should remain the rule.

On the other hand, the exceptional (and supplementary) nature of e-voting would strongly reduce the interest for innovation and for technologically supported participation in political processes. The evolution towards an information society has a significant impact on the ability of a citizen to exercise his/her rights and liberties. In the light of the political decision to improve e-government and e-participation, the introduction of an e-voting capability should be viewed as an institutionally equivalent and not as an exceptional option. In any case, such restrictions or other reservations do not seem to form an obstacle to the adoption of e-voting procedures [23].

3.2   Registration and identification as elements of equality and democracy

The voting right extends further to a right to exact composition of the electorate [2]. In this sense, eligibility is an element of peoples' sovereignty. (Secure) Registration and authentication of voters are the means of ensuring that the principles of universal and equal suffrage, summarized as "one voter, one vote", are respected and that elections cannot be rigged [41]. Voter registration systems and accurate voter registration lists are important for the integrity and the legitimacy of the election process. Any major compromise of the voter registration system could lead to election fraud.

Eligibility is primarily ensured through the registration of voters, who meet the requirements of eligibility, and through the identification of citizens at the moment of registration. In the context of a traditional election procedure, voters are identified and authenticated in the polling station by the use of adequate identification tokens. First level (phase) identification and authentication, which can take place at the moment of registration, is more reliable than online authentication; it could thus be considered as an additional guarantee for second level (phase) authentication. Providing a secure identification and authentication scheme of eligible voters is a *conditio sine qua non* for e-voting systems to be used in public elections. Identification and authentication of the voter are important at the time of the registration and/or request for e-voting, in order to avoid fraudulent possibilities ("first phase" authentication). Authentication at the time of casting a vote is another important procedure, which ensures that only eligible voters vote ("second phase" authentication).

An interesting question arising from this discussion is whether there is a need for a specific registration process in the case of e-voting and if such a procedure affects the principle of universal and equal suffrage. Taking into account that there will usually be no country-wide online voter register, a pre-registration for e-voting will be considered as necessary in order to avoid vote fraud. Thus, such a registration supports the integrity of elections and it cannot be considered as exclusion or discrimination. Registration and authentication procedures should not only be accurate, complete, immune from fraud, dynamic and up-to-date; from the principles pertaining to integrity, accessibility and equality it can be derived that it must be ensured that it will be easy for voters to register and authenticate themselves for e-voting, in other words that registration and authentication methods should not be a burden [7].

3.3 One voter, one vote

The principle of equality results not only in the right to equal accessibility to the election technology. It is furthermore required that each vote will be weighted equally towards the election outcome. An e-voting system must therefore ensure that the "one voter, one vote principle" is respected. In other words, such a system should prevent duplicability of the vote (either by the voter, or by a third person) as well as reusability of the vote (either by voting more than once online, or by voting online and offline) [15].

A critical issue, strictly related to equality, concerns the definition and duration of the voting period. Preventing multiple voting may require the definition of different voting periods for the various voting modes. Technical constraints and potential risks dissuade from limiting e-voting to one day only and especially to the election day, taking further into account that a possible unavailability of the system may deprive the voters of the capability to exercise their voting rights. Cutting off e-voting in advance of the election day is additionally advisable in order to avoid duplicability of the vote [6].

It is further suggested to extend the voting period to more than one day, so as to facilitate and encourage access to e-voting. However, the definition of a longer voting period may put in question the principle of equality [27] and raise constitutional issues, where it is provided that general elections shall be held simultaneously throughout the State. Where voting by mail has already been introduced, this problem has been solved by counting the mailed in ballots simultaneously with the physically cast ballots [12]. The possibility to cast an online vote should be temporally limited to the period in which postal voting is allowed [2]. However, such changes as the proposed extension of the Internet polling periods to three weeks, could and probably would have profound effects on both voting behaviour and political campaign techniques, with possibly further consequences to the integrity of elections [16].

3.4   e-equality of candidates

The role of political parties will inevitably be affected by the introduction of e-voting: the role and modus operandi of political parties will be changed dramatically insofar as new means result in immediate, but at the same time more complicated, political communication and possibly lead to a weakening of their influence potential [4].

The integrity and legitimacy of the voting act and, more generally of the elections, depends on safeguarding equal chances for parties and candidates who participate in public elections. This principle bears a number of implications and consequences for the organisation of e-voting procedures. Electoral equality requires that there are no deviations between the printed ballot and its electronic equivalent. A first requirement derived from the principle of equality is that electronic ballots should be edited and displayed in a way analogous to that used for the paper ballots. Changes to the electronic form of the ballot paper could be acceptable only if they are strictly necessary to facilitate the display of the electronic form [40]. Furthermore, the placement of electronic ballots in the (public) voting site (i.e. on the screen of the e-voting site) should ensure equal accessibility. Thus, the structure and appearance of site and ballots should not favour or discriminate against any of the participating parties. Major consideration must be given to the (organizational rather than technical) requirement that all parties should have equal access to the components of the voting system and procedures to control and ensure that it is functioning in a transparent and equal way [15].

4.   FREE AND SECRET SUFFRAGE

4.1   Free formation and expression of political choices

Freedom of voters includes two main aspects: the freedom of voters to form their opinion and the free expression of this opinion. The principle of free elections requires that the whole election process take place without any violence, coercion, pressure, manipulative interference or other influences, that may be exercised by the state, an organization, or by one or more individuals. The voter must be able to vote personally and without any extraneous influence.

By providing voters with an additional channel and easily accessible information and communication facilities, the introduction of e-voting has the potential to improve the quality of the choice. Some propose to provide voters with links to the sites of political parties and interest groups and argue for the provision of clearly designed menus, which allow them to rapidly locate the specific information they are looking for, before casting their votes, in order to promote the appearance of a more informed and active citizen [2].

Without denying the significance of information and deliberation for the ability to exercise political rights, it should be emphasized that the interactive and informative use/usability of the e-voting site could result in an undue influence of voters. Through the design of the portal or the site, de facto organized and controlled by the party in power, information and choice could be guided into a specific direction. Moreover the temporal proximity of information and vote casting could result in emotional options [4]. The requirements concerning free elections are applied in relation to the "online environment" of the voter. The freedom of decision may also be violated if a campaign message is blended on the computer screen, while the voter is casting her/his electronic ballot. In existing election schemes it is not allowed to advertise in (the vicinity of) the polling place. Thus, the e-voting procedure should make technically infeasible the advertisement of political parties/candidates on the e-voting website [4,12].

The democratic legitimatization of e-voting relies on satisfying the generic voting criteria of a democratic election system. This includes the free expression of the preferences of the voter, even through casting a non-valid or a "white" paper ballot [29]. In order to preserve the freedom of voter decision, the possibility for casting a consciously invalid vote must be provided and guaranteed [23,40]. However it is advisable that the voters be warned before casting a blank ballot, in order to avoid mistakes due to a possible lack of technical capacity and experience [39].

Coercion, vote buying and extortion are of great concern in connection with other methods of remote or absentee voting [14]. Where remote voting methods have been constitutionally accepted, regulators and judges have attributed major importance to the attestation that the voter has filled out the ballot personally. Providing an attestation declaration through a digital signature, instead of a handwritten declaration, could serve as an institutionally equivalent and feasible solution.

4.2 Secrecy as precondition of freedom

E-voting procedures may indeed pose new threats to the freedom and integrity of voter decision, beyond those that postal voting does [22,26]. The vulnerability of free choice is strongly related to the question of secrecy in e-voting. Secrecy is the precondition of a free political decision, a defining principle of modern democracy [41]. The requirement for secrecy mainly relates to two potential risks: a) the cast vote should not be an object of control of political opinions through public authorities, b) no person should know how a voter intends to vote or/and has voted [2].

In order to face the first risk, the secrecy of the vote, physically protected by traditional voting procedures, has to be guaranteed during the casting, transfer, reception, collection and tabulation of votes. None of the actors involved in the voting process (organizers, election officials, voters, etc.) should be able to link a vote to an identifiable voter or even to a group of voters. E-voting is a unique online "transaction", by which traceability should be excluded, while preserving the verification of the authenticity of the cast ballot: A further requirement is the existence of a clear and evident separation of registration and authentication procedures and casting-transfer of the vote, although the combination of secure authentication of eligible voters and guaranteed secrecy of the vote seems to be a hard requirement to comply with [31]. An additional difficulty is the need to reconcile secrecy on the one side and transparency, auditability and verifiability on the other.

The secrecy of a vote constitutes a fundamental principle, which can be satisfied through the personal and anonymous nature of the voting act [9]. As secrecy is intended to protect freedom of choice, no voter should be able to prove that he/she has voted in a particular way [18]. Confirmation of the vote, after the ballot has been transferred and received, enforces the confidence in the system and ensures the rights of the voter [6,30,41], but it cannot relate to the content of the vote [12]. Excluding the individual verifiability [1] of the vote casting process may appear - in view of the potential of new technologies - as a restriction of voters' options, but in fact it constitutes a protection against duress and undue influence.

Secrecy is predicated on voting being a private act in which the individual, in isolation and free from the immediate influence of others, makes up his/her political choice [22]. Coercion in workplaces or homes cannot be excluded. In workplaces, even if the employer, the supervisor, or the colleague are not looking over the shoulder of the employee-voter, intranet system administrators may monitor or record the activity at each workstation and obtain a copy of the ballot [18,20]. Since the employment relationship is not balanced, it is therefore suggested to avoid e-voting from the workplace.

But also "home voting" and the preservation of secrecy and freedom seem to be contradictory in terms [41], taking in account not only the spatial and social dimension of home voting but also the digital divide between generations: a conceivable scenario is a household that gives all its PIN numbers to the computer literate minor, who casts the votes for the whole family [16]. The French Data Protection Authority (CNIL) has recently rejected the application for a trial of internet voting for the French Presidential Election on the grounds that there were insufficient safeguards against impersonation and that home voting was susceptible to influence and pressure being placed upon voters [9].

These phenomena could not only violate the principles of secrecy and freedom but furthermore jeopardize the integrity of an elections outcome. It is an inherent risk of any form of remote voting. Coercion and influence can hardly be prevented by technology. Keeping e-voting as a supplementary option to traditional voting, as well as making available publicly accessible infrastructure, in sites monitored by public officials, allow voters to exercise their rights free of coercion of a third party [23]. Moreover, measures should be taken at the policy and regulatory levels, in order to impose compelling and enforceable measures against coercion and to sanction illicit behaviour.

4.3   Secrecy, data protection and confidentiality

Breaches of secrecy constitute not only a violation of political rights but also an infringement of personal freedoms and privacy rights. Privacy is not simply a refuge for individuals but an expression of self-determination and a prerequisite for the capacity to participate in social and political discourse [36]. Informational privacy is an integral part of the political process. Deliberative autonomy, meant as the underlying capacity for decision-making, plays a critical role in promoting deliberative democracy [35].

Political privacy [14] pertains not only to the requirements of secrecy, as analyzed above, but also to the use of data produced by e-voting procedures. In this respect, every processing of voter data during an election procedure should be conceived and organized in a way that privacy and confidentiality are preserved and guaranteed and the respective legislation, if any, is respected. At this point there is a strong overlap between data protection legislation and several constitutional clauses relating to privacy and confidentiality. Parties and individual candidates actively seek voter registers for a number of reasons, such as campaigns. Election data would undoubtedly be very valuable for political consultants, election system vendors and marketing firms [18]. Besides, some legislations explicitly allow or implicitly tolerate the practice of selling electoral registers to direct sales companies, credit reference agencies, charities etc. [41]. In our view, personal data and especially those relating to participation and electoral behavior, such as data necessary for registration, authentication or verification of calculation, should not be considered as a simple source of revenue for authorities [15]. These practices infringe Article 21 of the Universal Declaration on Human Rights, as well as Article 8 of the European Convention of Human Rights.

In addition, personal data related to, needed for or produced by election procedures must be used only for the defined purpose, i.e. for organizing and holding elections, and in a way compatible with this purpose [11,25]. Unauthorized transmission or disclosure of personal data to third parties is not allowed. Data collection and processing are subject to constraints, derived from the - worldwide, even with great discrepancies - admitted principles of finality and proportionality. Unauthorized access and secondary use of data may restrain voters from exercising their rights and consequently pose a threat to democracy. From the finality principle we can derive the obligation to take all technical measures, in order to anonymize all data that relate to an identified or identifiable voter, as soon as the objectives of their processing, including verification and control of the procedures, have been achieved. The proportionality principle imposes the processing of data, which are adequate and relevant for the e-voting procedures and they are not excessive wit respect to this purpose.

Specific issues are raised in connection with the use of sniffing software (or hardware), which permits the monitoring of traffic on a network: the data controller, in our case the election authorities, should take all necessary measures to prevent such a use. For the same reason, the use of cookies on polling sites should strictly be prohibited, taking into consideration that it may reveal personal information related to the e-voting procedure. Furthermore, concerns are expressed with reference to the use of mobile phones as a means to exercise voting rights: special legal measures should be taken in order to guarantee the confidentiality of voting data as well as of traffic and location data, not only for the authorities involved in an e-voting process but also for the providers of WAP (and similar) connections [15].

5.   EVALUATION THROUGH DEMOCRATIC CRITERIA

Elections are political events and e-voting constitutes a new mode of participation in political processes. Evolutions and innovations of voting systems must be evaluated on the basis of democratic criteria including transparency, controllability, accountability and - last but not least - legitimacy.

5.1   The transparency and control element

A key element of democratic, free and fair elections is the trust and legitimization that is gained by having a transparent vote casting and counting procedure. The traditional voting "technology" operates in a way that is transparent to the voters and to the other election actors, since in most countries votes are cast and counted in the presence of the parties' representatives. Openness is lost in online voting procedures: Electronic voting machines are completely closed [7]. Many of the processes are not visible: "one cannot see the voters ... nor their names being marked on the register. One cannot see the ballot boxes being sealed ... or the ballots being counted into piles" [39]. Note that ballot counting in public is among the factors which foster trust in the procedure [24]. The counting procedure in particular must be verifiable, transparent and open to scrutiny. Therefore, verification procedures of the accuracy and soundness of hardware and software used for counting ballots must be provided. A recount, as well as re-production of results and procedures should be possible, in order to guarantee the accuracy of results while protecting the identity of voters and preventing the traceability of their behavior [6,32].

In the case of online voting, neither the average voter nor the average party representative has the knowledge necessary to understand how the system works. Moreover, whereas traditional systems have the important advantage of decentralisation, which is a factual obstacle to large-scale fraud brake [24], online voting systems are inevitably centralised and rely on equipment handled by some experts in the absence of public scrutiny [7]. The loss of visibility, seen as a loss of (direct) controllability, may undermine the confidence in election procedures and may result in the loss of legitimacy of the outcome. Voters, parties and candidates must be ensured that there has been no malpractice. But trust in an online voting system means having confidence in the machinery and infrastructure rather than simply in the physical and administrative process [39]. As a result, in the case of e-voting much more trust in the technology is needed, as well as in the roles and characteristics of the persons involved (election officials, technology providers, etc.) [14,20].

Because voting is a public good, public control is essential. The regularity of the voting procedure, as well as the control of this regularity, are decisive and irreplaceable elements of democratic legitimization [3]. The regularity of elections must not only be affirmed by specialists but should also be confirmed in a way that creates public confidence. Openness must be preserved and encouraged [7]. All operations (authentication, vote recording, tabulation etc.) should be logged and monitored, while secrecy should be preserved. Infrastructure and equipment should be open to inspection by authorized bodies and parties' representatives [23]. An e-voting system should be developed in such a way as to preserve its controllability. Due to the increased complexity of hardware and software the degree of controllability remains questionable. In order for the voting process to be accepted, it is absolutely essential that all the software used during the operation is fully transparent. Non open-source software is secret by definition and there hardly is a way for anyone to be sure that the software does not include a hidden module, which is secretly aiming at manipulating election results. The question of an open source code appears to be dealt with as an element of an open and revitalized (e-) democracy [3].

5.2   Liability and accountability

Strictly related to the issue of controllability is the question of liability and accountability. As voting systems increasingly rely on software and network technologies, it is no longer possible for election officials to be personally knowledgeable or accountable for possible failures [18]. Liability is being "transferred" to other categories of actors and its nature is deeply changing. Furthermore, the fact that in e-voting a number of intermediaries, who are mostly private companies and who are inevitably involved in a public procedure [3], is involved must be taken into consideration; this complicates the issues of liability and accountability. Even if companies providing equipment and software could be made liable and controllable through appropriate contract clauses, the liability of other intermediaries, such as access, service, and network providers, remains a problem.

A critical problem is raised in relation to the nature of the network used for e-voting applications and its institutional implications. Global communication networks challenge the way interactions are regulated, implemented and controlled. The global nature of networks as well as trans-border online transactions challenge sovereignty paradigms [28] and constitute an obstacle to the control of voting procedures. The French Data Protection Authority (CNIL) has denied its "favorable opinion" to the application for trial of e-voting on the grounds that the server being used was situated abroad and was not subject to supervision by national authorities. Internet, an international medium, which is not governed by a sovereign entity [4], introduces the possibility of automated fraud and attacks that can be launched across national borders, and raises serious jurisdictional issues [18]. Voting online requires a degree of protection from fraud way beyond the current standards for everyday Internet use.

5.3   Reliability and security as constitutional requirements

Reliability and security requirements are derived from the democratic need to ensure that the outcome of an election correctly reflects the voters' will. A reliable system must ensure that the outcome of the voting process corresponds to the votes cast, i.e., that it guarantees eligibility, secrecy, equality and integrity [23]. Voting online requires a degree of security beyond the current standard for everyday Internet use [8].

Security is a multidimensional notion in the context of e-voting. It primarily refers to the (technically guaranteed) respect for secrecy and freedom, but in reality it covers the entire range of functions and election components such as registration, eligibility and authentication. The ballot being transmitted to the vote counting equipment must be an accurate and non-modifiable copy of the voter's real choice, with no possibility of modification anywhere in the transmission path, in any of the intervening networks and devices, including the infrastructure used by the voter (integrity). This is an extremely difficult requirement to comply with, given that the opportunity for an external attack would be significantly increased, particularly in view of the vulnerability of personal computers. Security further pertains to the availability of the system and to its protection against accidental or intentional denials of service, which could result in the loss of the capability of the voter to exercise his/her fundamental political rights.

Some researchers and practitioners argue that there is no reason to demand absolute security, whereas this is not the case in the other voting modalities. By invoking the proportionality principle, they support "optimum security", under given circumstances, which are necessarily subject to change, as opposed to "maximum security"[2]. However, security is not a purely technical, but a political issue as well. A threat to security would undermine not only the public trust in and the democratic legitimization of elections, but the election process as such, with wide-ranging institutional, political and economic implications [31].

Security aims at protecting the integrity, generality, equality, freedom, secrecy and fairness of elections. Security must of course not jeopardize the voting principles that it is called upon to guarantee; it has to comply with the requirements of transparency and verifiability. In conflict with other interests, such as the convenience of voting at a given level of technology, security remains, together with probity and accuracy, an integral component of the vitality and credibility of democracy. Security and confidence are not only means of making elections secure, but also means of convincing citizens that the system is secure [22].

6.   CONCLUSIONS

Voting systems have evolved in response to specific problems and needs of political systems. Virtually there is a dialectic/interactive relation between political systems and election systems, as the latter influence and reflect the way the former function and evolve. Technology could and should serve as a means of coping with the crisis of participation and confidence that democracy is facing in our days [10]. It could serve towards making democracy more accessible to citizens but it is not a panacea; it cannot itself revitalize democracy and redress the drift, just as convenience and "mouse-click voting" cannot replace participation.

Changes must be assessed and evaluated on the basis of criteria embedded in democratic constitutions and liberal political culture: equality, freedom, transparency and accountability. We should resist changes that would fail to achieve public confidence or to meet the highest democratic standards. Unequal access to ICT infrastructure and capabilities remains a crucial problem to solve, in order to enable all citizens to have an impact on political life and to avoid a re-construction of new political elites and a "restoration" of (aristocratic?) "two-thirds democracies".

REFERENCES

[1].   Adler J., *Internet Voting Primer*, www.votehere.net/adacompliant/whitepapers/primer.

[2].   Auer A./Trechsel A., *Voter par Internet? Le projet e-voting dans le canton der Genève dans une perspective socio-politique et juridique.*

[3].   Auer A., von Arx N., *La légitimité des procédures de vote: les défis du e-voting,* Genève 2001, http://c2d.unige.ch/vote

[4].   Bundesrat (Schweiz), *Bericht über den Vote électronique – Chancen, Risiken und Machbarkeit elektronischer Ausübung politischer Rechte.*

[5].   Burkert H., *Elektronische Demokratie: Einige staats- und verfassungsrechtliche Anmerkungen,* http://www.gmd.de/People/Herbert.Burkert/archiv

[6].   California Internet Voting Task Force, *A report on the Feasibility of Internet Voting,* January 2000.

[7].   CALTECH/MIT, *Voting Technology Project, Voting: What is? What could be?,* July 2001.

[8].   Coleman K., *Internet Voting: Issues and Legislation*, Congressional Research Service, Report for Congress, November 2001; http://usinfo.state.gov/topical/rights/democracy/inetvot110701.pdf

[9].   Commission Nationale de l' Informatique et des Libertés (CNIL), *Avis a des experimentations de vote électronique (Commune de Vandoeuvre-les-Nancy Societé election.com,)*, www.cnil.fr/actu/communic

[10]. Council of Europe, Parliamentary Assembly, *Impact of the new communication and information technologies on democracy, Report* (1) Doc 7772.

[11]. Council of Europe, *Convention for the protection of individuals with regard to automatic processing of personal data – Explanatory memorandum*, 1981.

[12]. Cybervote Project, *Report on electronic democracy projects, legal issues of Internet voting and users requirements analysis*, European Commission, IST Programme, 2000.

[13]. Digital Voting Group (Harvard University), *Legal issues*, http://www.ksg.harvard.edu/stp-307/group8/legal.htm

[14]. Dix A., "Electronic democracy and its implication for political privacy", in *Proc. of the 23rd International Conference of Data Protection Commissioners*, September 2001, Paris, www.cnil.fr

[15]. e-vote: *An Internet based electronic voting system, Legal and regulatory issues on e-voting and data protection in Europe*, EU-IST-2000-29518 (D. 3.4.).

[16]. Green P., *The Politics of the Future: The Internet and Democracy in Australia* (P. Green, Electoral Commissioner, to the Australian Political Science Association's Politics of the Future Seminar at the Australian National University, October 2000), www.elections. act.gov.au/adobe/PolFut.pdf

[17]. Hasen R., *Absentee Voting: Legal Issues and Unintended Consequences*, www.hss. caltech.edu/~voting/hasen_present.ppt.

[18]. Internet Policy Institute, *Report of the National Workshop on Internet Voting – Issues and Research Agenda* (March 2001).

[19]. Jones D.W., *E-voting: Prospects and Problems*, www.cs.uiowa.edu/~jones/voting/taubate.html

[20]. Kim A., "*Ten things I want people to know about voting technology*", Democracy Online Project's National Task Force, California Voter Foundation, January 2001.

[21]. Kubicek H., Wind M., *Wie modernisiere ich Wahlen? Der lange Weg vom Pilotprojekt zum Online Voting bei einer Bundestagswahl,* http://polbil.uibk.ac.at/pat/iud/pap/AK3 % 20Kubicek%20Wind.pdf

[22]. Local Government Association, *The implementation of electronic voting in the UK*, May 2002.

[23]. Mitrou L., Gritzalis D., Katsikas S., "Revisiting legal and regulatory requirements for e-voting, in *Proc. of the 17th IFIP International Information Security Conference*, M. El Hadidi (Ed.), Kluwer Academic Publishers, Egypt, May 2002, pp. 469-480.

[24]. Müller B., *Voter par Internet – Ein paar Bemerkungen*, http://c2d.unige.ch/vote.

[25]. OECD, *Privacy and Data Protection: Issues and Challenges*, OECD 1994.

[26]. Parliamentary Office of Science and Technology (United Kingdom), *Online Voting* (Postnote Nr. 155, May 2001) www.parliament.uk/post/home.htm

[27]. Phillips D., von Spakovsky H., "*Gauging the risks of Internet elections*", in *Com. of the ACM,* Vol. 44, no. 1, pp. 73-85, January 2001.

[28]. Reidenberg J., *Governing Networks and Rule-Making in Cyberspace*, 45 Emory Law Journal 911 (1996).

[29]. Rüß O., *Wahlen im Internet, quelle multimedia und recht*, http://www.Internetwahlen. de/project/ruess.html

[30].   Safevote, *Voting System Requirements*, Newsletter - February 28, 2001.

[31].   Schily O., *Politische Partizipation in der Informationsgesellschaft*, Speech in Congress „Internet-eine Chance für die Demokratie", Berlin, May 2001.

[32].   Schoenmakers B., *Compensating for a lack of transparency*, http://citeseer.nj.nec.com/ schoenmakers00compensating.html.

[33].   Schreiber W., *Handbuch des Wahlrechts zum Deutschen Bundestag. Kommentar zum Bundeswahlgesetz*, Köln/Bonn/München 1997.

[34].   Schwartz P., *Voting Technology and Democracy*, New York University Law Review, 2002 (to appear).

[35].   Schwartz P., Reidenberg J., *Data Privacy Law*, Charlotsville 1996.

[36].   Simitis S., *Reviewing Privacy in an Information Society*, University of Pennsylvania Law Review, Vol. 135 (1987), p. 707 ff.

[37].   Stephanidis C., *Editorial*, Universal Access in the Information Society (International Journal 1/2001).

[38].   Tauss J., Kollbeck J., *e-vote: Die elektronische Briefwahl als ein Beitrag zur Verbesserung der Partizipationsmöglichkeiten*, www.tauss.de/bn/e-vote.html

[39].   The Independent Commission on Alternative Voting Methods, *Elections in the 21st Century: from paper ballot to e-voting*, (UK, January 2002).

[40].   The Legislative Assembly for the Australian Capital Territory – Electoral Amendment Bill 2000 No. 2 – Explanatory Memorandum.

[41].   Watt B., *Implementing Electronic Voting - A report addressing the legal issues raised by the implementation of electronic voting* (Essex, May 2002).

Part II

TRENDS AND PERSPECTIVES

Chapter 5

TOWARDS SECURE AND PRACTICAL E-ELECTIONS IN THE NEW ERA

Mike Burmester[1], Emmanouil Magkos[2]

[1]*Dept. of Computer Science, Florida State University, USA*
  burmester@cs.fsu.edu

[2] *Dept. of Informatics, University of Piraeus, Piraeus, Greece*
  emagos@unipi.gr

Abstract: We overview the main e-voting schemes currently proposed in the literature and assess their security and practicality. We also analyze the security risks and discuss methods to minimize them.

Key words: E-voting, I-voting, security, cryptography, uncoercible protocols.

1. INTRODUCTION

There is concern in many democracies about the declining rates in voter turnout and more generally, the (perceived) trend towards political apathy. To reverse this, and to promote political activity, political reform is needed. One of the measures considered is to simplify the election procedure by introducing electronic voting, and in particular Internet voting. It is expected that this will increase voter convenience and voter confidence in the accuracy of election results.

Electronic voting (e-voting) uses digital data to capture the voter selection. With Internet voting (I-voting) we also get remote connectivity via the Internet. A few Internet-based elections have already taken place[1], while

---

[1] Examples are: the Arizona Democratic party's election (legally binding), March 2000 [36]; the Military personnel Presidential election in the US and overseas (legally binding), 2000 [21]; the Alaska Republican party's election (non-binding), January 2000 [35]; the UK local and mayoral elections (non-binding), May 2002 [18].

pilot elections are scheduled in several countries. Broadly speaking, each election involves four distinct stages:

- Registration. Prior to the election, voters prove their identity and eligibility. An electoral roll is created.
- Validation. During the election, voters are authenticated before casting their vote. Only one vote per voter is authorized.
- Casting. Voters cast their vote.
- Tallying. At the end of the voting period, all votes are counted.

Each of the above stages can take place by using *physical* or *electronic* procedures. In this paper we consider e-voting and focus on those types that involve at least one remote interaction via an open network such as the Internet. We distinguish two types of e-voting: polling place voting and Internet voting (see Fig. 1).

Polling place voting. In a polling place, both the voting clients (voting machines) and the physical environment are supervised by authorized entities. Depending on the type of polling place (precinct or kiosk [6]), validation may be either physical (e.g. by election officials) or electronic (with some kind of digital identification). Casting and tallying are electronic: the voting clients may be Direct Recording Electronic devices[2] (DRE's) or they may send their tallies electronically to a central site (e.g. by using a "secure" Internet connection, a dedicated line or an ATM[3] network [28]).

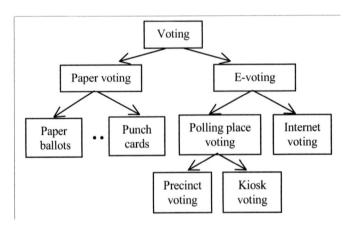

Figure 1. Different types of voting

[2] With such devices voters make their choices on a computer. Votes are locally tabulated and internally stored on a removable cartridge and/or hard drives.

[3] ATM networks have several highly desirable security features (privacy, well-equipped tamper-resistant terminals, national distribution etc). However there are reservations about their appropriateness for voting [32].

Internet voting. The vote is cast over the Internet and the voting client is unsupervised during voting (the voting client may be at home, at work, in a library, etc). Registration may be either physical (at the elections office) or electronic (with some form of digital identification). Validation, casting and tallying are electronic.

The security requirements for I-voting are more complex than those for e-commerce. Indeed, while checking the eligibility of voters and ensuring secrecy and anonymity of the ballot are no more difficult than meeting the security requirements of an e-commerce application, *ensuring these* and meeting other requirements such as a universally verifiable audit trail and uncoercibility, has been difficult to achieve in a practical and affordable way.

In this paper we assess e-voting from various security and practicality aspects, analyse security risks and discuss methods to minimize them. We also discuss cryptographic models and protocols that have been proposed to establish security in large-scale I-voting protocols.

2.   AN ASSESSMENT OF E-VOTING

To design an e-voting system that can be used for large-scale elections, it is important to identify a set of publicly acceptable and technologically neutral criteria. A system should be [28, 14]:

- **Secure**[4]. That is,
  - o *Democratic.* Only eligible voters can cast votes, and no voter can cast more than one vote.
  - o *Accurate.* No vote can be altered, duplicated or eliminated without being detected.
  - o *Private.* All votes remain secret while the voting takes place, and each individual vote cannot be linked to the voter who cast it.
  - o *Uncoercible.* No voter can prove the value of his/her vote to another party.
  - o *Universally verifiable.* Any observer can be convinced that the election is accurate and that the published tally is correctly computed from votes that were correctly cast[5].

---

[4] The cryptographic security of electronic elections is also discussed in Section 3.

[5] *Atomic* verifiability is a weaker version of universal verifiability in which voters can only check their own votes and correct mistakes without sacrificing privacy. It is useful when the cost of achieving universal verifiability outweighs its benefit.

o *Robust.* All security requirements are fully satisfied, despite failure and/ or malicious behaviour by any (reasonably sized) coalition of parties (voters, authorities, outsiders).

- **Practical.** That is, convenient, compatible with a variety of standard platforms and technologies, and accessible to the disabled. It should support a variety of ballot formats, its performance not drastically affected by the size of the election, and be tested extensively so that officials and the public have confidence in it.

2.1 Advantages

E-voting. Traditional voting systems are not perfect. In the US 2000 elections, a large number of residual votes (under votes, spoiled votes, uncounted votes, etc) were cast [7]. E-voting promises to ameliorate this error rate substantially. It also promises to improve accessibility for disabled voters. Furthermore, election results will be calculated quickly and efficiently, with less chance of human error, and long-term costs will be reduced by eliminating the expense of printing ballots.

I-voting. Uniform Internet access will soon be a fact of life for most developed countries. I-voting is very likely to increase voter convenience and therefore the potential voter turnout. Computers and equipment in public facilities can be made available to the voting public during an election period. I-voting could also play an important role in small-scale elections.

2.2 Disadvantages

While current paper-based voting systems carry a potential for small-scale vote fraud, with e-voting the potential for large-scale vote fraud is considerable because of automation and network connectivity [6, 11, 28, 44].

E-voting. E-data is likely to be more easily altered or destroyed than physical ballots. In addition, all kinds of e-voting systems are susceptible to a certain extent to *insider attacks* and *Denial of Service* (DOS) attacks. It is widely known that current e-voting systems have poor audit trails. Even worse, although there are strong cryptographic algorithms we do not have systems (e.g. platforms, operational systems) with adequate security into which the cryptography can be embedded [43].

I-voting. This type of voting will only become democratically acceptable when most eligible voters have easy access to the Internet. I-voting systems may also introduce high costs in terms of buying and up-keeping voting servers, standardized databases and routing systems. From a security point of view, I-voting is more susceptible to coercion attacks. Voters may also be required to secure their own machines before they vote, to guarantee accuracy for the election results. Testing and certification of I-voting systems may be difficult as such systems will likely rely on third-party (secret-source) components, such as operating systems and browsers. I-voting is more vulnerable to attacks than polling place voting:

- *At the voting client.* Worm-like viruses or Trojan horses may alter the vote before any encryption or authentication is applied to the data. An attacker may (remotely) exploit security holes at the operating system or at the web browser level [44].
- *At the communication level.* During a spoofing attack, an attacker could feed a voter with a seemingly legitimate web page. This may be enough to change the voter's vote. Communication may also be threatened by other network-based attacks (e.g. TCP SYN spoofing, IP fragmentation, etc).
- *At the election server.* Attacks at this level are similar to attacks at the voting client. Denial of Service (DOS) attacks are also possible. The *bottleneck* problem is similar to a DOS attack except that the jam is caused by an overwhelming number of legitimate contacts occurring simultaneously.

2.3 Security Precautions

There are several issues, both technical and policy related, that must be resolved before e-voting is publicly acceptable. Strong cryptographic methods must be employed to establish auditability and thus public confidence in e-voting systems, and voters need to be educated regarding the very nature of cryptographic assurances. Observe that if the voting clients and the physical environment are carefully supervised, such as with polling place voting, then e-voting may be feasible [6, 11, 28] even with an Internet connection[6] between clients and election servers. However for large-scale I-voting, additional precautions should be taken.

I-voting will become fully electronic (from registration to tallying) only when a secure and uniform Public Key Infrastructure for digital signatures becomes available. Accuracy and privacy over the Internet should be protected with strong digital signatures and encryption techniques. Browsers that allow both the encryption and digital signing at the browser level should be designed. Furthermore, research is needed on secure implementation of technologies such as SSL/TLS and SSH to deal with spoofing attacks [45].

---

[6] With tools such as *encrypting firewalls* and VPN (Virtual Private Networks) technologies, secure and authenticated channels can be built over the Internet.

Strong recount and auditing procedures, anti-virus systems at the host side, firewalls and Intrusion Detection Systems (IDS) at the server side should be employed. Furthermore, the use of redundancy and failover procedures (e.g. power backup systems) in election servers, as well as in communication traffic (e.g. high bandwidth connections) and strong analysis techniques, such as thorough testing and high-assurance methods, should be supported.

Finally, a robust security policy must be carefully designed to deal with all possible attacks and threats. New laws need to be enacted to protect the right to cast a secret vote and to criminalize behaviours such as coercion of the voter, hacking voting systems or individual votes, jamming a voting system or preventing access to the system, etc.

3.   CRYPTOGRAPHIC MODELS AND PROTOCOLS

Currently four election models are used: the mix-net model [10], the blind signatures model [23], the Benaloh's model [3], and the homomorphic encryption model [13]. We briefly describe these.

The mix-net model. Chaum [10] was the first to introduce the concept of a *mix-net*, which is a cryptographic alternative to an anonymous channel. A mix net is composed of several linked servers called *mixes*. Each mix takes a batch of messages (e.g. encrypted votes), randomises it and then outputs a batch of permuted messages such that the input and output messages are unlinkable. In the original proposal, a vote is first encrypted with the public key of each mix (in reverse order). It is then decrypted, shuffled and forwarded to the next mix. This type of mix-net is referred to as a *decryption net*. Another type is the *re-encryption net* [29], in which all votes are encrypted with the public key of the first mix, and then randomised re-encryption takes place at each layer in a verifiable way.

A useful property of mix-nets, especially in large-scale elections, is their universal verifiability. Mix-nets are also quite efficient (provided there are not too many mixes). Several methods to improve mix-nets in both terms of correctness and efficiency have been proposed in the literature (e.g. [30, 37]) No election system based on mixes has been implemented so far.

The blind signatures model. The concept of blind signatures[7] was introduced by Chaum [9] as a method to digitally authenticate a message without

---

[7] Blind signatures are the equivalent of signing carbon-paper-lined envelopes. A user seals a slip of a paper inside such an envelope, and later gets it signed on the outside. When the envelope is opened, the slip will bear the carbon image of the signature.

knowing the contents of the message. A distinguishing feature of blind signatures is their unlinkability: the signer cannot derive the correspondence between the signing process and the signature, which is later made public. This method, originally conceived for e-cash applications, was used by Fujioka et al. [23] to solve the problem of validating votes without sacrificing privacy: each voter encrypts his/her vote and then gets the encryption blindly signed by a *validator*. The voter un-blinds the signature and sends the encryption and the signature to a voting authority (this could be the validator) via an *anonymous channel* (Section 3.1), for privacy. At the end of the voting period the authority posts all encrypted votes and their blind signatures on a *bulletin board* (Section 3.1). Each voter checks that his/her encrypted vote is on the board and then sends the decryption key to the authority, also anonymously. The authority decrypts the votes and posts the tally on the board.

Several election schemes based on blind signatures have been proposed (e.g. [38, 40]). There are also several systems that have been piloted in small -scale elections[8]. An advantage of blind signature election schemes is that their communication and computation overhead is fairly small even when the number of voters is large. Furthermore, these schemes can easily be managed and realize elections with multiple candidates. However, they only offer *atomic verifiability*[5] and require that every eligible voter should not abstain after the registration phase, or else a corrupted validator can add extra votes on behalf of abstaining voters [14]. This is an impractical assumption. To get robustness, the power of the validator can be distributed by using *threshold cryptography* [17]. An implementation is given in [19].

Benaloh's model. This model uses a *homomorphic secret sharing* scheme. With such schemes there is an operation $\oplus$ defined on the share space, such that the "sum" of the shares of any two secrets x_1, x_2 is a share of the secret $x_1 \oplus x_2$.

In the voting scheme proposed by Benaloh [3] each voter shares his/her vote among n voting authorities. The shares are encrypted with the public key of the receiving authority, authenticated, and posted on a bulletin board.

At the end of the voting period each authority adds all the received shares to get a share of the sum of the tally. Finally the authorities combine their shares to get the tally. For robustness, a (t, n) homomorphic threshold scheme is used: then only t authorities need to combine their (true) shares. Results are universally verifiable.

---

[8] The SENSUS system [14] was the first to be implemented. The Davenport et al. system [16] was used to conduct student governmental elections. The EVOX system [25] was used at MIT for undergraduate association elections.

Schemes of this type (e.g. [46]), although structurally quite simple, have a high communication cost: each voter must cast his/her vote over n communication channels.

The homomorphic encryption model. This election model, proposed by Cramer et al [13], uses the special properties of homomorphic encryption algorithms to establish universal verifiability in large-scale elections, while retaining privacy for individual votes. With homomorphic encryptions, there is an operation $\oplus$ defined on the message space and an operation $\otimes$ defined on the cipher space, such that the "product" of the encryptions of any two votes v_1, v_2: $E(v_1) \otimes E(v_2)$, is the encryption $E(v_1 \oplus v_2)$ of the "sum" of the votes.

In [13], a variant of the ElGamal encryption scheme [20] is used. For this scheme the votes are *+1* or *-1* (*yes/no*). We shall briefly describe it. Let p, q, be large primes such that q is a factor of $p-1$, and let $g \in Z_p$ be an element of order q. The secret encryption key is $x \in Z_q$ and the public encryption key is $y = g^x \bmod p$. The encryption of a vote $v \in \{-1, +1\}$ is given by: (z, w) where $z = g^k \bmod p$, and $w = y^k g^v \bmod p$, where k is a random number in Z_q. (z, w) is decrypted by taking $w / z^x \bmod p$, and by comparing the result with $g^{-1} \bmod p$ and $g^{+1} \bmod p$.

Each voter encrypts his/her vote with the public encryption key of a voting authority and then publishes the encryption on a bulletin board, together with a proof of correctness: that the encryption contains a valid vote –we shall discuss such proofs in Section 3.1.

At the end of the voting period the authorities "multiply" all the received encryptions to get an encryption of the tally –see Fig. 2. The authorities then jointly decrypt this. The final tally can be checked for accuracy by all parties. So we have universal verifiability. For robustness the encryption procedure is distributed among n authorities using threshold cryptography [17] (Section 3.1).

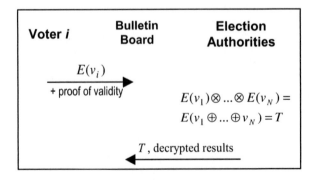

Figure 2. The flow diagram of a basic homomorphic encryption voting system

An election system based on the Cramer et al. scheme [13] has been implemented (the VoteHere system [1]) and piloted on a limited basis. A drawback of such schemes is their reduced flexibility, as the votes are essentially limited to yes/no values. In addition, the Cramer et al. scheme, which uses ElGamal encryption, has a relatively high computational complexity, if the number of candidates is large. Indeed, since there is no known trapdoor for the discrete logarithm, the only way to get the decrypted tally T from the decryption $g^T = w/z^x \bmod p$, is by exhaustive search. If λ is the number of voters and r the number of candidates, the complexity (number of multiplications) of an exhaustive search is exponential in the number of candidates $(\Omega(\lambda^{(r-1)/2}))$.

Alternative homomorphic encryption voting schemes have been proposed for which the computational complexity is either *linear* [2], or even *logarithmic* [15]. These schemes are based on the Pallier cryptosystem [39].

3.1 High-Level Primitives

Bulletin boards. These are public broadcast channels that enable voters to communicate with the voting authority(ies) in public. By using digital signatures, the communication is authenticated. A practical implementation of a bulletin board was proposed in the Rampart toolkit project [41]. Public key verification can be integrated into a web browser environment by using an established Public Key Infrastructure.

Anonymous channels. These assure the anonymity of voters. Besides mix-nets, which we discussed earlier, proxy-based systems such as the Anonymizer [12] and the LPWA system [33] have been proposed. A different approach, which combines several characteristics of both mix-nets and proxy-based systems is the CROWDS system [42].

Threshold cryptography. Threshold cryptosystems [17] distribute the functionality of cryptographic protocols to establish robustness. In the election paradigm, the tallying process can be shared among n voting authorities by using a (t, n) threshold public-key encryption system. In this case there is only one public encryption key, while each of the n authorities has a share of the private decryption key. Each voter posts his/her vote encrypted with the public key of the authorities. The final tally is decrypted by the voting authorities jointly. Privacy of the votes and accuracy of the tally are assured provided at least a threshold of t authorities is not faulty (or corrupted). Threshold cryptosystems can be further enhanced to deal with dynamic attacks by using *proactive* mechanisms [26] and *strong forward security* [5].

Zero-knowledge proofs. These are prover-verifier interactive protocols, in which a Prover proves to a Verifier the correctness of a statement in such a way that the Verifier learns nothing from the Prover that he could not learn by himself, apart from the fact that the statement is correct [24]. Zero-knowledge proofs have been used extensively in e-voting schemes. For example, to prove correctness of permutations in mix-nets (e.g. [27]), to prove the validity of encrypted votes in homomorphic elections (e.g. [13]), to prove correctness of encryptions in uncoercible protocols [34], and to prove correctness of blind signatures [45]. Interactive zero-knowledge proofs are *non-transferable*. However, it is possible to transform such proofs into non-interactive proofs that *are* transferable (universally verifiable), by using the Fiat-Shamir heuristic [22].

3.2 Uncoercibility

The notions of receipt-freeness and uncoercibility were introduced to deal with vote-selling and coercion in e-voting systems [4]. These notions are similar in many respects, however there are subtle differences. With receipt-freeness the voter is the adversary: the voter should not be able to convince a third party of the value of the vote, even if the voter wants to (e.g. for reward). With uncoercibility, the adversary is a coercer: the coercer should not be able to extract the value of the vote from the voter, even if the voter is forced to (e.g. threatened). In fact receipt-freeness is stronger than uncoercibility, in the sense that there are e-systems that are uncoercible but not receipt-free (e.g. *deniable encryptions* [8]). This is because, although a voter can succeed in fooling a coercer (uncoercibility), the voter is also able to sell the vote by pre-committing to the random choices made during its encryption [27]. For simplicity, we shall assume that uncoercibility extends to receipt-freeness. In particular, that voters can also be "self-coercers", i.e. information sellers.

Most of the solutions for uncoercibility presented so far in the literature involve two basic premises: the existence of *voting booths* (e.g. [4, 38]) and the existence of *untappable channels* (e.g. [27]). However solutions based on these premises affect the mobility of the system and can be quite cumbersome to implement, particularly with large-scale I-voting [34].

To avoid the use of untappable channels the voting scheme in [34] uses a probabilistic homomorphic encryption, with randomness chosen jointly by the voter and a tamper-resistant token. That is, the voter first encrypts his/her vote and then the token randomises the encryption without affecting the encrypted vote (see Fig. 3). The voter must be convinced that the token has not altered the vote during its randomisation. For this purpose a zero-knowledge proof is used: the token proves correctness to the voter in a non-transferable way (the proof must be non-transferable to prevent vote selling) [34]. Finally the token and the voter jointly prove (in zero-knowledge) that the encryption is indeed an encryption of a valid vote [34].

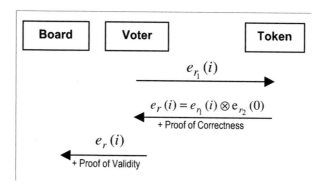

Figure 3. An uncoercible election based on tokens

Even in a vote-selling scenario, where the voter may conspire with a coercer, they will not succeed without the randomness of the token. Observe that in schemes with tamper-resistant tokens (e.g. smart cards), the tokens should incorporate strong identification mechanisms (e.g. biometric techno-logies).

Probabilistic homomorphic encryptions are also used in [2], only this time the randomness for the encrypted vote is jointly chosen by the voter and *self-scrambling anonymizers*. These are trusted external entities. As previously, the anonymizers must prove correctness of their encryption in a non-transferable way. In this case a *designated-verifier* proof [31] is used. However, this approach (as well as the one in [27]) requires an untappable channel between voter and anonymizers.

To gain social acceptance, I-voting systems must prevent voters from constructing a receipt for their vote. Policy makers and security experts often neglect uncoercibility, the main argument being that if voters can use a computer to vote via the Internet, then there is no way to prevent a coercer from watching them while they vote. The goal of I-voting protocols however should not be to prevent such attacks, but to prevent a voter from getting, or being able to construct, a receipt. In a *massive coercion* attack such receipts could easily be sent via the Internet to a coercer.

4.   CONCLUSION

Due to our increased reliance on the Internet, it is inevitable that ultimately e-voting, and especially I-voting will replace traditional voting. However this will only happen when security issues such as privacy, voter identification and uncoercibility are first addressed.

In the cryptographic literature on e-voting only few protocols offer provable security. Furthermore, the demands placed on voters are usually impractical for large-scale environments. There is an urgent need for more research on secure and efficient cryptographic techniques to support electronic elections.

A well-designed e-voting system should produce an audit trail that is even stronger than that of conventional systems (including paper-based systems). Future of e-voting systems will exploit current technologies and tools including *smart cards*, *biometrics* (e.g. voice, fingerprint, retinal recognition - for identification), as well as *mobile* voting clients (e.g. hand-held organizers, cell phones, etc). Research is needed to determine to what extent such technologies are viable for e-voting.

REFERENCES

[1]   Adler, J., Dai, W., Green, R., Neff, A., "Computational Details of the VoteHere Homomorphic Election System". November 2000, http://www.votehere.net/ada_ compliant

[2]   Baudron, O., Fouque, P., Pointcheval, D., Poupard, G., Stern, J. "Practical Multi-Candidate Election System". In *20th ACM Symposium on Principles of Distributed Computing*, ACM, pp. 274-283, 2001.

[3]   Benaloh, J. "Verifiable Secret-Ballot Elections". PhD Thesis, Yale University, 1987.

[4]   Benaloh, J., Tuinstra, D. "Receipt-Free Secret-Ballot Elections". In *26th Annual ACM Symposium on Theory of Computing*, ACM, pp. 544-553, 1994.

[5]   Burmester, M., Chrissikopoulos, V., Kotzanikolaou, P., and Magkos, E. "Strong Forward Security". In *IFIP-SEC '01*, Kluwer Academic Publishers, pp. 109-119, 2001.

[6]   California Internet Voting Task Force. *A Report on the Feasibility of Internet Voting*, Jan 2000. http://www.ss.ca.gov/executive/ivote/

[7]   CALTEC/MIT. *Voting Technology Project*, 2001, http://www.vote.caltech.edu/reports/

[8]   Canetti, R., Dwork, C., Naor, M., Ostrovsky, R. "Deniable Encryption". In *CRYPTO '97*, LNCS 1294, Springer-Verlag, pp. 90-104, 1997.

[9]   Chaum, D. "Blind Signatures for Untraceable Payments". In *CRYPTO '82*, Plenum Press, pp. 199-203, 1982.

[10]   Chaum, D. "Untraceable Electronic Mail, Return Addresses, and Digital Pseudonyms". In *Com. of the ACM*, 24(2), pp. 84-88, 1981.

[11] Coleman, S. "Elections in the 21st Century: From Paper Ballot to E-Voting". Report by the Independent Commission on Alternative Voting Methods, London, Electoral Reform Society, February 2002.

[12] Community ConneXion, Inc., http://www.anonymizer.com

[13] Cramer, R., Gennaro, R., Schoenmakers, B. "A Secure and Optimally Efficient Multi-Authority Election Scheme". In *EUROCRYPT '97*, Springer-Verlag, pp. 103-118, 1997.

[14] Cranor, L., Cytron, R. "Sensus: A Security-Conscious Electronic Polling System for the Internet". In *Hawaii International Conference on System Sciences*, Hawaii, 1997.

[15] Damgard, I., Juric, M. "A Generalization, a Simplification and Some Applications of Pallier's Probabilistic Public-Key System". In *Public Key Cryptography '01*, LNCS 1992, Springer-Verlag, pp. 119-136, 2001.

[16] Davenport, B., Newberger, A., Woodard, J. "Creating a Secure Digital Voting Protocol for Campus Elections". Princeton University, 1996. http://www.princeton.edu/

[17] Desmedt, Y. "Threshold Cryptography". In *European Transactions on Telecommunications*, 5(4), pp. 449-457, 1994.

[18] DTLR News Release. "May Elections to Trial Online Voting", 2002, http://www.press. dtlr.gov.uk/pns/DisplayPN.cgi?pi_id=2002_0033

[19] Durette, B. W. "Multiple Administrators for Electronic Voting". Bachelor's Thesis, MIT, May 1999.

[20] ElGamal, T. "A Public-key Cryptosystem and a Signature Scheme Based on Discrete Logarithms". In *IEEE Transactions on Information Theory*, 31(4), pp. 469-472, 1985.

[21] Federal Voting Assistance Program. *Voting Over the Internet Project*, www.fvap.ncr. gov/voireport.pdf.

[22] Fiat, A., Shamir, A. "How to Prove yourself: Practical Solutions to Identification and Signature Problems". In *CRYPTO '86*, LNCS 263, Springer-Verlag, pp. 186-194, 1987.

[23] Fujioka, A., Okamoto, T., Ohta, K. "A Practical Secret Voting Scheme for Large Scale Elections". In *AUSCRYPT '92*, LNCS 718, Springer-Verlag, pp. 244-251, 1993.

[24] Goldwasser, S., Micali S., Rackoff, C., "The Knowledge Complexity of Interactive Proof Systems". In *SIAM Journal on Computing*, 18(1), pp. 186-208, 1989.

[25] Herschberg, M. "Secure Electronic Voting Using the World Wide Web". Master's Thesis, MIT, June 1997. http://theory.lcs.mit.edu/~cis/theses/herschberg-masters.pdf

[26] Herzberg, A., Jakobsson, M., Jarecki, S., Krawczyk H., Yung, M., "Proactive Public-key and Signature Schemes". In *4th ACM Annual Conference on Computer and Communications Security*, ACM, pp. 100-110, 1997.

[27] Hirt, M., Sako, K. "Efficient Receipt-Free Voting Based on Homomorphic Encryption". In *EUROCRYPT 2000*, LNCS 1807, Springer-Verlag, pp 539-556, 2000.

[28] Internet Policy Institute. *Report of the National Workshop on Internet Voting*, March 2001, www.internetpolicy.org.

[29] Jakobsson, M. "Flash Mixing". In *18th ACM Symposium on Principles of Distributed Computing PODC '99*, ACM, pp. 83-89, 1999.

[30] Jakobsson, M., Juels, A., Rivest, R. L. "Making Mix Nets Robust for Electronic Voting by Randomized Partial Checking", 2002. http://theory.lcs.mit.edu/~rivest

[31] Jakobsson, M., Sako, K., Impagliazzo, R. "Designated Verifier Proofs and their Applications". In *EUROCRYPT '96*, LNCS 1070, Springer-Verlag, pp. 143-154, 1996.

[32] Jefferson, D. "ATM Network Voting: A non-Starter". The Risks Digest, 21(15), 2000, http://catless.ncl.ac.uk/Risks/21.15.html#subj2

[33] The Lucent Personalized Web Assistant, http://lpwa.com

[34] Magkos, E., Burmester, M., Chrissikopoulos V. "Receipt-Freeness in Large-scale Elections without Untappable Channels". In *1st IFIP Conference on E-Commerce/E-business/E-Government*, Kluwer Academic Publishers, pp. 683-693, 2001.

[35] May, P. "Alaskan Voters are Pioneers". Mercury News, Jan. 25, 2000, http://www.mercurycenter.com/svtech/news/indepth/docs/vote012600.htm

[36] Mohen, J., Glidden, J. "The Case for Internet Voting". In *Com.of the ACM*, 44(1), 2001.

[37] Neff, A. "A verifiable Secret Shuffle and its Application to E-voting". In *8th ACM Conference on Computer and Communications Security*, Philadelphia, 2001, http://www.votehere.net

[38] Okamoto, T. "Receipt-Free Electronic Voting Schemes for Large Scale Elections". In *5th Security Protocols Workshop '97*, LNCS 1163, Springer-Verlag, pp. 125-132, 1997.

[39] Pallier, P. "Public-Key Cryptosystems Based on Discrete Logarithm Residues". In *EUROCRYPT '99*, LNCS 1592, Springer-Verlag, pp. 223-238, 1999.

[40] Petersen, H., Horster, P., Michels, M., "Blind Multisignature Schemes and their Relevance to Electronic Voting". In 11th Annual Computer Security Applications Conference, IEEE Press, pp. 149-155, 1995.

[41] Reiter, M., "The Rampart Toolkit for Building High-Integrity Services". In *Theory and Practice in Distributed Systems*, LNCS 938, Springer-Verlag, pp. 99-110, 1995.

[42] Reiter M., Rubin A. "Crowds, Anonymity for Web Transactions", DIMACS Technical Report 97-15, April 1997, http://www.research.att.com/projects/crowds/

[43] Rivest, R. "Electronic Voting". In *Financial Cryptography '01*, http://theory.lcs.mit.edu/~rivest/Rivest-ElectronicVoting-ppt.pdf

[44] Rubin, A. "Security Considerations for Remote E-Voting over the Internet", AT&T Labs Research, June 2001. http://avirubin.com/e-voting.security.html

[45] Schneier, B., *Applied Cryptography - Protocols, Algorithms and Source Code in C*. 2nd Edition, 1996.

[46] Schoenmakers, B. "A Simple Publicly Verifiable Secret Sharing Scheme and its Application to Electronic Voting". In *CRYPTO '99*, LNCS 1666, Springer-Verlag, pp. 148-164, 1999.

Chapter 6

THE THEORY AND IMPLEMENTATION OF AN ELECTRONIC VOTING SYSTEM

Ivan Damgård[1], Jens Groth[1,2], Gorm Salomonsen[2]

[1] *BRICS, Dept. of Computer Science, University of Aarhus, Denmark*
  ivan@brics.dk

[2] *Cryptomathic A/S, Århus C, Denmark*
  jens.groth@cryptomathic.dk, gorm.salomonsen@cryptomathic.dk

Abstract: We describe the theory behind a practical voting scheme based on homomorphic encryption. We give an example of an ElGamal-style encryption scheme, which can be used as the underlying cryptosystem. Then, we present efficient honest verifier zero-knowledge proofs that make the messages in the voting scheme shorter and easier to compute and verify, for voters as well as authorities, than in currently known schemes. Finally, we discuss various issues connected with the security of a practical implementation of the scheme for on-line voting. Notably, this includes minimizing risks that are beyond what can be handled with cryptography, such as attacks that try to substitute the software running on client machines.

Key words: Voting, Homomorphic Encryption, Zero-knowledge Proofs.

1.   INTRODUCTION

Voting schemes are one of the most important examples of advanced cryptographic protocols with immediate potential for practical applications. Such protocols should of course have security properties similar to those of ordinary paper based elections, but the fact that digital communication is used may also open up new possibilities. Informally, the most important goals for electronic voting schemes are: a) Privacy: Only the final result is made public, no additional information about votes will leak; b) Robustness: The result reflects all submitted and well-formed ballots correctly, even if some voters and/or possibly some of the entities running the election cheat; c) Universal verifiability: After the election, the result can be verified by anyone. Other properties may be considered as well, such as receipt-free-ness. In a receipt-free election voters are not able to prove that they voted for a particular candidate after the election, thereby discouraging vote-buying or coercing.

Various fundamentally different approaches to electronic voting are known in the literature. One may use *blind signatures and anonymous channels* [13], where the channels can be implemented using *MIX nets* (see [20,1] for instance) or be based on some physical assumption. The idea in such a scheme is that a voter prepares a ballot in cleartext, i.e., a message stating for whom he votes. He then interacts with an authority that can verify that he is eligible to vote and has not already voted. If this is the case, the authority issues a blind signature on the ballot. Informally, this means that the voter obtains the authority's digital signature on the ballot, without the authority learning any information about the contents of the ballot. On the other hand, a voter cannot obtain such a signature without interacting with the authority, and is therefore prevented from voting several times. Finally, all voters send their ballots to another authority that is responsible for counting votes. In order to preserve the privacy of voters, this must be done through an anonymous channel. Such a channel can be implemented based on cryptography, using a so-called MIX network or it may be based on physical assumptions. After all ballots have been received, votes can be counted directly. Ballots without the relevant authority's signature are ignored.

Another approach is to use several servers to count the votes and have voters *verifiably secret share* votes among the servers [8,6]. In such a scheme, the voter interacts with all servers. Each server gets a *share* of each voter's ballot. These shares are constructed with respect to a threshold t in such a way that the servers together have complete information on each ballot, but any set of at most t servers has no information at all. The voter must convince all servers that the shares were correctly constructed, and so he is prevented from voting twice or voting incorrectly. Once the votes have been cast, the set of all servers can interact and compute the result of the election without any side information becoming public.

A final approach is to use *homomorphic encryption* [9,11]. In such a system, a voter simply publishes an encryption of his vote, represented as a number. This encryption is done using a public-key cryptosystem, i.e., there is a public key known by everyone that can be used for encrypting each vote. When submitting his encrypted vote, the voter must identify himself to prove that he is eligible to vote and has not voted before. Furthermore, he must prove knowledge of the fact that his encryption contains a valid vote. Because all individual votes will remain encrypted and the proof is zero-knowledge, this does not violate privacy. On the other hand, because we use homomorphic encryption, the election result can be computed efficiently. This is because the cryptosystem comes with a method by which two encryptions of, say, numbers a and b can be combined to produce a new encryption that is guaranteed to contain a+b. By repeated use of this method, all votes can be "implicitly added" together without decrypting anything. This will produce an encryption of the result and so finally all that is needed is to decrypt this. This can be done securely assuming that the private key needed for this has been *secret-shared* among a set of authorities, each running a server responsible for helping computing the result. Each server holds a share of the private key. The shares have to be constructed with respect to a threshold value t so that no information about the private key leaks as long as at most t severs are corrupt, or are broken into by a hacker. On the other hand, if at least t+1 servers behave correctly, then a decryption operation can be executed. This is also known as *threshold decryption.*

If the total number of servers participating is n, then we can set t to just below n/2, i.e. $t = \lfloor (n-1)/2 \rfloor$. Then, we are guaranteed that if a majority of the servers are in operation and are not corrupted, the election result, and only that will be decrypted. In practice, one may imagine that some public institutions and political parties could be running these servers in order to create broad trust in the process.

The last approach seems the most practical of the three discussed: anonymous channels are quite difficult to implement. Even the best implementations (based on MIX nets) require that all votes have been cast before any processing can be done, and so they may introduce a significant delay in getting the final result. The second approach requires each voter to interact with every authority, and is hardly practical either. Hence this paper deals only with variants of the approach based on homomorphic encryption.

2.   WHICH CRYPTOSYSTEM CAN WE USE?

The introduction above shows that the approach on which we concentrate here requires a homomorphic public-key cryptosystem with threshold decryption. In addition, some other technical properties come in handy; we discuss those in more detail below.

In [9], the use of ElGamal encryption is suggested. This is possible, but leads to efficiency problems if the number of candidates is large. Most of these problems can be solved by using Paillier's cryptosystem [21], or the generalization suggested by Damgård and Jurik in [11]. In that case the zero-knowledge protocols and threshold decryption presented in [4,11] are also required. In this paper, we suggest an alternative cryptosystem. It is based on a different intractability assumption (a general form of the Decision Diffie-Hellman assumption) and has other properties that neither Paillier nor El Gamal can satisfy at the same time.

We present the system from a general point of view: let R be a ring, fix some $g \in R$ and let $G = \langle g \rangle$. We will assume that one can compute addition and multiplication efficiently in R and that a number T can be computed easily, so that $T \geq \text{ord}(g)^2$. This just requires that some upper bound on $\text{ord}(g)$ is publicly known. As for intractability assumption, we assume that a *generalized DDH assumption* holds with respect to R and g, i.e., given R, g, triples of form g^a, b^b, g^{ab} where a, b are random in $[0..T]$, and they are computationally indistinguishable from triples of form g^a, b^b, g^c where a, b, c are random in $[0..T]$. Note that the choice of T ensures that the distribution of elements such as g^a is statistically close to uniform in $\langle g \rangle$ as long as $\text{ord}(g)$ is large.

It is now clear that we can define an ElGamal style cryptosystem where the public key is $R, g, h = g^x$ where x is random in $[0..T]$, and where the private key is x. The message space is $\langle g \rangle$, and to encrypt a message m, choose $r \in [0..T]$ at random and output $E(m,r) = (g^r, m\, h^r)$. Decryption of a ciphertext (u,v) takes place by computing $v(u^x)^{-1}$. Clearly, this system is semantically secure under the generalized DDH assumption.

This system is not homomorphic as we required above. As a first step to solve this problem, we can redefine the system by fixing an element $w \in \langle g \rangle$, and letting the message space be instead $Z_{\text{ord}(w)}$. Now, we can define $E(m,r) = (g^r, w^m\, h^r)$. This does not affect the semantic security, but of course implies that we have the homomorphic property $E(m,r)E(m',r') = E(m+m' \bmod \text{ord}(w), r+r')$. But as the case was with the ElGamal variant used in [9], we have the problem that to decrypt, we must find discrete logarithms to the base w, since the basic decryption from above only allows us to compute w^m.

The point is that in some rings, one can find elements for which computing the discrete logarithm is in fact easy. Suppose we have $w = \alpha + \beta$. Then:

$$w^i = (\alpha + \beta)^i = \sum_{j=0}^{i} \binom{i}{j} \alpha^j \beta^{i-j}$$

using the standard binomial expansion. Since i will typically be exponentially large, this is normally not going to be useful towards computing i. But if α is nilpotent, that is $\alpha^j = 0$ for some small j, then most of the terms in the expansion disappear, and it may be feasible to compute i. As a concrete example of this, we can use let $R = Z_n^{s+1*}$, where $n = pq$ is an RSA modulus where $\gcd((p-1),(q-1)) = 2$. We let g have Jacobi symbol 1 and maximal order, that is $\text{ord}(g) = n^s(p-1)(q-1)/2$. Now, $n \in R$ is nilpotent, since $n^{s+1} = 0$. So we set $w = n+1$. By classical algebra and number theoretic results, we have $\text{ord}(w) = n^s$ and that discrete logarithms base w are easy to compute, along the lines just sketched. A concrete algorithm can be seen in [11]. The threshold decryption only requires that we can compute securely $u^x \bmod n^{s+1}$ given u and a secret sharing of x. A protocol for this is given in [11].

Our scheme can be described as simply the ElGamal solution from [9], but transplanted to a ring where it happens to be easy to compute discrete logarithms base the fixed element w. The Paillier and Damgård-Jurik schemes also use the ring $\mathbf{Z}_n^{s+1*}$ and (implicitly) the special properties of the element n+1, but as mentioned these are known results from algebra. The distinguishing feature of Paillier/Damgård-Jurik is that they propose a way to use the factorization of n as the trapdoor that makes decryption possible, while we use a secret discrete logarithm. Therefore, when keys are generated, a trusted party could choose n and g but then immediately delete the factorization. Then the private key x and the sharing of it can be generated independently of the factorization, perhaps in a distributed way. It also means that one can define several instances of the same system using the same n, i.e., several different public h-values. If one or more private keys are compromised, this does not affect the security of the other keys.

We note a couple of facts for later use: The cryptosystem satisfies a root opening assumption. If we are given the decryption of a ciphertext (u^e, v^e) for some e<p,q, then we can also find the message m contained in the ciphertext (u,v). The reason is that the plaintext corresponding to (u^e, v^e) must be em $\bmod n^s$, and so we can find m because e is always invertible modulo n^s. Another observation is that when using standard techniques, the zero-knowledge protocols for proving various claims on encrypted values from [11] can all be transplanted to our cryptosystem quite easily - basically because the plaintext space is the same, and both systems are homomorphic.

3.   ZERO-KNOWLEDGE PROOFS

In this section, we take a closer look at how the correctness of encrypted votes can be proved in zero-knowledge. We present an efficient zero-knowledge proof of knowledge for demonstrating the correctness of the vote in the case where each voter may select only one option or candidate. We then extend the proof system to cover the more complex elections where the voter on the same ballot may cast several votes with the restriction that they all are on different candidates.

We define two election parameters M and L. M is a strict upper bound on the number of voters participating in the election. L is the number of candidates or options each voter may choose from. Included in this number may be dummy candidates representing unused, blank, or invalid votes. In theory, only $O(\log L)$ bits are needed to convey the choice of the voter. This possibility was investigated in [12] where the tally servers transform the encrypted votes into encrypted votes in a more usable format. In practice, their scheme places too large a workload on the tally servers though. Currently, the best choice seems to be to represent votes in a format that can use the homomorphic property of the cryptosystem directly.

We represent the candidates by numbers $j \in \{0,...,L-1\}$. A vote on candidate j is represented as the number M^j. Notice that in this way the sum of several votes will be a number on the form $v_0 M^0 + ... + v_{L-1} M^{L-1}$ where v_j is the number of votes on candidate j. With this choice of vote representation the message space for the cryptosystem must be of size $\Omega(L \log M)$. When the number of candidates is large, the ciphertexts are correspondingly large, and in the cryptosystems we know the computational complexity of the encryption process is large too. The encryption process is not the heaviest part in generating a vote though. Looking closer at the schemes proposed in the literature [9,11,4] it turns out that the zero-knowledge proofs used to prove the correctness of the encrypted votes involve several encryptions. The really heavy part of generating a vote and tallying a vote, both in terms of communication complexity and computational complexity, is producing and verifying the zero-knowledge proof associated with it. It is therefore highly interesting to find efficient zero-knowledge proofs for the correctness of encrypted votes.

In the zero-knowledge proof, the prover (the voter) wants to convince the verifier (the tally servers) of the correctness of the encrypted vote. For this purpose, we use Σ-protocols that are a type of 3-move honest verifier zero-knowledge proofs that work in the following way: The prover and verifier know a common input x and the prover knows a witness w such that $(x,w) \in R$ where R is some relation. The prover sends an initial message a to the verifier, is then given a randomly chosen challenge e, and responds with an answer z. On basis of (a,e,z), the verifier decides whether to accept the claim that $x \in L$ where L is the language specified by the relation R. We call such a proof system a Σ-protocol when it satisfies the following criteria:

Completeness: Given w so that $(x,w) \in R$ the prover can make an honest verifier accept with overwhelming probability.

Special soundness: Given x and two acceptable proofs (a,e,z) and (a,e',z') with the same initial message but different challenges it is possible to extract a witness w so that $(x,w) \in R$. Note that special soundness makes a Σ-protocol a system for proofs of knowledge.

Special honest verifier zero-knowledge: Given $x \in L$ and any challenge e it is possible to simulate a proof (a,e,z) with the same probability distribution as the distribution of real proofs with any witness and conditioned on using the challenge e.

Using the Fiat-Shamir heuristic Σ-protocols can be made non-interactive by using a cryptographic hash function h and letting the challenge be created as e=h(x,a). In the random oracle model, the resulting hash value h(x,a) is completely random and we therefore have a non-interactive zero-knowledge proof of knowledge for $x \in L$.

Very efficient Σ-protocols exist for basic properties such as three cipher-texts being encryptions of plaintexts a,b,c so that c=ab, a ciphertext being an encryption of 0, two ciphertexts containing a,b so that a=b, etc. For more complex cases such as a ciphertext containing a vote on the form M^j, $0 \leq j < L$, it is possible to build a zero-knowledge proof from the more basic Σ-proto-cols. However, the basic Σ-protocols, while being efficient, do need a few extra encryptions in the process. When several basic proofs are needed, it all adds up to the use of several encryptions, which, in the context of voting, as mentioned before, can be heavy to deal with both in terms of communication and computational complexity. The ideas behind the basic Σ-protocols are quite general though and can be used not only in connection with homo-morphic public key encryption schemes but also with homomorphic commit-ment schemes. To improve the efficiency of the needed zero-knowledge proof for correctness of the vote, Lipmaa suggests in [18] to create a com-mitment to the vote and prove knowledge of the commitment and the cipher-text holding the same content. Using a homomorphic integer commitment scheme this carries two advantages: The commitments do not need to be un-conditionally binding as do the ciphertexts and so they can be much lighter to work with. By using an integer commitment scheme, we can potentially use special properties of this ring, in our case that of unique factorization.

Before proceeding, let us be more precise about the kind of commitment scheme we deal with. First, there is the key generation phase in which a public key is generated. In our case, the election authorities will be the ones generating the key. From now on we will just assume that some key K has been generated, and accordingly there is an associated message space M_K, a randomizer space R_K, an opening space $B_K \supset R_K$, a commitment space C_K, a commitment function $com_K(;):M_K \times R_K \to C_K$ and a verification function $ver_K(;;):M_K \times B_K \times C_K \to \{0,1\}$. Given the key, we can commit to an element $m \in M_K$ by selecting at random according to some distribution spe-cified by the commitment scheme $r \in R_K$ and letting the commitment be $c=com_K(m;r) \in C_K$. This (m,r,c) satisfies $ver_K(m,r,c)=1$.

To open a commitment, we reveal $m \in M_K$, $r \in B_K$ so that $ver_K(m,r,c)=1$. Note that we do allow for openings not corresponding to correctly formed commitments since the opening space and the randomizer space do not need to be identical. However, we still require that the binding property be satisfi-ed, i.e., that nobody can find a commitment in C_K and two correct openings of it with different messages m_1 and m_2.

In order for the commitment schemes to be useful in our voting protocol we have some additional requirements. One important thing is that the spaces associated with the commitment scheme shall be abelian groups[1], and furthermore that the message space is the entire set of integers. That means we have groups $M_K=\mathbf{Z},(R_K,+)\leq(B_K,+)$ and $(C_K,)$.

Homomorphic property: The commitment schemes we look at must be homomorphic, meaning that for all $m_1,m_2\in\mathbf{Z}$ and all $r_1,r_2\in B_K$:

$$\text{com}_K(m_1;r_1)\,\text{com}_K(m_2;r_2) = \text{com}_K(m_1+m_2;r_1+r_2).$$

Root opening: We demand that for any $c\in C_K$, if we can find $e\in\mathbf{Z}\setminus\{0\}$ and $m\in\mathbf{Z},z\in B_K$ so that $\text{com}_K(m;z)=c^e$ then we can compute an opening of c.

An example of such a commitment scheme is the following variant of the Damgård-Fujisaki commitment scheme from [10]. Here, the key consists of n chosen as a product of two large safe primes, and two squares g,h so that $\log_g h$ and $\log_h g$ is not known to the sender who is making the commitment.

A commitment to an integer m is formed by choosing r at random from a sufficiently large interval of integers and letting the commitment be $\text{com}_{(n,g,h)}(m;r)=g^m h^r \bmod n$. To open a commitment c we produce b,m,r such that $1=b^2 \bmod n$ and $c=bg^m h^r$.

The ElGamal style encryption scheme we presented before satisfies these requirements too, except for the root opening property. It satisfies a weaker root opening property. Given a valid ciphertext (u,v) we may extract the plaintext of (u,v) from an opening of (u^e,v^e), where $0<e<p,q$. In addition, we can simply check whether a ciphertext is valid by computing the Jacobi symbols of u and v. In the following, any homomorphic public-key cryptosystem with the above properties will work, even if the root opening property is only satisfied for $e\in\{0,...,2^t-1\}$, where t is some security parameter. Therefore, we describe the protocols in general terms in what follows. We shall always write pk for the public key of the cryptosystem, and let C_{pk} be the corresponding ciphertextspace, consisting of only *valid* ciphertexts.

Given a homomorphic integer commitment scheme, we can now use the following Σ-protocol for proving knowledge that a commitment and a ciphertext contain the same element modulo n where the message space for the cryptosystem is $\mathbf{Z}_n$.

Proof of commitment and encryption holding same element mod n

Common input: A commitment $c\in C_K$ and an encryption $E\in C_{pk}$.

Private input for the prover: $m\in\mathbf{Z}_n$, $r_c\in R_K$ and $r_E\in R_{pk}$ so that $c=\text{com}_K(m;r_c)$ and $E=E_{pk}(m;r_E)$.

Initial message:

---

[1] We assume that both the group and the elements in the groups we work with can be represented in a suitable manner, the binary operations and inversions can be computed efficiently, and that we can readily recognize whether an element belongs to a particular group.

Pick $d \in \mathbf{Z}$ as a shadow[2] of em, $r_c' \in R_K$ as a random shadow of er_c and $r_E' \in R_{pk}$ as a random shadow of er_E. Let $a_c = com_K(d;r_c')$ and $a_E = E_{pk}(d \bmod n; r_E')$. The initial message is (a_c, a_E).

Challenge:

The challenge consists of e chosen at random from $\{0, \ldots, 2^t - 1\}$.

Answer:

Set $D = em + d$, $z_c = r_c' + er_c$, $z_E = r_E' + er_E$. The answer to the challenge is (D, z_c, z_E).

Verification:

The verifier checks that $(D, z_c, z_E) \in \mathbf{Z} \times R_K \times R_{pk}$, $com_K(D; z_c) = a_c c^e$ and $E_{pk}(D \bmod n; z_E) = a_E E^e$.

Having an integer commitment to the vote, the next question is how to prove that it has the correct form. Lipmaa [18] suggests selecting M as a prime and using a zero-knowledge proof of knowledge to demonstrate that the following commitments $c_v = com_K(v; r_v), c_b = com_K(M^L/v; r_b)$, $c_c = com_K(M^L; 0)$ satisfy a multiplicative relationship. This implies that the absolute value of the content in c_v, $|v|$, is a divisor in M^L. Subsequently using a range proof, see [18] or Boudot's article [2], we can then prove that $v \geq 0$. Combining these two pieces of information we see that v is of the desired form.

This idea can be improved upon. Proving that a committed integer is positive is not that simple. In [18], the fact that all positive integers can be written as a sum of four squares, and, of course, no negative number can be written as such a sum, is used. In other words four commitments are provided and it is proven that all of them contain squares. The commitment to the vote v is the product of these four commitments, by the homomorphic property giving us that the commitment contains a non-negative integer. According to [18], the range proofs in [2] are 20% more efficient but still in the same ball park.

As an alternative, we propose letting M be the square of a prime. Any legal vote is now a square, and we simply have to prove it a square in order to show that it is non-negative. So let $M = p^2$ with p prime and provide a commitment c_v to M^j. We show that c_v contains the square of the contents of

---

[2] Let us informally explain the concept of shadowing and random shadowing. In this proof we will at some point reveal D=d+em where $e \in \{0, \ldots, 2^t - 1\}$. To preserve the zero-knowledge property we must therefore choose d such that revealing D does not give away any knowledge about m. In the particular case here we know that $m \in \mathbf{Z}_n$ and $0 \leq e < 2^t$. Thus by selecting d at random from $\{-2^{k+2t}, \ldots, 2^{k+2t}\}$, where $k = |n|$, we ensure that the secrecy of m is preserved. Similarly we will at some point reveal an element $z_c = r_c' + er_c \in R_K$. This should not give away knowledge about r_c. In addition r_c' should be chosen such that we cannot distinguish it from a properly chosen random element from R_K. We call r_c' chosen in this way a random shadow for er_c. We can speak of computational, statistical and perfect shadowing depending on how the shadow hides the underlying element. In the protocols we know of the most common case is statistically hiding shadows and random shadows.

a commitment c_a to p^j. Furthermore, we prove that the content of c_a multiplied by the content of another commitment c_b equals p^{L-1}. All in all this proves that c_v contains a vote of the correct form, and it replaces the somewhat complex range proof with a single squaring proof. Further improvements can be achieved but they require that we dig into the proof system we use for proving multiplicative relationships between commitments. Let us therefore first present a general Σ-protocol for making proofs of the contents of some commitments having a multiplicative relationship with each other.

Proof of multiplicative relationship

Common input: $c_a, c_b, c_c \in C_K$.

Private input for the prover: $a, b \in \mathbf{Z}, r_a, r_b, r_c \in R_K$ such that $c_a = com_K(a;r_a)$, $c_b = com_K(b;r_b)$, $c_c = com_K(ab;r_c)$.

Parallel proof:

Make in parallel with the rest of the protocol a proof of knowledge of commitment opening of c_b or c_c using a Σ-protocol.

Initial message:

Select d such that it shadows ea. Choose $r_d, r_{db} \in R_K$ as random shadows of er_a and $-(ea+d)r_b+er_c$, and send $c_d = com_K(d;r_d)$ and $c_{db} = com_K(db;r_{db})$ to the verifier.

Challenge:

Select at random $e \in \{0,\ldots,2^t-1\}$.

Answer:

Respond with $f = ea + d$, $z_1 = er_a + r_d$, $z_2 = fr_b - er_c - r_{db}$.

Verification:

Accept if and only if $f \in \mathbf{Z}$, $z_1, z_2 \in R_K$, $com_K(f,z_1) = c_d c_a^e$ and $c_{db} c_c^e com_K(0;z_2) = c_b^f$ and the parallel proof of knowledge is acceptable.

The proof of this being a Σ-protocol is standard and we do not go through it here. We would, however, like to point out the little detail that we allow the parallel proof to be a proof of knowledge of an opening of c_c. The reason for this is that we make a multiplication proof where we already know the opening of $c_c = com_K(p^{L-1};0)$ and thus we can save ourselves from having to do the parallel proof. The price for this change is that the root opening assumption on the commitment scheme needs to be slightly stronger than usual. Usually, one only requires that knowing an opening of c^e for a commitment c with $e \in \{1,\ldots,2^t-1\}$ makes it possible to open c itself. We require that knowing an opening of c^f with $f \in \mathbf{Z}\backslash\{0\}$ makes it is possible to find an opening of c. Another thing worth noting is that in the proof of the commitment c_v containing M^j the commitment c_a to p^j is involved in two multiplication proofs. It is used both in the multiplication proof that shows it is a factor in p^{L-1} and in the multiplication proof where it is shown that the square of its content is contained in c_v. Selecting the same challenge e in both the multiplication proofs, something that we can do and still preserve zero-knowledge because the proof system is special honest verifier zero-knowledge, allows us to recycle d, c_d, f and z_1 in the two proofs.

As a final improvement, we shall see that we do not at all need c_v in the proof of the correctness of the vote. We may entirely skip this commitment and jump directly to proving that the encryption of the vote contains the square of the content in c_a. This is due to the fact that on the commitment side, we use c_v to hold M^j as the result of squaring the content of c_1. However, we may as well use $c_1^f = c_1^{ep^j+d}$ directly since this by the homomorphic property of commitments is a commitment to $ep^{2j}+dp^j$ and thus contains the interesting $p^{2j}=M^j$ itself.

It is time to combine all our ideas into an actual protocol.

Proof of knowledge for a ciphertext containing a valid vote

Common input for prover and verifier: Prime p such that $M=p^2$ and an encryption $E \in C_{pk}$.

Private input for the prover: $0 \leq j < L$ and $r_E \in R_{pk}$ such that $E = E_{pk}(M^j; r_E)$.

Initial message:

Choose first r_a, r_b at random from R_K and form commitments $c_a = com_K(p^j; r_a)$ and $c_b = com_K(p^{L-j-1}; r_b)$.

Choose d such that it shadows p^j. Choose γ such that it shadows eM^j+dp^j. Choose $r_d, r_{db}, r_\gamma \in R_K$ and $r_\gamma' \in R_{pk}$ as random shadows of $er_a, (ep^j+d)r_b, (ep^j+d)r_a, er_E$ respectively.

Send $c_d = com_K(d; r_d)$, $c_{db} = com_K(dp^{L-j-1}; r_{db})$, $c_\gamma = com_K(dp^j+\gamma; r_\gamma)$ and $E_\gamma = E_{pk}(dp^j+\gamma \bmod n; r_\gamma')$ to the verifier.

Challenge:

Select e at random from $\{0,\ldots,2^t-1\}$.

Answer:

Send $f = ep^j+d$, $z_1 = er_a+r_d$, $z_2 = fr_b-r_{db}$, $z_3 = fr_a+r_\gamma$, $z_4 = er_E+r_\gamma'$ and $D = eM^j+dp^j+\gamma$ to the verifier.

Verification:

Check that $c_d, c_{db}, c_\gamma \in C_K$, $E_\gamma \in C_{pk}$, f, $D \in Z, z_1, z_2, z_3 \in R_K$ and $z_4 \in R_{pk}$. Verify that $com_K(f; z_1) = c_d c_a^e$, $c_{db} com_K(p^{L-1}; 0)^e com_K(0, z_2) = c_b^f$, $com_K(D; z_3) = c_a^f c_\gamma$ and $E_{pk}(D; z_4) = E^e E_\gamma$.

Theorem 1 *The proof system above is a Σ-protocol for proving that E is a ciphertext holding a vote on the correct form. It is statistical special honest verifier zero-knowledge if the commitment scheme is statistically hiding and the shadows are statistically hiding.*

Proof. Theorem 1 follows as a corollary to Theorem 2 proven later.

Compared to the scheme from [11], which until now is the most efficient voting scheme based on homomorphic encryption, we asymptotically get an improvement in the order $\log L$ both in terms of communication complexity and computational complexity on the voter's side. Furthermore we note that the constants in this scheme are smaller than the constants in the schemes of both [11] and [18]. An additional advantage of the approach is that it can be extended to cover the situation where each voter is allowed to cast several votes in the same session. We define a new election parameter N to be the number of candidates a voter may vote for. Moreover, we demand that the votes must be cast on different candidates. A simple approach would be to cast N votes and proving them all to be different, but we can do much better than this. The first thing we notice is that it is sufficient for the voter to provide an encryption of the sum of his votes and proving this sum correct. We write the candidates in increasing order $0 \leq j_1 < ... < j_N < L$. We encrypt $M^{j}_1 + ... + M^{j}_N$ and wish to have a Σ-protocol for proving that a ciphertext E contains a vote of this form. To do so, we may form commitments $c_1,...,c_N$ to $p^{j}_1,...,p^{j}_N$, and furthermore make commitments $c_1',...,c_N'$ to $p_2^{-j}{}_1^{-1},...,$ $p^{L-1-j}{}_N^{-1}$. Using multiplication proofs we can demonstrate knowledge that for i=1,...,N, the contents of c_i and $(c_i')^p$ multiplied with each other equals the content of c_{i+1}, where we let $c_{N+1}=E_{pk}(p^L;0)$. This shows that all the commitments $c_1,...,c_N$, except for a sign difference, contain powers of p, that all the exponents are different, and that the exponents lie in the interval $\{0,...,L-1\}$.

We can proceed by forming commitments $c_1'',...,c_N''$ to $M^{j}_1,...,M^{j}_N$. We prove for i=1,...,N knowledge that the contents of $c_1'',...,c_N''$ contain the square of the content of $c_1,...,c_N$. Finally, we form the commitment $c_1''...c_N''$. This is a commitment to the intended vote, which proofs show contains an element on the form $M^{j}_1 + ... + M^{j}_N$, where $0 \leq j_1 < ... j_N < L$. What is left is to encrypt this vote to a ciphertext E and prove knowledge of the equality with the content of $c_1''...c_N''$.

We can make similar improvements as we did in the voting scheme for the single candidate scenario. We note that the commitments $c_1,...,c_N$ are all involved in two multiplication proofs and obtain a more efficient proof system by using the same challenge e in all the proofs allowing us to recycle the d,c_d,f,z_l parts in the multiplication proofs.

Furthermore, we do not need to start each multiplication proof with a parallel proof of knowledge for some opening. Throughout the proofs, we do have knowledge of an opening to the commitment to the product of the contents, since we know how to open $c_{N+1}=com_K(p^L;0)$ of course. The multiplication proof involving c_N and c_N' proves knowledge of how to open c_N. This in turn means that the multiplication proof involving c_{N-1} and c_{N-1}' proves knowledge of how to open c_{N-1}, etc. Finally, since we use the same challenge in all the proofs, we may avoid supplying the commitments $c_1'',...,c_N''$ in a manner similar to the single candidate scheme. Let us write the entire scheme down

Proof of knowledge for a ciphertext containing a valid vote on multiple candidates

Common input: Prime p such that $M=p^2$ and $E \in C_{pk}$.

Private input for the prover: $0 \leq j_1 < \ldots < j_N < L$ and $r_E \in R_{pk}$ such that $E=E_{pk}(M^{j_1}+\ldots+M^{j_N};r_E)$.

Initial message:

Choose at random $r_1,\ldots,r_N,r_1',\ldots,r_N'$ from R_K, and form commitments $c_1=com_K(p^{j_1};r_1),\ldots,c_N=com_K(p^{j_N};r_N),c_1'=com_K(p^{j_2-j_1-1};r_1'),\ldots,c_N'=com_K(p^{L-j_N-1};r_N')$

Choose $d_1,\ldots,d_N$ such that they shadow $ep^{j_1},\ldots,ep^{j_N}$, and γ such that it shadows $ep^{2j_1}+d_1p^{j_1}+\ldots+ep^{2j_N}+d_Np^{j_N}$.

Choose $r_{d1},\ldots,r_{dN}$ as random shadows of $er_1,\ldots,er_N$. Choose $r_{d1b},\ldots,r_{dNb}$ as random shadows of $-p(ep^{j_1}+d_1)r_1'+er_2,\ldots,-p(ep^{j_N}+d_N)r_N'+er_{N+1}$, where $r_{N+1}=0$. Choose r_γ as a random shadow of $(ep^{j_1}+d_1)r_1+\ldots+(ep^{j_N}+d_N)r_N$, and $r_\gamma' \in R_{pk}$ as a random shadow of er_E.

Send $c_{d1}=com_K(d_1;r_{d1}),\ldots,c_{dN}=com_K(d_N;r_{dN})$, $c_{d1b}=com_K(d_1p^{j_2-j_1}_1;r_{d1b}),\ldots,$ $c_{dNb}=com_K(d_Np^{L-j_N}_N;r_{dNb})$, $c_\gamma=com_K(\gamma;r_\gamma)$ and $E_\gamma=E_{pk}(d_1p^{j_1}+\ldots+d_Np^{j_N}+\gamma \bmod n;r_\gamma')$ to the verifier.

Challenge:

Select e at random from $\{0,\ldots,2^t-1\}$.

Answer:

Send $f_1=ep^{j_1}+d_1,\ldots,f_N=ep^{j_N}+d_N,z_{1,1}=er_1+r_{d1},\ldots,z_{1,N}=er_N+r_{dN},z_{2,1}=pf_1r_1'-er_2-r_{d1b},\ldots,z_{2,N}=pf_Nr_N'-er_{N+1}-r_{dNb},z_3=f_1r_1+\ldots+f_Nr_N+r_\gamma,z_4=er_E+r_\gamma',D=e(M^{j_1}+\ldots+M^{j_N}+d_1p^{j_1}+\ldots+d_Np^{j_N}+\gamma$ to the verifier.

Verification:

Check that $c_{d1},\ldots,c_{dn},c_{d1b},\ldots,c_{dNb},c_\gamma \in C_K$, $E_\gamma \in C_{pk}$, $f_1,\ldots,f_N$, $D \in Z$, $z_{1,1},\ldots,z_{1,N},z_{2,1},\ldots,z_{2,N},z_3 \in R_K$ and $z_4 \in R_{pk}$. Verify that $com_K(f_1;z_{1,1})=c_{d1}c_1^e,\ldots,com_K(f_N;z_{1,N})=c_{dN}c_N^e$, $_2{}^ec_{d1b}com_K(0;z_{2,1})=(c_1')^{pf_1},\ldots,$ $c_{N+1}{}^ec_{dNb}com_K(0;z_{2,N})=(c_N')^{pf_N}$, $com(D;z_3)=c_1^{f_1}\ldots c_N^{f_N}c_\gamma$, where $c_{N+1}=com_K(p^L;0)$. Finally check that $E_{pk}(D \bmod n;z_4)=E^eE_\gamma$.

Theorem 2 *The proof system above is a Σ-protocol proving that E encrypts a correct vote on multiple candidates. If the commitments are statistically hiding and the shadows and random shadows are statistically hiding, then the proof system is statistical special honest verifier zero-knowledge.*

Proof.

Completeness: Easy to see.

Special Soundness: Assume that we have two acceptable proofs to two different challenges e and e' to the same initial messages. This means we have answers $f_1,\ldots,f_N$, $z_{1,1},\ldots,z_{1,N},z_{2,1},\ldots,z_{2,N},z_3$, D, z_4 and $f_1',\ldots,f_N',z_{1,1}',\ldots,$ $z_{1,N}',z_{2,1}',\ldots,z_{2,N}',z_3',D',z_4'$ to the respective challenges satisfying the criteria specified in the verification step.

Starting with the encryption side of the proof we have:

$$E_{pk}(D;z_4)=E^eE_\gamma \wedge E_{pk}(D';z_4')=E^{e'}E_\gamma.$$

This gives us

$$E_{pk}(D-D';z_4-z_4')=E^{e-e'}.$$

Using the root opening assumption of the homomorphic cryptosystem we may now extract the plaintext of E. We call this plaintext v.

Going to the commitments we see that

$$com_K(f_1;z_{1,1})=c_{d1}c_1^e \wedge com_K(f_1';z_{1,1}')=c_{d1}c_1^{e'}.$$

This gives us

$$com_K(f_1-f_1';z_{1,1}-z_{1,1}')=c_1^{e-e'}.$$

Using the root opening assumption on the commitment scheme we may from this extract an opening of c_1. In a similar manner we can extract openings of $c_2,\ldots,c_N$. We call the contents of the commitments for $a_1,\ldots,a_N$.

From the other part of the multiplication proofs we see that:

$$c_{N+1}^e c_{dNb} com_K(0,z_{2,N})=(c_N')^{pf}{}_N \wedge c_{N+1}^{e'} c_{dNb} com_K(0,z_{2,N}')=(c_N')^{pf}{}_N{}'$$

giving us

$$com_K(0;z_{2,N}-z_{2,N}')com_K(p^L;0)^{e-e'}=(c_N')^{p(f_N - f_N{}')}.$$

We now know an opening of the commitment on the left hand side. We have $f_N' \neq f_N$ since $1=com_K(0;0)$, and the left hand side cannot be opened as zero by the binding property of the commitments. Accordingly we argue by the root opening assumption on the commitment scheme that we can extract an opening of c_N'. The opening must furthermore be non-zero since the left hand side opens to something non-zero. We can now in a quite similar manner go backwards finding non-zero openings of $c_{N-1}',\ldots,c_1'$. We call the contents of the commitments for $b_N,\ldots,b_1$.

We now have openings of the commitments $c_1,\ldots,c_N,c_1',\ldots,c_N'$ and E. Furthermore, by the binding property of the commitment scheme, these openings must be the only ones that the prover can produce. Therefore, we can speak of *the* content of $c_1,\ldots,c_N,c_1',\ldots,c_N'$ and E in the rest of the proof.

What is left to argue is that the opening of the encryption satisfies the requirements of the proof. In that case, we have extracted a witness for the vote being on the correct form. We get from

$$com_K(f_N-f_N';z_{1,N}-z_{1,N}')=c_N^{e-e'}.$$

that

$$f_N-f_N' = a_N(e-e') \Rightarrow a_N = \frac{f_N-f_N'}{e-e'} \in \mathbf{Z}.$$

From

$$(c_N')^{p(f_N-f_N')}=com_K(0;z_{2,N}-z_{2,N}')com_K(p^L;0)^{e-e'}.$$

we see that

$$p(f_N-f_N')b_N=(e-e')p^L.$$

This implies that

$$a_N b_N = p^{L-1}.$$

This means that $|a_N|=p^j_N$ where $0{\leq}j_N{<}L$. In a similar fashion, we deduce $|a_1|=p^j_1,\dots,|a_{N-1}|=p^j_{N-1}$ with $0{\leq}j_1{<}\dots j_{N-1}{<}j_N$.

We proceed to the link between the commitments and the encryption. We have

$$com(D;z_3)=c_1^{f_1}\dots c_N^{f_N}c_\gamma \wedge com(D';z_3')=c_1^{f_1'}\dots c_N^{f_N'}c_\gamma$$

implying that

$$com(D-D';z_3-z_3')=c_1^{f_1-f_1'}\dots c_N^{f_N-f_N'}.$$

Recall that for all i we have $a_i=[(f_i-f_i')/(e-e')]$. This means that the equation above gives us

$$D-D'=(e-e')(p^{2j}_1+\dots+p^{2j}_N).$$

On the encryption side the equation

$$E_{pk}(D-D';z_4-z_4')=E^{e-e'}$$

shows that the content v satisfies

$$D-D' \equiv (e-e')v \bmod n.$$

Since $(e-e')$ is invertible modulo n we deduce that

$$p^{2j}_1+\dots p^{2j}_N=v \bmod n.$$

In other words, the witness (v,r_E) consists of a correctly formed vote on the form $M^j_1+\dots+M^j_N$, where $0{\leq}j_1{<}\dots{<}j_N{<}L$, and the randomness involved in the encryption. This concludes the demonstration of the special soundness. **Special honest verifier zero-knowledge:** Given the common input and a challenge $e\in\{0,\dots,2^t-1\}$ we wish to simulate a proof of the encryption containing a vote on the right form.

We start by picking at random $r_1,\dots,r_N,r_1',\dots,r_N'$ from R_K. We form the commitments $c_1=com_K(p^0;r_1),\dots,c_N=com_K(p^{N-1};r_N),c_1'=com_K(1;r_1'),\dots,c_N'=com_K(1;r_N')$. Due to the hiding property of the commitment scheme these commitments are indistinguishable from properly formed initial message commitments to $p^j_1,\dots,p^j_N$ and $p_2^{-j_1-1},\dots,p^{L-j_N-1}$.

We now pick $f_1,\ldots,f_N$ as shadows for $ep^j_1,\ldots,ep^j_N$ and D as a shadow for $f_1p^j_1+\ldots+f_Np^j_N$. With this choice of $f_1,\ldots,f_N,D$ they are indistinguishable from the $f_1,\ldots,f_N$ and D of a real proof by the definition of shadows. We may also pick $z_{1,1},\ldots,z_{1,N},z_{2,1},\ldots,z_{2,N},z_3 \in R_K$ and $z_4 \in R_{pk}$ as random shadows so that they are indistinguishable from those in a real proof. We compute $E_\gamma = E_{pk}(D;z_4)E^{-e}$ and $c_\gamma = c_1^{-f}{}_1\ldots c_N^{-f}{}_N com_K(D;z_3)$. We set $c_{d1} = com_K(f_1;z_{1,1})c_1^{-e}$, $\ldots,c_{dN} = com_K(f_N;z_{1,N})c_N^{-e}$ and $c_{d1b} = com_K(0;z_{2,1})^{-1}c_1^{pf}{}_1c_2^{-e}$, $\ldots,c_{dNb} = com_K(0;z_{2,N})^{-1}c_N^{pf}{}_Nc_{N+1}^{-e}$.

With these choices, we have a simulated proof that due to the hiding property of the commitment scheme and the semantic security of the crypto-system looks entirely like a normal proof with challenge e. This means that we have demonstrated the special honest verifier zero-knowledge property of the proof system.

Finally, we see from the proof of special honest verifier zero-knowledge that if the commitments $c_1,\ldots,c_N,c_1',\ldots,c_N'$ are statistically hiding and that all the shadows and random shadows are statistically hiding, then the entire proof system is statistical special honest verifier zero-knowledge. The possibility of a voter voting on less than N candidates is obtained by includeing N dummy candidates. If we remove the exponentiation to the power p and let $c_1',\ldots,c_N'$ be commitments to $p^{j_2-j}{}_1,\ldots,p^{L-j}{}_N$ instead, we get a proof system for the correctness and knowledge of the vote where the voter does not need to vote on different candidates. Here, p must, of course, be chosen large enough to accommodate for the larger number of votes a candidate can obtain.

So far, we have presented methods to make the zero-knowledge proofs that accompany an encrypted vote easy to form for the voter. On the server side, things are also much easier since the verification of these proofs is much easier than the more involved Σ-protocols used in [11]. We present a further speedup by presenting a randomized verification algorithm where we only need to compute one commitment instead of several of them. One thing that is common in the verification procedure of the proofs we have presented above is that we compute two elements in C_K in two different ways, for instance as $com_K(f,z_1)$ and ac^e, and then, after this computation, we check whether they are identical. Since the computations involved in the computation of the two elements may be complicated, for instance requiring large exponentiations, we wish to reduce the time used in this process. When having many such pairs of elements, we may reduce the computational time involved in the verification of the proofs, taking advantage of the fact that we are working in a group.

Let us say we are given multiple pairs $(c_1,d_1,\ldots,c_n,d_n)$ in C_K. We wish to check that the elements are pairwise identical. Choose $s_1,\ldots,s_n$ at random from $\{0,\ldots,2^t-1\}$. Here t may be a smaller security parameter than in the Σ-protocols since the computation happens only on the verifier's side and thus the prover is incapable of trying actively to cheat. Provided C_K is a group with no non-trivial elements of order less than 2^t we have with probability at least $1-2^{1-t}$ that $c_1{}^s{}_1...c_n{}^s{}_n \neq d_1{}^s{}_1...d_n{}^s{}_n$ if $\exists i: c_i \neq d_i$.

The reason why this is interesting is the homomorphic group structure of the commitments we are investigating. Note that the proofs we presented are in a form where one side has the form of a commitment $c_i = com_K(m_i;r_i)$, with m_i and r_i known to the verifier. Let us say that $c_1,...,c_n$ are commitments. We can compute $c_1{}^s{}_1...c_n{}^s{}_n$ as $com_K(s_1 m_1+...+s_n m_n; s_1 r_1+...+s_n r_n)$. If the binary operations in the groups M_K and R_K are faster to compute than the binary operations in C_K this makes verification more efficient.

Furthermore, depending on the groups in use we may take advantage of exponentiation techniques allowing us to compute $d_1{}^s{}_1...d_n{}^s{}_n$ roughly at the price of one exponentiation. This was the emphasis in [5] where a somewhat similar technique for fast batch verification of signatures was investigated.

Since the probability of catching any cheating grows exponentially with t, we can typically choose t reasonably small. Accordingly, the extra computational effort required to compute the additional exponentiations to $s_1,...,s_n$ is dwarfed by the savings we get by not having to verify each commitment opening by itself.

The technique is presented in quite general terms above since indeed it can be used in many contexts. Furthermore note that it works in all contexts where the message space is some group without small annihilators, not just where the message space is the integers.

In the voting scheme for multiple candidates, the verification procedure after some calculating becomes the following:

Verification: Check that $c_{d1},...,c_{dn},c_{d1b},...,c_{dNb},c_\gamma \in C_K$, $E_\gamma \in C_{pk}$, $f_1,...,f_N$, $D \in Z, z_{1,1},..., z_{1,N}, z_{2,1},...,z_{2,N}, z_3 \in R_K$ and $z_4 \in R_{pk}$. Select at random $s_1,...,s_N,s_1',...,s_N',s \in \{0,...,2^t-1\}$. Verify that

$$com_K(s_1 f_1+...+s_N f_N + sD + es_N'p^L; s_1 z_{1,1}+...+s_N z_{1,N}$$

$$+s_1'z_{2,1}+...+s_N'z_{2,N}+z_3)$$

$$= c_\gamma{}^s\, c_{d1}{}^s{}_1...c_{dN}{}^s{}_N (c_{d1b}{}^{-1})^{s'}{}_1...(c_{dNb}{}^{-1})^{s'}{}_N c_1{}^{es}{}_1{}^{+sf}{}_1 c_2{}^{e(s}{}_2{}^{-s}{}_1{}^{')+sf}{}_2 ..$$

$$c_N{}^{e(s}{}_N{}^{-s}{}_{N-1}{}^{')+sf}{}_N (c_1')^{pf}{}_1{}^{s'}{}_1...(c_N')^{pf}{}_N{}^{s'}{}_N$$

Finally, check whether $E_{pk}(D \bmod n; z_4) = E^e E_\gamma$.

4. SECURING AN IMPLEMENTATION IN PRACTICE

We have had the opportunity to work with practical aspects of implementing an e-voting system in connection with the EU project, e-Vote. Several challenges beyond the scope of the cryptographic protocols have been identified and solutions have been found. These challenges are partly due to security aspects special to voting solutions, which cannot be solved by technical means alone, and partly due to standard problems with providing a satisfactory combination of security and usability of the authentication mechanisms used. We dedicate some subsections to the individual problems and solutions. We use the bulletin board model. All entities, persons as well as servers, will have at least one public/private key pair to enforce the model. However, we will only include the aspects of PKI having to do with authentication of voters here. We do not propose a total solution, but give solutions to sub-problems, some of which can be adopted for any particular voting system according to relevant tradeoffs for each individual system.

4.1   Taking Requirements Seriously

In the newspapers, a considerable amount of the debate on electronic voting is dedicated to suggestions for voting systems tailored at selling large amounts of expensive equipment of one kind or the other. Examples are chip-cards and biometric devices. It is, however, our belief that the competition will rapidly make such approaches obsolete. In order to have success with voting technology, it has to be tailored to meet the requirements of election organizers and voters rather than those of the vendors. Shortly expressed, voting systems are like all other systems. In order to implement a successful system it is not only necessary to understand the requirements correctly; it is also necessary to respect them.

4.2   Deployment of a PKI

After having stated some concerns in Section 4.1, we must, however say that we see no alternative to using PKI for authentication of voters. The main reason is that unless a public/private key pair is used, anybody who can verify authentication information can also fake it. In particular, universal verifiability of an election with a decent level of security is very significantly simplified by using PKI. If a public PKI is in place and most voters have signature keys, it will be most natural to use that PKI. In practice, this is usually not the case today though. We are working with two approaches to overcome the limitation of a potentially lacking PKI: Having the voters generate one-time key pairs on their web browsers and having certificates on those keys issued on-line. In practice we work with the model that each voter receives a cryptic user identity and a one-time password, based on which the certificate is issued on-line. The user identity and the password must be received through two different channels in order to provide a decent level of security. We consider two physical letters with some days in between as the most realistic option. Using a virtual chip-card. This means that the keys of the voters are stored in secure hardware by a pair of trusted organizations. Usage of the keys can be requested by providing two means of authentication to two servers located in different organizations. Again, both means of authentication can be very cheap and simple-minded.

As for the approaches mentioned above, the first one is appropriate if there is a long period of time between elections, and the PKI is not used for other purposes. The last one is appropriate if regular elections take place or the PKI is to be used for other purposes as well. The last approach has the advantage that voters already in the system can be notified about new elections by means of an insecure email only. Thus the cost of arranging additional elections is very low.

4.3   Protection against Hackers

In [11] Damgård and Jurik proposed a scheme for protecting internet voters against hackers. We will understand the word hacker in a broader sense so that it includes system administrators, who can completely legitimately observe and control computers of voters remotely, as well as hackers breaking in without permission. The proposed solution is to provide each voter with a paper ballot with a list of candidates listed in some natural ordering, and, in addition, numbered corresponding to a permutation π of the candidates. The voter then enters the number $\pi(c)$, where c is the number of the candidate selected according to the natural ordering. If a hacker observes the voting process, he will not gain any information about the candidate chosen, even if he has full control of the computer of the voter. Furthermore, if he tampers with the vote, the outcome will be uniformly distributed on all candidates. Combining this protection with homomorphic encryption in an efficient way is quite difficult. The scheme suggested in [11] for the generalized Paillier system is too slow to be feasible with the current band-with on the Internet and performance of computers.

In [16] we will propose another scheme, where we trade security and performance. In short, by restricting the possibilities of the hacker slightly less than for the original scheme, performance properties of the integration with the homomorphic cryptosystem improves sufficiently to make this sort of protection feasible. The paper ballot with permutations can also contain one piece of authentication information and possibly more.

4.4   Server Authentication

Server authentication is normally obtained by a SSL connection between a web server and a web browser. Technically, this works well, but in practice most web browsers are wrongly configured and most voters will be unable to tell, whether a server has been correctly authenticated or not. As a solution to this problem we propose that the paper ballot with permutations and one piece of authentication information shall also contain a piece of graphics, different for each voter. Furthermore, it will include instructions for the voter about how to verify that the same graphics appears on the web page from where he votes. When the voter enters the first piece of authentication means, he will be confronted with graphics on the screen. If it is not identical to the graphics on his paper ballot, he will have instructions to exit the faked web server.

4.5   Voters **Being Looked over the Shoulder**

A concern that for example journalists have expressed to us, and that we will have to take very seriously, is that of a voter being looked over the shoulder while he/she votes. The person looking over the shoulder can, for example, be a husband or an employer. This problem is not solved by the solution that protects against hackers because also physical items can be seen by the person looking over the shoulder. The best solution to this problem that we have encountered was suggested by the local community of Høje Tåstrup, a suburb of Copenhagen, which had worked with the problem in connection with an early voting pilot. The solution is to provide a facility where the voter can go discretely to have his/ her electronic vote replaced by a manual vote. In a transition period, where manual voting (voting at election sites) exist side by side with Internet voting, this can be by providing the opportunity for voters to vote at election sites before and after they have cast their Internet vote. In order to integrate this with a voting scheme based on homomorphic encryption and protection against hackers, cancellation/ replacement of votes must be implemented in such a way that it cannot be detected, which votes have been replaced. When this is combined with universal verifiability, the need for new cryptographic primitives arises. We will treat this subject in a separate paper.

4.6   Long Term Privacy

The universal verifiability means that anybody can connect each voter to the ciphertext. Security is based on the assumption that it is infeasible to decrypt the ciphertext and see what the voter has voted. In order to protect the privacy of the voter, not just at the time of the election but also several years into the future, the keys used for the cryptosystem must be large. For the same reason, we suggest proving the correctness of the vote using a zero-knowledge proof that is statistical zero-knowledge. If this suggestion is followed, the zero-knowledge proof will not reveal which vote has been cast even if the commitment scheme is broken. The key used for the homomorphic cryptosystem must be sufficiently strong to be supposed to remain unbroken for an extended period, whereas the strength of the key for the commitment scheme will only have to be strong enough to remain unbroken for a shorter period, provided that the zero-knowledge proofs are statistical zero-knowledge.

4.7   Legal Considerations

Most countries have rather precise regulations, specifying how public elections of various types must be performed. Thus laws, but usually not constitutions, may have to be changed before an electronic voting system can be used in elections covered by these laws. For elections performed internally in an organization other than a state, similar challenges may be encountered-parts of the internal rules of the organization may have to be changed. Today, most developed countries have a signature law. It seems to be a wise decision to study, which messages in a voting system must be secured in particular ways in order to make the decisions imposed by election organizers legally binding. For example, in order to provide non-repudiation, it may be necessary to have some messages independently time stamped. This can be reformulated in the way that the system must be designed so that predictable conflicts can be resolved successfully in court using the local signature law. We refer to [19] and the national signature laws for more details.

REFERENCES

[1]   Abe: *Universally verifiable MIX net with verification work independent of the number of MIX centers*; proceedings of EuroCrypt 98, Springer Verlag LNCS.

[2]   Boudot: *Efficient Proof that a Committed Number Lies in an Interval*, Proc. of Euro-Crypt 2000, Springer Verlag LNCS series 1807.

[3]   J. Bar-Ilan, D. Beaver: *Non-Cryptographic Fault-Tolerant Computing in a Constant Number of Rounds*, Proc. of the ACM Symposium on Principles of Distributed Computation, 1989, pp. 201-209.

[4]   Baudron, Fouque, Pointcheval, Poupard and Stern: *Practical Multi-Candidate Election Scheme* (manuscript), May 2000.

[5]   Bellare, Garay, Rabin: *Fast Batch Verification for Modular Exponentiation and Digital Signatures*; proceedings of EuroCrypt 98.

[6]   B. Schoenmakers: *A simple publicly verifiable secret sharing scheme and its application to electronic voting*, Advances in Cryptology-Crypto '99, vol. 1666 of LNCS, pp. 148-164.

[7]   R. Cramer, I. Damgård, J. Nielsen: *Multiparty Computation from Threshold Homomorphic Encryption*, Proc. of EuroCrypt 2001, Springer-Verlag, vol. 2045 of LNCS, pp. 280-300.

[8]   R. Cramer, M. Franklin, B. Schoenmakers, M. Yung: *Multi-authority secret ballot elections with linear work*, Advances in Cryptology - EuroCrypt '96, vol. 1070 of LNCS, pp. 72-83.

[9]   R. Cramer, R.Gennaro, B.Schoenmakers: *A Secure and Optimally Efficient Multi-Authority Election Scheme*, Proc. of EuroCrypt 97, Springer Verlag LNCS series, pp. 103-118.

[10] Damgård and Fujisaki: *An Integer Commitment Scheme based on Groups with Hidden Order*, Manuscript, 2001, available from the ePrint archive.

[11] Damgård and Jurik: *A Generalisation, a Simplification and some Applications of Paillier's Probabilistic Public-Key System*, Proc. of Public Key Cryptography 2001, Springer Verlag LNCS series.

[12] Damgård and Jurik: *Client/server tradeoffs for online elections*; proceedings of PKC'02.

[13] A. Fujioka, T. Okamoto, K. Otha: *A practical secret voting scheme for large scale elections*, Advances in Cryptology - AusCrypt '92, pp. 244-251.

[14] Fujisaki and Okamoto: *Statistical Zero-Knowledge Protocols to prove Modular Polynomial Relations*, Proc. of Crypto 97, Springer-Verlag, Vol. 1294 of LNCS.

[15] O. Goldreich, S. Micali, A. Wigderson: *How to play any mental game or a completeness theorem for protocols with honest majority*, in *Proc. of the 19th Annual ACM Symposium on Theory of Computing*, pp. 218-229, New York, May 1987.

[16] J. Groth, G. Salomonsen: *A practical Protocol for protecting Internet Voters against Hackers* (work in progress).

[17] M. Hirt, K. Sako: *Efficient Receipt-Free Voting based on Homomorphic Encryption*, Proc. of Euro Crypt 2000, Springer-Verlag, LNCS series, pp. 539-556.

[18] Lipmaa: *Statistical Zero-Knowledge Proofs from Diophantine Equations*; Cryptology ePrint Archive, Report 2001/086.

[19] L. Mitrou, D. Gritzalis, S. Katsikas, S. Revisiting legal and regulatory requirements for secure e-voting. *Proc. of the 16th International Information Security Conference*, M. Hadidi, et al. (Eds.), Egypt, May 2002. Kluwer Academics Publishers.

[20] Ohkubo and Abe: *A Length-Invariant Hybrid Mix* Proc. of Asia Crypt 2000, Springer Verlag LNCS.

[21] P. Pallier: *Public-Key Cryptosystems based on Composite Degree Residue Classes*, Proc. of Euro Crypt 99, Springer Verlag LNCS series, pp. 223-238.

[5]   Bellare, Garay, Rabin: *Fast Batch Verification for Modular Exponentiation and Digital Signatures*; proceedings of EuroCrypt 98.

[6]   B. Schoenmakers: *A simple publicly verifiable secret sharing scheme and its application to electronic voting*, Advances in Cryptology-Crypto '99, vol. 1666 of LNCS, pp. 148-164.

[7]   R. Cramer, I. Damgård, J. Nielsen: *Multiparty Computation from Threshold Homomorphic Encryption*, Proc. of EuroCrypt 2001, Springer-Verlag, vol. 2045 of LNCS, pp. 280-300.

[8]   R. Cramer, M. Franklin, B. Schoenmakers, M. Yung: *Multi-authority secret ballot elections with linear work*, Advances in Cryptology - EuroCrypt '96, vol. 1070 of LNCS, pp. 72-83.

[9]   R. Cramer, R.Gennaro, B.Schoenmakers: *A Secure and Optimally Efficient Multi-Authority Election Scheme*, Proc. of EuroCrypt 97, Springer Verlag LNCS series, pp. 103-118.

[10]   Damgård and Fujisaki: *An Integer Commitment Scheme based on Groups with Hidden Order*, Manuscript, 2001, available from the ePrint archive.

[11]   Damgård and Jurik: *A Generalisation, a Simplification and some Applications of Paillier's Probabilistic Public-Key System*, Proc. of Public Key Cryptography 2001, Springer Verlag LNCS series.

[12]   Damgård and Jurik: *Client/server tradeoffs for online elections*; proceedings of PKC'02.

[13]   A. Fujioka, T. Okamoto, K. Otha: *A practical secret voting scheme for large scale elections*, Advances in Cryptology - AusCrypt '92, pp. 244-251.

[14]   Fujisaki and Okamoto: *Statistical Zero-Knowledge Protocols to prove Modular Polynomial Relations*, Proc. of Crypto 97, Springer-Verlag, Vol. 1294 of LNCS.

[15]   O. Goldreich, S. Micali, A. Wigderson: *How to play any mental game or a completeness theorem for protocols with honest majority*, in *Proc. of the 19th Annual ACM Symposium on Theory of Computing*, pp. 218-229, New York, May 1987.

[16]   J. Groth, G. Salomonsen: *A practical Protocol for protecting Internet Voters against Hackers* (work in progress).

[17]   M. Hirt, K. Sako: *Efficient Receipt-Free Voting based on Homomorphic Encryption*, Proc. of Euro Crypt 2000, Springer-Verlag, LNCS series, pp. 539-556.

[18]   Lipmaa: *Statistical Zero-Knowledge Proofs from Diophantine Equations*; Cryptology ePrint Archive, Report 2001/086.

[19]   L. Mitrou, D. Gritzalis, S. Katsikas, S. Revisiting legal and regulatory requirements for secure e-voting. *Proc. of the 16th International Information Security Conference*, M. Hadidi, et al. (Eds.), Egypt, May 2002. Kluwer Academics Publishers.

[20]   Ohkubo and Abe: *A Length-Invariant Hybrid Mix* Proc. of Asia Crypt 2000, Springer Verlag LNCS.

[21]   P. Pallicr: *Public-Key Cryptosystems based on Composite Degree Residue Classes*, Proc. of Euro Crypt 99, Springer Verlag LNCS series, pp. 223-238.

Chapter 7

SECURE ELECTRONIC VOTING: THE CURRENT LANDSCAPE

Costas Lambrinoudakis[1], Dimitris Gritzalis[2], Vassilis Tsoumas[2],
Maria Karyda[2], Spyros Ikonomopoulos[1]

[1] *Dept. of Information and Communication Systems Engineering, Univ. of the Aegean, Greece*
{clam,ikono}@aegean.gr

[2] *Dept. of Informatics, Athens University of Economics and Business, Athens, Greece*
{dgrit,bts,mka}@aueb.gr

Abstract: This paper presents the security requirements and the system wide properties
              that the voting protocol of an electronic voting system is expected to fulfil.
              Then, an overview of the existing voting protocols, together with a brief
              analysis of their characteristics, is provided. The aim is to investigate and
              discuss the extent to which current voting protocols comply with the identified
              requirements and thus examine the feasibility of organising and conducting an
              Internet based election in a secure, efficient and reliable way.

Key words: E-voting, I-voting, Security Requirements, Voting Protocols.

1.   INTRODUCTION

*"Voting is ...an indispensable feature of democracy because, however
the goals of democracy are defined, its method involves some kind of
popular participation in government. Although participation can take
many forms, historically - and probably logically - it invariably includes voting"* [1]

Democratic societies are founded on the principle of elections and on
opinion expression capabilities. However, often many eligible voters do not

---

[1] William H. Riker, 1982

participate in elections. One of the common reasons for not participating is that voters find it inconvenient to go to the designated voting places; they may be out of town, on work, or even on vacation.

With the rapid growth of the Internet, online voting provides a reasonable alternative and in future may even replace conventional elections and opinion expression processes, attaining, also, economies of scale. Internet voting would support "voter mobility", allowing them to participate in an election from any location that provides Internet access.

Let us concentrate, for a while, to the main characteristics that such a system should exhibit. It should:

- Support all the required services for organising and conducting an opinion expressing process (poll, decision making-referendum, internal election, general election). Depending on the election process these services may be voter registration, voter authentication, vote casting, calculation of the vote tally and verification of the election result.
- Support all actors involved; namely election organisers, party representatives, candidates, voters and system administrators (ballot generation and management, management of voting districts and eligible voters, monitoring the voting centre and the remote voting districts etc).
- Provide a user-friendly environment that for Internet based systems is accessible through a conventional WWW browser.
- Support co-operative techniques for assisting the voter, taking into account all related sociological and behavioural aspects.
- Automatically calculate the final vote tally (after the election has ended).

It becomes evident, however, that there are numerous opportunities for corruption during the performance of each of the above mentioned tasks -for instance election organisers may "cheat" by knowingly allowing ineligible voters to register, allowing registered voters to cast more than one vote, or systematically miscounting or destroying ballots. Especially in cases where the Internet is utilized for realizing large-scale electronic voting systems, the task of simultaneously achieving security and privacy becomes even more difficult and if the system is not carefully designed it will be easily compromised, thus corrupting results or violating voter's privacy.

To this end an electronic voting system should implement a voting protocol that can prevent opportunities for fraud or for sacrificing the voter's privacy. The security (non-functional) requirements that the voting protocol should fulfil are presented in the following section. Furthermore, a brief overview of the system wide properties (requirements) that are closely related to the characteristics of the voting protocol is provided. It is emphasised that all remaining non-functional system requirements (the ones that do not affect in any way the design of the voting protocol), as well as the entire list of functional requirements for an electronic voting system are outside the scope of this paper.

Section 3 provides a rough classification and a brief overview of the electronic voting protocols that have been proposed since 1981. Also, an analysis of the most important characteristics exhibited by each protocol family is provided. Finally, Section 4 demonstrates the degree to which each protocol family fulfils the security requirements identified (in Section 2) for an electronic voting system.

2. REQUIREMENTS FOR ELECTRONIC VOTING

Despite the numerous advantages of an electronic voting system, both for the organising state but also for the voters, the decision to build such a system in order to conduct elections over public networks (i.e. Internet) is neither an easy nor a straightforward one. The reason being that a long list of legal, societal and technological requirements must be fulfilled [16,18]. A further difficulty is that the vast majority of the system requirements has been produced by transforming *abstract formulations* (i.e. laws, or principles like "preserve democracy") to a concrete set of functional and non-functional requirements.

The functional requirements of an e-voting system specify, in a well-structured way, the minimum set of services (tasks) that the system is expected to support, highlighting at the same time their desired sequence and all possible interdependencies. For instance, the number and type of elections processes (e.g. polls, referenda, general elections, etc.) supported by an e-voting system is determined by its set of functional requirements. Furthermore, functional requirements are related to many of the *usability properties* of the system, dominating the properties and characteristics of its interaction model with the user.

On the other hand, non-functional requirements are related to the underlying system structure, in principle they are invisible to the user and they normally have a severe impact on architectural decisions. *Security requirements* and several *system wide properties* like flexibility, voter convenience, efficiency etc, are derived through the set of non-functional requirements.

In principle, functional requirements for e-voting systems may vary a lot, since each system is aiming to fulfil the specific requirements of the market segment that it is targeting. On the contrary, the vast majority of security requirements and system wide properties are common to all e-voting systems since they determine the required compliance of the system with the election principles (democracy) and the security and privacy issues dictated by the international legal frameworks. Security requirements are, at a large extent, fulfilled by the *voting protocol* adopted by the system. Furthermore, the voting protocol dominates the majority of the system wide properties (for instance the performance, flexibility, scalability etc. of an electronic voting system are affected by the respective properties of the voting protocol).

2.1 Security Requirements

The chapter of this book, which is co-authored by Mitrou et al., provides a detailed analysis of the constitutional and legal requirements for electronic voting, concluding that "*Security aims at protecting the integrity, generality, equality, freedom, secrecy and fairness of elections. Security.... has to comply with the requirements of transparency and verifiability*". On the ground of this analysis, the current section addresses the properties that the voting protocol of an electronic voting system should exhibit. The brief description provided for each one aims to highlight, in a slightly technical way, the *attributes* - that can be later verified and evaluated both in a qualitative and quantitative way - associated with each property.

2.1.1 Accuracy

Accuracy, also referred to as *correctness* in [6], demands that the announced tally exactly matches the actual outcome of the election. This means that no one can change anyone else's vote (inalterability), all valid votes are included in the final tally (completeness) and no invalid vote is included in the final tally (soundness).

2.1.2 Democracy

A system is considered to be "democratic" if only eligible voters are allowed to vote (eligibility) and if each eligible voter can only cast a single vote (unreusability). An additional characteristic is that no one should be allowed to duplicate anyone else's vote.

2.1.3 Privacy

According to this requirement nobody should be able to link a voter's identity to his vote, after the latter has been cast. Computational privacy is a weak form of privacy ensuring that the relation between ballots and voters will remain secret for an extremely large period of time, assuming that computational power and techniques will continue to evolve in today's pace. Information-theoretic privacy is a stronger and, at the same time, harder to obtain form of privacy, ensuring that no ballot can be linked to a specific voter as long as information theory principles remain sound.

2.1.4 Robustness

This requirement guarantees that no reasonably sized coalition of voters or authorities (either benign or malicious) may disrupt the election. This includes allowing abstention of registered voters, without causing problems or allowing other entities to cast legitimate votes on their behalf, as well as preventing misbehaviour of voters and authorities from invalidating the election outcome by claiming that some other actor of the system failed to properly execute its part. Robustness implies that security should also be provided against external threats and attacks, e.g. denial of service attacks.

2.1.5 Verifiability

Verifiability implies that there are mechanisms for auditing the election in order to ensure that it has been properly conducted. It can be provided in three different forms: a) Universal or public verifiability [22] meaning that anyone (voters, authorities, external auditors) can verify the election outcome after the announcement of the tally, b) Individual verifiability with open objection to the tally [20] which is a weaker requirement allowing every voter to verify that his vote has been properly taken into account and file a sound complaint, in case the vote has been miscounted, without revealing its contents and c) Individual verifiability which is an even weaker requirement since it allows for individual voter verification but forces voters to reveal their ballots in order to file a complaint.

2.1.6 Uncoercibility

The terms *receipt-freeness* and *uncoercibility* for electronic voting have appeared in [4]. According to [15], a receipt-free scheme convinces the voters that their vote has been counted without providing them with a receipt. An uncoercible scheme does not allow the voters to convince any other participant (e.g. a coercer) on what they have voted. More specifically, in an uncoercible voting scheme a voter neither obtains, nor is able to construct, a receipt proving the content of his vote. While the concept of uncoercibility is stronger than receipt-freeness, the latter term has been used in the literature as the prevalent expression to denote the security resulted by both the receipt-freeness and uncoercibility properties.

2.1.7 Fairness

This property ensures that no one can learn the outcome of the election before the announcement of the tally. Therefore acts like influencing the decision of late voters by announcing an estimate, or provide a significant but unequal advantage (being the first to know) to specific people or groups, are prevented.

2.1.8 Verifiable participation

This requirement, often referred as declarability [13], ensures that it is possible to find out whether a particular voter actually has participated in the election by casting a ballot or not. This requirement is necessary in cases where voter participation is compulsory by law (as in some countries, e.g. Australia, Belgium, Greece) or social context (e.g. small or medium scale elections for a distributed organisation board) where abstention is considered a contemptuous behaviour.

2.2   System Wide Properties (Requirements)

In addition to the security requirements, an electronic voting system should comply with several other non-functional requirements. For example the system must be *reliable* (resistant to randomly generated malfunctions), *user friendly*, it must promote the principle of *"equal election"*, it must be based on *open computer architectures* and *open-source software* etc. In this section, *only* the system wide properties that are closely linked to the voting protocol implemented by the system, namely the *voter convenience*, *voter mobility*, *flexibility* and *efficiency*, are addressed.

2.2.1 Voter convenience

Voter's convenience imposes the need for the walk-away property. As in conventional elections, voters should be able to quickly cast their ballot and then "walk away", without having to return for a new round of communication with the voting authorities in order to complete the voting procedure. Clearly, this requirement is only related to the "vote casting" process and not to any other election activities like voter registration or tally verification. Furthermore, the specific property ensures that only standard hardware (i.e. no additional equipment other than a networked device) is necessary for participating in the elections. Normally this is a PC, but a PDA or a digital TV set could be also considered.

2.2.2 Voter mobility

In order to waive the limitations that apply to conventional elections, there should be no restrictions on the location from which a voter can cast a vote. Although it appears that this requirement simply imposes the need for a properly secured centralised voter database, it actually poses significant obstacles to many election schemes that rely on physical assumptions (e.g. voting booths or untappable channels) for combining contradictory security properties, such as verifiability and privacy or receipt-freeness.

2.2.3 Flexibility

A system should allow a variety of ballot question formats, in various languages and adaptable to many types of election processes. The ability to handle open-ended questions (i.e. write-in candidates) can be also claimed through this property but, as pointed out in [17], this is not compatible with receipt-freeness.

2.2.4 Efficiency

Taking into account the present figures for hardware performance and network capacity, it becomes clear that performance is a property that cannot to be neglected. In fact, almost every election scheme proposed so far employs many processing-intensive cryptographic operations, while communication volume tends to increase as more voters are participating, or more authorities are engaged in their protocols. Thus the complexity of a scheme becomes a crucial system parameter.

The time needed by a voter to cast a ballot poses an upper boundary to the number of voters that are allowed to participate in a specific election (scalability), given the election window (the period of time that online voting in allowed) and resources (servers, network availability and capacity, etc.) available.

2.3 Comments on the Identified Requirements

2.3.1 Contradicting Properties

Clearly some of the requirements listed above are contradicting each other, while others cannot be fulfilled given the available technology. Voter privacy, for example, demands that a ballot cannot be linked to the voter. On the other hand, in order to comply with the verifiability property, it should be possible to verify - inter alia - that each and every ballot, included in the tally, was cast by an eligible voter. Since preserving privacy breaks the linkage between the voter and the ballot, after the latter is cast, this is definitely not an easy task.

Individual verifiability contradicts uncoercibility. In order for the voters to be able to object, in case they notice that their vote has been miscounted, a receipt describing the way they voted should be supplied to them. But the same receipt may be utilised for selling their vote, just by presenting the receipt to the buyer, or make them subject to coercion, since the coercer will be able to verify the way they voted.

Moreover, fairness demands that no intermediate results are available to anyone, the election organisers included, before the election has ended. This often reduces voter convenience and eliminates the "walk-away" property, as it will be explained later, since the voter has to further interact with the organisers, possibly for sending a decryption key or otherwise allowing access to his ballot.

Finally, efficiency often falls for obtaining other properties, especially universal verifiability and uncoercibility, since computationally complex and communication intensive solutions are necessary.

2.3.2 Interrelating Properties

Although many of the security requirements for an electronic voting system are conflicting at the same time they are closely interrelated, forming different pairs, since the existence of one property implies the second or simply cannot exist without it. An example is uncoercibility and privacy. As already mentioned, the former is a stronger requirement than the latter, since it protects voter's beliefs from disclosure, even if he voluntarily wishes to prove his vote to a third person. An uncoercible voting system ensures voters' privacy, by definition.

Verifiability is a powerful supporter to the accuracy of a voting system. Such a system, possessing strong verification mechanisms, thwarts attackers wishing to disrupt an election, since their efforts will have no chance of affecting the result.

In some cases, where voters' identities remain attached to the ballot, lack of fairness may cause breach of voters' privacy. This can only happen if an intermediate result of the election can be computed, thus making possible to find out how a particular voter voted, by computing a partial tally immediately before and after his voting.

Robustness supports in an indirect way, fairness and often privacy. Fairness is benefited since intermediate results are not leaked when an election is abruptly stopped due to a malicious action. As stressed in the literature, this could lead into producing different results when the election is repeated, even in exactly the same context.

Finally, voter mobility and convenience are closely related, since in most cases the requirement for additional hardware also implies that the voter has cast his vote from a certain place, appropriately equipped. For example, untappable channels, often required to obtain receipt-freeness, can be only implemented in certain places (e.g. polling places). A scheme offering voter mobility is almost certain to provide for convenience as well.

2.3.3 Uncoercibility

Whether uncoercibility is necessary or not is under question. Certainly, it is possible that someone will be watching over the shoulder of a voter while he is filling out an Internet ballot and there are no technical measures to prevent that. A voter willing to sell her vote could simply supply the buyer with the credentials necessary to cast the vote herself, instead of the receipt. However, such a possibility applies also to someone filling out a paper absentee ballot, so Internet voting is no less private.

The idea behind both the absentee voting and remote Internet voting is to provide voters with the ability to cast a ballot in situations where this would be impossible otherwise. Coercion is inevitable, but it is deemed acceptable due to the reduced potential of influencing the outcome of the election, since the coercer must be present at the time the voting takes place. However, in the case of remote Internet voting the danger of massive coercion or vote buying is much greater, since ballot receipts could be collected and processed off-line. Receipt-freeness is necessary to prevent the latter from happening, not to eliminate occasional coercion. Currently, it seems that nothing can be done to avert this kind of threat in a remote Internet voting context.

However, it should be emphasised that an objection could in practice reveal in which way the voter voted, as pointed out in [21]. Even though the exact vote itself is not revealed, it can be more or less deduced from the conjecture that someone would not go into trouble, making an objection, if the result of the election is favourable, despite of the treatment of his vote.

3. VOTING PROTOCOLS

A large number of protocols and more generalised schemes for electronic voting have been proposed since 1981. Many of them share some common characteristics, a fact that has been utilised as the criterion for their rough classification presented next. For each *"protocol family"* an analysis[2] of the most promising protocol, in terms of its suitability to support electronic voting as a result of satisfying the majority of the previously mentioned requirements, that is currently available is provided.

3.1 Trusted Authorities

One of the most common approaches to e-voting depends on the involvement of an independent third party, namely a trusted authority. Protocols capitalising on the concept of trusted authorities attempt to build on the same principle that conventional elections do; that is the existence of one or more trusted agents that will faithfully administer the election. Voters interact with those authorities to register and submit their ballots and rely on them to produce the correct tally, without compromising their privacy.

3.1.1 A six-authority protocol

In [14], Karro and Wang proposed a practical and secure voting protocol for large-scale elections based on trusted authorities, which attempts to solve most of the problems that other protocols relying on this concept face.

The specific protocol employs six distinct voting authorities, namely the registrar, the authenticator, the distributor, the counter, the matcher, and the verifier. The communication model is based on the use of off-the-shelf secure communication protocols, like HTTPS, between the voters and the authorities. However, rather complicated methods are used for filtering suspicious communication among the authorities, in order to prevent collusion.

The way that this protocol can be utilised for conducting an electronic voting process is presented in the following sections.

3.1.1.1 Registration Phase

A voter must register with the registrar, identifying himself as an eligible voter. Upon registering, the registrar assigns a unique identification number to the voter, places the voter's name and ID in the registered voter list, and sends the ID without the name to the authenticator. The authenticator generates a unique pair of public/private keys for the ID it received, stores them in a list, and sends the pair of the public key s and the ID to the registrar. The registrar then sends the pair back to the voter (in so doing, the authenticator will not know whom the given key belongs to without conspiring with the registrar).

---

[2] The analysis has been based on the claims, comments and remarks published by the designers of the protocols, or by other researchers in the area.

The registrar sends the number of eligible registered voters to the counter. The counter, in turn, generates a larger number of ballots than the number of registered voters. Each one consists of each of the choices on the ballot, an encrypted version of each choice, and a ballot ID. The counter keeps record of the decryption key and the ballot ID for each ballot, so that the counter can later decrypt the cast votes. The counter sends the ballots to the distributor, a copy of the decryption table to the verifier and the match pairings (pairs of a ballots encrypted and decrypted choices) to the matcher. The registrar sends the authenticator a list of ID's that are eligible for the given election. If desired, the registrar may publish the names of these voters and the verifier can check the ballots and pairings to confirm that they were properly generated.

3.1.1.2 Voting Phase

In order to vote, the voter contacts the distributor and asks for a ballot. The distributor randomly selects a ballot and sends it to the voter, who, in turn, requests and receives the matching pair for the received ballot from the matcher. The voter then signs the encrypted version of the desired vote using his signature key and sends them to the authenticator, along with the ballot's ID number and the voter's own ID. The voter informs the distributor that the ballot with the given ballot ID has been cast (doing so, the distributor has a record of how many votes are actually cast and by which ballots, thus preventing any facility from generating votes for unused ballots). The voter also informs the registrar that he has cast a vote but it is not required to tell the registrar which ballot ID it used. The authenticator checks the signature to authenticate the voter and verifies that the authenticated voter is permitted to vote in the given election. Once authenticated, the authenticator passes only the legitimate encrypted vote and the ballot's ID to the counter. The voter gets a receipt, confirming that the authenticator has received the ballot packets.

3.1.1.3 Tallying and Verification

For producing the vote tally, the counter simply decrypts the votes it has received. After the tallying of the votes, each authority releases certain information to the public. To verify the integrity of the election, the verifier compares certain published lists. An individual voter could also compare some of these lists. The integrity of the election does not require a voter to do so, but allowing a voter to perform such checks increases the election security. The authenticator publishes the list containing the encrypted ballots and the ballot ID. The counter publishes its version of the same list and the verifier confirms that these lists are identical. To prevent cover-ups, it may be desirable to have the lists be sent to the verifier before they are published.

The verifier also uses this list and the decryption table produced by the counter during registration to confirm the results published by the counter. The voters can look at the two identical lists to see their votes on them. The distributor also looks at these lists to make sure that only legitimate ballots appear. Any illegal ballots can than be removed and the results recalculated. The distributor could also release its list of ballot ID's, but this should be done after the authenticator and the counter released their encrypted ballot lists. The authenticator also publishes a list consisting of all voter IDs that cast ballots (in numerical order) and the registrar looks at this list and confirms that only eligible voters voted. This list may be published, if desired.

3.1.2 Analysis of the protocol

The security of this protocol is based on mutual auditing and checkout. Each authority participates in an internally executed communication protocol, designed to prevent collusion. After the election is over, each of them is publicly audited by the others. According to the authors, their construction fulfils democracy, provided that no cheating occurs in the registration phase. Accuracy is obtained because voters are given a receipt and they are allowed to view the published lists at the verification phase. A legitimate vote cannot be altered, duplicated, or removed without being detected. No authority can generate votes for unused ballots without being detected, because of the lists published by the end of the election.

Regarding privacy, the only authority that can see the voters' names is the registrar. The registrar, however, can only see the encrypted ballot cast by a particular voter's ID and has no way to decrypt this vote without collaborating with the counter, but the communication model does not allow them to conspire. Voters can be sure that their votes were tabulated by verifying that their IDs and encrypted keys are in the lists posted by the authenticator and the counter, therefore the scheme supports individual verifiability.

Although the protocol is not designed to be receipt-free (each voter obtains a receipt, proving the way he or she voted), it allows the voter to change his or her vote. This means that a coercer can only ensure that the voter has cast the desirable vote by forcing her/him to vote just before the closing time of the election. The registrar is aware of the voters that have participated in the election. A list of them can be easily prepared and published, so verifiable participation is obtained.

The protocol also fulfils the voter convenience and voter mobility properties. Furthermore, it can be considered efficient, since only limited computation is necessary. Finally, since there are no restrictions on the ballot form, this protocol may accommodate any type of election and it is therefore flexible.

3.2   Anonymous Voting

Another widely used approach to electronic voting relies on the concept of anonymity. The main idea behind protocols following this approach is to allow voters to anonymously submit their ballot, in order to preserve their privacy. Since this would allow for fraud, the notion of an "eligibility token", in a variety of forms, has been introduced. These tokens are analogous to voter ID cards or handbooks used during conventional elections for certifying that the bearer or the person depicted in the attached photograph is an eligible voter.

The eligibility tokens are provided by the authorities to all eligible voters during the registration phase and after their credentials have been verified. The voters subsequently attach this token to their ballot, thereby validating it, and send them both to the authority through an anonymous channel. It is important to emphasise at this point that the token is assigned to a voter in an untraceable manner, meaning that the issuing authority has no way to correlate tokens with voters. On the contrary, finding whether a token is valid or not is a trivial task. Obviously, eligibility tokens should be very carefully handled, since anyone who possesses a token is allowed to cast a legitimate ballot.

The main differentiation between the protocols of this family is in the way that tokens are generated.

3.2.1 Improved Multi-Authority Scheme

In [11] a multi-authority protocol using blind signatures and bit-commitment on the ballot to form an eligibility token, is presented. The token is subsequently submitted via an anonymous channel. This scheme is suitable for large-scale elections, since the communication and computation overhead is fairly small even if the number of voters is large. It is a classical protocol, in the sense that it has been the basis for numerous enhancements and implementations. According to this scheme the participants are the voters, a validator and a tallier. Finally, it is assumed that an anonymous communication channel exists, utilised by the tallier and the voters for their communication.

An electronic voting protocol, proposed in [3] ("A practical electronic voting protocol using threshold schemes"), extends the one proposed by Fujioka, et al. in [11]. This scheme includes the candidates in the voting process, each computing a partial tally, in order to prevent malicious authorities from rejecting ballots or stuffing the ballot box. The final tally is produced by the tallier using a t-out-of-N threshold scheme.

The model of the original protocol has been further modified with the addition of a trusted third party, whose role is limited to the newly introduced "preparation (announcement) phase". Furthermore, in addition to the anonymous channels, a bulletin board is utilised for communication.

3.2.1.1 Announcement Phase

A list of eligible voters that is universally accepted by the candidates and the voting authorities is prepared. This list is stored in a read-only memory and is only available to the administrator. The trusted party generates a pseudo-random identity for each of the listed voters, using a secure pseudo-random generator. This identity is then stored, in scrambled order, in a read-only memory, accessible only to the counter, which, however, is unable to establish any relation between this list and the list of voters. The trusted party generates N partial keys of a threshold encryption scheme for the candidates, as well as the correct decryption key for the counter and delivers them securely to their holders. The threshold parameter, the candidates' partial secret keys and the decryption key are kept secret. The pseudo-identities are digitally signed and sent to the voters using an untraceable and secure channel.

3.2.1.2 Registration

Each voter selects his vote and produces his ballot (actually, a bit commitment to it) using a random key. He blinds the ballot, using another random value, signs the blinded ballot and sends them both to the validator, together with his identity.

The latter checks that the voter is eligible to vote, that he has not voted before and that the signature on the bit commitment is valid. It then adds the message on its public board, signs the blinded bit commitment and sends this certificate back to the voter.

3.2.1.3 Voting Phase

Each voter retrieves and checks the validator's signature on the ballot. If the check is successful, he sends the certificate together with his pseudo-identity to every candidate, through anonymous communication channels. If the check failed, he publishes the validator's response as an invalid certificate.

Each candidate checks that he has not received this certificate before and that it is a valid one, by checking validator's signature. If both checks are successful, he encrypts the certificate and the voter's pseudo-identity with his threshold key; he then appends both ciphertexts to the certificate and sends them all to the counter. Finally, he publishes the entire received message on his board. At the end of the voting phase, every candidate publishes the number of the valid votes he processed.

The counter, in turn, selects all messages received from the candidates having the same certificate as a prefix. If they are less than the threshold parameter t, he publishes that certificate as invalid, otherwise he extracts both ciphertexts from each message until t of them have been recovered. Using his secret key and the threshold decryption algorithm, he extracts the encrypted certificate and the voter's pseudo-identity and checks that the certificate's signature is valid, the certificate has not been received before and that the pseudo-identity is a valid one (it can be found in his list). He then publishes the certificate on his own public board.

At the end of voting process, the validator publishes the number of registered voters, while the counter publishes the number of the valid votes received.

3.2.1.4 Tallying Phase

Each voter checks that at least t of the candidates' published totals are equal to the counter's published total and less than the validator's total. She also checks that hers certificate is in the list published by the counter and notes its position (index) in it. If both checks are successful, he sends her random key and the index to the counter through an anonymous communication channel. Otherwise, she opens the certificate as the valid ballot and its signature.

The counter extracts the ballot from the certificate, retrieves the vote using the key received from the voter and appends to its public board next to the certificate, allowing everyone to see the vote. Finally, she counts the votes and announces the result.

3.2.2 Analysis of the Protocol

The checks performed by the candidates and the counter, during the voting phase, ensure that a valid ballot will always be accepted by the honest candidates, and the counter and hence this scheme can be considered as accurate. The privacy of the votes is preserved even if the administrator, the counter and the candidates conspire. The scheme is also universally verifiable, since if a voter claims disruption by the validator or the counter, he can keep his vote secret and present the certificate instead.

Moreover, if the majority of the candidates are honest, a voter or a conspiring group of the candidates cannot disrupt the election, making the scheme robust. Given that the blind signature scheme and the threshold scheme are secure, only eligible voters are able to vote and no voter can vote more than once, so the scheme can be also characterised as democratic. Finally, since counting is done only after the voting phase is completed the scheme can be considered to be fair.

However, it is emphasised that the fulfilment of all security requirements by the specific protocol strongly relies on the assumption that the trusted authority is functioning as expected. Furthermore, the inherent problem of forcing the voters to interact twice with the authorities inhibits the fulfilment of the "walk-away" property. Finally, receipt-freeness is not supported and thus a voter can easily sell his vote or a coercer can easily extort a voter.

3.3   Homomorphic Encryption

This broad class of electronic election schemes follows a different approach. Instead of hiding the identity of the voters using eligibility tokens and anonymous voting methods, they hide the contents of the ballot itself. The ballot is submitted in a traceable manner, attached to the voter identity, so that the verifiability property is easily satisfied. However, at some certain moment, the tally of the election has to be computed and this implies that the ballot must be decrypted, thereby violating voter's privacy. This is avoided by encrypting the ballot using a homomorphic encryption function. Briefly, a cryptographic function E is called $(\otimes, \oplus)$-homomorphic if the equation: $E(T_1)\otimes E(T_2) = E(T_1 \oplus T_2)$ holds for any two plaintext T_1, T_2. Usually, but not necessarily, the operators $\otimes$ and $\oplus$ represent modular multiplication and addition, respectively.

Although this property represents a weakness to the strength of this function, it is very important for e-voting applications, since if the encrypted ballots are "multiplied" together they produce a result that is the encrypted tally of the election. In other words the vote tally can be calculated without decrypting any of the ballots. However, the addition used limits the votes to a "yes" or "no" option (1 or 0, respectively), whereas a proof is required that the encrypted ballot indeed contains such a vote and not an arbitrarily large value.

It is clear that the above scenario may fail under a corrupt authority. In order to tolerate a misbehaved "teller", the encryption of the tally can be distributed to several authorities in such a way that only coalitions of a certain size can decrypt the tally. Schemes adopting this approach are presented in [7,8]; the concept being originally introduced by Benaloh, et al. [1,5,6]. Interesting variations were proposed by Schöenmakers [22] (improved in [[23]]) replacing the homomorphic encryption by publicly verifiable secret sharing, by O. Baudron et al. [2] who propose a hierarchical multi -candidate election system, and by Damgård and Jurik (see next section).

3.3.1 Generalised Pailler scheme

In [9,10] I. Damgård and M. Jurik propose a generalisation of Paillier's scheme [19] using computations modulo N^{s+1}, for any $s \geq 1$, allowing reducing the expansion factor from 2 for Paillier's original system to almost 1. They also propose a threshold variant of it, which is subsequently used to construct an electronic voting scheme along the lines of the one proposed in [8].

Their scheme involves M voters $V_1, \ldots, V_M$, and N authorities $A_1, \ldots, A_N$. The initial scheme only allows for "yes" or "no" voting, but it was later expanded to allow 1-out-of-L elections, essentially by holding L elections in parallel. A bulletin board is used for communication among the participants.

3.3.1.1 Announcement phase
Security parameters k (the size of N in bits) and t as well as a g are selected in advance. A key for the threshold generalised Paillier encryption is generated and the public key is published on the bulletin board for all to see, while the shares for the private key are secretly given to the corresponding authorities $A_1, \ldots, A_N$.

3.3.1.2 Voting phase
Each voter chooses a random r_i, encrypts his vote v_i as $E_i = E(v_i, r_i) = g^{v_i} r_i^N \bmod N^2$ and attaches a proof that it encrypts 0 or 1. The proof is generated using the Fiat-Shamir heuristic, incorporating voter's identity to prevent vote copying and it is actually a zero-knowledge proof that either E_i or E_i/g is a n^s'th power mod n^{s+1}. The resulting vote consisting of the ciphertext and the proof is published on the message board.

3.3.1.3 Tallying and verification
Each authority reads the posts on the bulletin board submitted by the voters, and checks for each voter that he has only posted one ciphertext belonging to $Z^*_{n^{s+1}}$ accompanied by a valid proof that is an encryption of either 0 or 1. It then calculates the product of the ciphertext in the valid votes. The number of voters as well as the resulting product of ciphertext, c, is published on the message board. Each authority decrypts c with its key share and posts the result on the message board together with a proof that the decryption was correctly performed.

Having completed these two steps, an appointed authority locates the first t authorities that have posted a decryption share together with a valid proof of it being legal. Using these shares the authority computes the product of the published ciphertext to get the result of the election and posts it on the bulletin board. The final tally consists of the number of valid votes and the number of "yes" votes.

Anyone can verify that the votes that have been taken into account are valid, by checking the proof of validity accompanying them. Correct partial decryption by each authority can be verified by the proof of correct decryption posted with the computed share. Finally, the actual result of the election can be computed by anyone, by multiplying the published shares - there is no need for a key in order to do this.

3.3.2 Analysis of the protocol

The scheme preserves all properties of [8], but improves dramatically the tallying time, since the use of brute force for finding the discrete logarithm corresponding to the result is no more necessary. Receipt-freeness is not considered, but the authors are claiming that combining the framework presented in [12] with their scheme would allow the fulfilment of the specific property.

4.   PROTOCOL SUMMARY

Table 1 summarises the requirements fulfilled by the protocols and schemes presented above. A legend, at the bottom of the table, provides an explanation of the symbols appearing in each property column.

In order to assess a specific protocol it is essential to evaluate the "requirement fulfilment matrix" in conjunction with the assumptions made by the protocol. For example, some schemes based on the trusted authority model appear to fulfil most of the requirements, but the assumption that every authority remains honest (especially when no cross-controls exist) is very strong and, thus, unlikely to be true in a real environment. Also, receipt-freeness is often obtained under strong assumptions, which render impractical the respective voting protocols.

5.   CONCLUSIONS

The employment of electronic voting systems for organising and conducting large-scale elections in a secure way is feasible, provided that certain deficiencies of existing voting protocols are successfully addressed. Specifically, it has been demonstrated that several security requirements are contradicting each other, thus requiring special treatment, while there are requirements that can either not be fulfilled, given the currently available technology, or they can be handled provided that a substantial increase in cost and complexity is accepted.

This (current) situation is also demonstrated by the fact that none of the existing voting protocols supports in an acceptable way (meaning with reasonable cost and complexity or/and by avoiding strong and unrealistic assumptions) the entire list of requirements with which the voting protocol of a secure electronic voting system is expected to comply.

Voting Protocols and Schemes	Security Requirements											System Wide Properties		
	Accuracy			Democracy										
	Inalterability	Completeness	Soundness	Eligibility	Unreusability	Privacy	Robustness	Verifiability	Uncoercibility	Fairness	Verifiable participation	"Walk-away"	Voter mobility	Flexibility
TRUSTED AUTHORITIES														
[14]	Yes	Yes	Yes	Yes	Yes	Cmp	No	Indi	No[1]		Yes	Yes	Yes	Yes
ANONYMOUS VOTING														
[11]	Yes	Yes	No	Yes	Yes	Cmp	No	Opn	No	Yes	No	No	Yes	Yes
[3]	Yes	Yes	Yes	Yes	Yes	Cmp	Yes	Univ	No	Yes	No	Yes	Yes	Yes
HOMOMORPHIC ENCRYPTION														
[22]	Yes	Yes	Yes	Yes	Yes	Cmp	Yes	Univ	No	Yes	Yes	Yes	Yes	No
[12]	Yes	Yes	Yes	Yes	Yes	Cmp	Yes	Indi	Yes	Yes	Yes	Yes	No	No
[10]	Yes	Yes	Yes	Yes	Yes	Cmp	Yes	Univ	No[3]	Yes	Yes	Yes	Yes	No[2]
[2]	Yes	Yes	Yes	Yes	Yes	Cmp	Yes	Univ	No[3]	Yes	Yes	Yes	Yes	No[2]

[1] Allows multiple ballots, only the last is taken into account.
[2] Allows extension to multi-way elections, with increased complexity and cost.
[3] Can be obtained by applying framework presented in [12].

Privacy: Inf= information-theoretical, Cmp = computational.
Verifiability: Indi = individual, Opn = individual with open objection, Uni = universal.

Table 1: Security requirements fulfilled by protocols and schemes

It is clear that the solutions are not straightforward, in particular since handling specific requirements (such as uncoercibility or universal verifiability) may have side effects on the complexity of the voting protocol, which in turn may affect the performance of the system and thus limit its scalability.

However, the extensive research work in the area of cryptographic algorithms and distributed systems is expected to produce, soon, exploitable results. Furthermore, the use of advanced computer architectures exhibiting increased number crunching capability should be investigated.

REFERENCES

[1]. Benaloh J., "Verifiable secret-ballot elections", *Ph.D. Dissertation*, Yale University, YALEU/CDS/TR-561, December 1987.

[2]. Baudron O., Fouque P., Pointcheval D., Poupard G., "Practical multi-candidate election system", in *Proc. of the 20th ACM Symposium on Principles of Distributed Computing*, August 2001, USA, pg. 274-283, ACM Press.

[3]. Baraani A., Pieprzyk J., Safavi R., "A Practical electronic voting protocol using threshold schemes", Centre for Computer Security Research, Dept. of Computer Science, University of Wollongong, Australia, May 1994.

[4]. Benaloh J., Tuinstra D., "Receipt-free secret-ballot elections", Clarkson University, 1994.

[5]. Benaloh J., Yung M., "Distributing the power of a Government to enhance the privacy of votes", in *Proc. of the 5th ACM Symposium on Principles of Distributed Computing*, pg. 52-62, August 1986.

[6]. Cohen J., Fischer M., "A robust and verifiable cryptographically secure election scheme", in *26th Annual Symposium on Foundations of Computer Science*, IEEE Press, pg. 372-382, October 1985.

[7]. Cramer R., Franklin M., Schöenmakers B., Yung M., "Multi-authority secret-ballot elections with linear work", in *Advances in Cryptology – EUROCRYPT'95*, LNCS 1070, pg. 72-83, Springer-Verlag, May 1996.

[8]. Cramer R., Gennaro R., Schöenmakers B., "A secure and optimally efficient multi-authority election scheme", in *Proc. of EUROCRYPT'97*, Germany, Springer-Verlag, LNCS 1233, pg. 103-118.

[9]. Damgård I., Jurik M., "Efficient protocols based on probabilistic encryption using composite degree residue classes", *RS-00-5*, Dept. of Computer Science, University of Aarhus, March 2000.

[10]. Damgård I., Jurik M., "A generalisation, a simplification and some applications of Paillier's probabilistic public-key system", in *Proc. of the Fourth International Workshop on Practice and Theory in Public Key Cryptography*, LNCS 1992, 2001, pg. 119-136.

[11]. Fujioka A., Okamoto T., Ohta K., "A practical secret voting scheme for large-scale elections", in *Advances in Cryptology, Proceedings of AUSCRYPT'92*, LNCS 718, pg. 244-251, Springer-Verlag, 1992 .

[12]. Hirt M., Sako K., "Efficient receipt-free voting based on homomorphic encryption", *Theory and Application of Cryptographic Techniques*, pg. 539-556, 2000.

[13]. Kiong N., "Electronic election", *Proceedings of ITSim 2000*.

[14]. Karro J., Wang J., "Towards a practical, secure and very large-scale online election", *in Proc. of the 15th Annual Computer Security Applications Conference*, IEEE Press, USA, 1998.

[15]. Magkos E., Burmester M., Chrissikopoulos V., "Receipt-freeness in large-scale elections without untappable channels", in *Proc. of the 1st IFIP Conference on E-Commerce/E-Business/E-Government*, Zurich, October 2001, Kluwer Academic Publishers, pg. 683-693, 2001.

[16]. Mitrou L., Gritzalis D., Katsikas S., "Revisiting legal and regulatory requirements for secure e-voting", in *Proc. of the 17th IFIP International Information Security Conference,* pg. 469-480, Egypt 2002.

[17]. Mürk O., "Electronic voting schemes", Semester Work, Tartu University, 2000.

[18]. Ikonomopoulos S., Lambrinoudakis C., Gritzalis D., Kokolakis S., Vassiliou K., "Functional requirements for a secure electronic voting system", in *Proc. of the 17th IFIP International Information Security Conference,* pg. 507-520, Egypt 2002.

[19]. Paillier P., "Public-key cryptosystems based on discrete logarithms residues", in *EUROCRYPT'99, LNCS 1592*, Springer- Verlag, 1999.

[20]. Riera A., Borell J., Rifà J., "An uncoercible verifiable electronic voting protocol", in *Proc. of the IFIP International Information Security Conference*, Vienna-Budapest, pg. 206-215, 1998.

[21]. Riera A., "An introduction to electronic voting schemes", *Unitat de Combinatòria i de Comunicació Digital*, Universitat Autònoma de Barcelona, 1998.

[22]. Schöenmakers B., "A simple publicly verifiable secret sharing scheme and its application to electronic voting", in *Advances in Cryptology - CRYPTO'99*, LNCS 1666, pg. 148-164, Springer-Verlag 1999.

[23]. Yung A., Young M., "A PVSS as hard as discrete log and shareholder separability", in *Proc. of 4th International Workshop on Practice and Theory in Public Key Crypto-systems,* Korea, LNCS 1992, p. 287, 2001.

Part III

CAPABILITIES AND LIMITATIONS

Chapter 8

PUBLIC CONFIDENCE AND AUDITABILITY IN VOTING SYSTEMS

Roy G. Saltman, M.S., M.P.A.

Consultant on Election Policy and Technology, Columbia, USA
rsaltman@alum.*mit.edu*

Abstract: Methods of achieving public confidence in ballot-tallying and non-ballot voting systems through auditability are discussed. Systems using ballots may use ballots as documents if strict control of all ballots is maintained and if voters are fully cognizant of ballot contents. Non-ballot systems require that software and hardware are assured to be logically correct through testing, and that full accounting of undervotes is made. System designs must be sensitive to human factors.

Keywords Auditability; Ballots, Direct Recording; Elections; Human Factors.

1. INTRODUCTION

There are two basic types of voting systems: ballot and non-ballot. Both types have been in use for a long time and continue to be used now.

1.1. Voting With Ballots or Other Artifacts

This type of voting began with the use of artifacts such as pebbles or beans. In ancient Greece, a vote using shards or shells was used to determine if a person was to be ostracized (from "ostracon," shell), that is, banished from a city. For binary decisions in olden times and even into modern times, voting might be carried out with black and white balls; the word "ballot" comes from the Italian "ballotta" for little ball. More recently, ballots began to be made of paper on which voters could write the names of their chosen candidates. Eventually, paper ballots containing the names of all candidates were printed and issued by a neutral election administration. In the US, before the adoption of the party-neutral and fully secret "Australian" ballot for voting for public offices, political parties printed and distributed their own ballots. Ballots distributed by the parties were not fully secret because of their differences in color or size; the selection and use of a particular party's ballot by a voter could be noted by those standing in the vicinity of the ballot box. The fully secret ballot was adopted state-by-state, beginning in 1888. In that year, Kentucky approved it for the city of Louisville and Massachusetts required its use statewide [1]. Some other democratic nations, obviously including Australia, had previously accepted it.

The use of artifacts such as ballots for voting brings confidence in the reported election outcomes to some election observers, as it provides a hard-copy record of the vote. Ballots can provide a meaningful count and recount, if the use of each ballot that was printed is fully accounted for, if the ballots are a true representation of the choices of the electorate, and if the ballots are properly guarded and the counting system assures an honest count. Investigators of the scandals of the Tweed Ring in New York City in the 1870s reported that Boss Tweed had stated that the ballots themselves did not matter; it was only the persons who did the counting who mattered.

In the US, the type of voting system used has varied widely among local jurisdictions. About 71% of US voters used a voting system with ballots in 2000, i.e., pre-scored punched cards (33%), non-pre-scored punched cards (4%), mark-sense paper ballots (30%), all of which were computer-readable, or hand-counted, hand-marked paper ballots (4%).

1.2   Non-Ballot Voting

Voting without ballots had begun, probably, with a so-called *viva voce* system, that is, with public announcements by the members of the electorate, whether divided only by ayes versus nays, or individually polled for specific preferences. A raising of hands, when all members of the electorate are gathered in the same place, is similarly non-artifactual. Clearly, in these cases, the persons who do the recording really matter, as there are no artifacts to be counted. With non-ballot voting, no recount is possible in the same sense as a ballot recount.

In the US, closely following the widespread adoption of the Australian ballot, non-ballot voting for public offices began to be used again with the introduction of the mechanical lever voting machine in the last years of the 19th century. Lever machines began to be increasingly used in the early 20th century as the population of cities burgeoned, and the cost and time of counting the ballots grew prohibitively in densely populated areas. The

American consolidated ballot, involving many contests at the three levels of government (federal, state and local), favored the use of machines on which all contests could be voted by a single voter within a few minutes. By the middle of the 20th century, almost one-half of US voters were voting on this type of machine. The machines are constructed so that each candidate is selected by the moving of a small lever to point to the name of a candidate listed on the machine's face. Each lever is connected to its own vote accumulator, but the latter is not seen by the voter. With the voter's final action at the machine, the levers are returned to their neutral positions and the selections for each contest are added to the sum of all previous selections for the chosen candidates. The machine retains only the accumulated totals of all voters and cannot store an individual voter's choices. However, the machine has an advantage over a ballot-counting system in that interlocks prevent overvotes (i.e. casting more votes than is lawfully permitted).

While the use of mechanical lever machines prevents ballot frauds, since there are no ballots, other frauds or errors may be perpetrated that are peculiar to the machines themselves. For example, if there is a disconnection between a lever assigned to a candidate and its associated vote accumulator, no vote will be recorded and the voter will be none the wiser. In fact, a serious logical limitation of the machines is that the recorded values of votes do not distinguish between a vote not cast and a vote intended to be cast but not recorded due to a machine malfunction [2]. In 2000, about 29% of US voters used a non-ballot voting system, either mechanical lever (19%) or computer-based, direct-recording electronic (10%).

2. CONFIDENCE IN VOTING SYSTEMS

"Voter confidence" is the level of certainty in a particular voter's mind that his/her desired election choices were actually transcribed as intended into the equivalent computer-readable indicators. The voter's confidence may be said to be determined following a personal review (a self-audit) of the voter's own candidate selection and vote-casting activity. The voter would also want to be assured that his/her choices were also summed correctly with all other voters' choices, but this is not completely knowable by the voter from his/her personal experience. "Public confidence," on the other hand, is the level of acceptance by the general public, taken as a whole, that the reported election results actually represent the collective choices of the voters. The level of public confidence includes the sum of all individual voter confidences, plus other factors such as assurance of computer program correctness, the announced result of an audit and reports of election difficulties and their causes.

Voter confidence in the method of voting and public confidence in the reported outcomes are essential in a democratic nation. Democratic theory, as expressed in the US Declaration of Independence that "governments derive their just powers from the consent of the governed" requires that these confidences be assured. Voter confidence may be increased with the use of voting systems that have superior human-factors capability, coupled with education and familiarization of the voters with the voting process and equipment. Public confidence may be additionally addressed with the implementation of auditing techniques.

3.   AUDITABILITY

To carry out an audit of an accounting system is to examine the system in order to determine if the results it reports are justified by the input data and by the actions of the process. A voting system for determining the outcome of an election is a type of accounting system. An audit may be used to determine if the summary of votes calculated by the system as received by each of the competing candidates is justified by the number and assignment of votes cast by the individual voters and by the arithmetic process of summation to obtain the candidates' results. It is assumed that the audit will be carried out by auditors whose independence is certain and respected.

Auditability is the determination of whether the data on which an audit is based are available to be applied so that a conclusive determination of correctness of reported results can be made. A problem of auditability occurs when the necessary data may not be available at all, or might be very difficult or expensive to obtain. In the latter cases, which are often the real-world situation, an audit might result in a level of confidence less than 100% in the correctness of the system outputs, rather than an certainty of correctness.

4.   PURPOSES OF AN AUDIT

An audit attempts to determine if applicable law and regulations have been followed in the steps of the voting process leading up to and including the release of the final counts. In addition, it may provide evidence of administrative errors, either deliberate or accidental, that were committed in the course of the voting process. Finally, the audit, if it demonstrates that the reported counts are correct, or corrects them if wrong, significantly contributes to public confidence in the administration of the process that results in the selection of the community's leaders. Public confidence in governmental operations is an essential component of the social contract that permits a society that is organized in a democratic manner to continue in that way for the foreseeable future.

5. AUDITABILITY IN A DOCUMENT-BALLOT SYSTEM

In a voting system in which each voter is issued a hard-copy blank ballot, each voter marks, punches or otherwise records his/her choices on the ballot. The blank ballot is thus converted into a document providing an input to the voting process. The essential condition of the document-ballot is that, even if some intermediation of the voting system is employed to create the ballot, the review and acceptance by the voter of the completed ballot before voting it renders the ballot an independent input to the election process. The inability of a voter to easily analyze a pre-scored punch card ballot (used by 33% of US voters in 2000) just before voting it, because the names of the candidates are not on the ballot, reduces the quality of this type of ballot as an independent input document.

The document-ballots provide the essential information necessary to assure that an audit of the reported results can be made (we assume that the voter's intent on each ballot is clear, or that a binding judgment about each questionable ballot has been made, so that the contribution of each ballot to the determination of the results can be unambiguously assigned.)

5.1 Auditing Around the Computer - Using Independent Input Documents

There are several ways in which an audit of a document-ballot voting system may proceed. One method of auditing is for 100% of the ballots to be counted manually or counted on an independently programmed and maintained system. Excepting for consideration of the inaccuracies of the ballot-sensing mechanisms and the impermanence of the conditions of voted pre-scored punch card ballots that occur with ballot handling and reading (should that type of ballot be used), the second count should exactly match the first if the system being audited is producing the correct results.

A second possible procedure is to select a sample set of ballots from the total quantity of ballots and to recount the sample, again either manually or on an independently programmed and maintained system. In the latter case, the audit cannot provide an absolute certainty that the reported results are correct, but instead, can provide a level of confidence in the correctness, depending on the percent of ballots recounted and the closeness of the reported difference between the two leading candidates. Some of the mathematics associated with the selection of the quantity of the sample, when determined by the closeness of the count, have been previously analyzed [2]. The analysis demonstrates that as the two main candidates become closer together in vote totals, the percent of precincts to be recounted grows, for a constant level of confidence. In the limit, when the two candidates are nearly tied, a full recount needs to be done. Note that the auditing methods just described ignore the actual equipment used to determine the count that is to be audited, i.e., the ballot-sensor, the computer, and the program. Instead, the audits employ substitute systems (either manual or electronic) under the control of the independent auditor or of an organization trusted by the auditor.

One method of auditing that cannot be used is that often used in banks in which there are accounts held in the names of customers and the bank is serving as the custodian of those accounts. Typically, each depositor is sent a statement of the value of his/her account on a certain date, with a list of transactions that have occurred since the distribution of the previous statement. The customer is sometimes specifically asked to verify the correctness of the account value and the transactions shown on the statement. In a voting system, the voter is depositing votes, not in his/her own account, but into a candidate's account, and the voter has no way of personally verifying how many votes in total were cast for the candidate. However, the voter may be part of the auditing process by submitting anecdotal evidence of personal observations and experiences, and by reporting the confidence that he/she has, based on observations, that the desired choices were transcribed as intended on to or into the corresponding computer-readable indicators.

5.2   Auditing Through the Computer - Analyzing Program Correctness

An alternate auditing method is to attempt to prove the correctness of the computer program that calculates the results of the voting. This analysis and testing should be carried out before the voting starts, with assurance that the program actually performing the calculations is exactly the same as the one that was tested for correctness. Ordinarily, auditors work after the fact. The program analysis and testing should be done beforehand by the election administration conducting the election, or by approved testing organizations as required under the Federal Election Commission (FEC) voluntary standards [3], with extensive documentation retained and made available to the auditors when requested. In order to attempt to prove program correctness, the program may be provided with simulated ballots with a wide variety of choices indicated, to determine if the program produces a pre-determined result. It is difficult to provide the program with all possible variations of ballots, so that an absolute certainty may not be possible. In addition, the paths of the program need to be analyzed to determine if there are any loops that were not exercised in the simulation. Such loops may contain "hidden" code, intended to operate under certain conditions and have malicious intent.

If the vote-counting program is to be run on a multi-programmed computer, then the effect of any other program also running on the computer must be considered. In vote-counting that is done at the precinct, the computers are typically doing nothing else but counting ballots, so that multi-programming is not an issue. However, the correctness of the compiler, the program that converts the application program from source code to object code, also must be considered. Testing of the program, by exercising it against many inputs of ballots containing a variety of choices, should be carried out directly on the object code, in order to assure that the effects of the compiler and other support programs are included in the tests.

5.3 Voter Contributions to the Auditing Effort

The voter can attempt to verify the votes recorded by reviewing the ballot before it leaves his/her control. After the voter relinquishes the ballot to the counting process, exits the polling area and then receives additional information from other voters or the media, the voter may conclude that the ballot, as submitted, did or did not reflect his/her intention. Then, a certain level of voter confidence will result, and the voter's level of confidence may be part of the auditing effort. An improved personal audit can be promoted before the polls are open by training of the voters to help them to carry out the voting instructions without error and to understand what a fully filled-out ballot that will be correctly sensed will look like. Voter confidence is likely to be higher if the names of the candidates are on the ballot to be cast, so that the voter may directly ensure that the marks or punches made correspond exactly to the choices that the voter intended to make. The PPC voting system is defective in this regard.

Documented errors by voters in using PPC ballots have demonstrated the depth of this problem. The peculiar presentation of the Presidential candidates on the ballot-holder in Palm Beach County, Florida, (the so-called "butterfly ballot") in the 2000 general election caused some voters to mistakenly vote for another candidate instead of their intended choice. However, after these voters withdrew their ballots from the ballot holder in order to deposit their ballots in the computer reader, they could not see for whom they had voted and therefore did not realize that they had made a crucial error. It was the lack of review capability, as much as the confusing presentation, that resulted in miscast ballots. Voters have been known also to punch holes in locations in pre-scored punch card ballots that represent no candidate whatsoever and not recognize that they have done so. In Wisconsin (1993) a documented situation of this type caused the Wisconsin State Board of Elections to order its municipalities not to procure any additional PPC voting systems. In the aborted review of Miami-Dade County ballots that was started in Leon County by court order following the 2000 Presidential election, it was reported by the supervisor of the recount process that literally "hundreds" of these ballots showed punches in ballot locations not corresponding to any candidate. The inability of voters to recognize the content of their voted ballots caused these errors.

Even with a mark-sense system, difficulties are possible. Some voters, misunderstanding instructions, will vote for a listed candidate and also vote on the write-in line, having written in the same name as the previously selected candidate. In that manner, an inadvertent overvote is cast. Clearly, precinct-count of ballots, including return for correction of overvoted ballots, rather than central-count of ballots where such return is not possible, will enable voters to be more certain that the submitted ballots accurately represent their intentions. Inadvertent undervotes are also possible. Voters who mark their mark-sense ballots in an unapproved manner risk the ballot-sensor not recording their votes. There has been some discussion and controversy as to whether precinct-located, ballot-sensing computers should return undervoted ballots to the voter. As it is lawful to undervote any contest, some election observers believe that returning undervoted ballots for "second chance" voting would cause unnecessary delays and violate voters' privacy. Some experimentation might contribute to the resolution of this issue.

6.   AUDITABILITY IN NON-BALLOT SYSTEMS

The more difficult problem of auditability in non-ballot voting systems arises because there are no document-ballots. There are no ballots created by the voters that form independent records and can be independently recounted, either fully or partially. Thus, the process of auditing using independent input documents cannot be carried out. Additionally, as with document-ballots, voters cannot be queried as to whether "deposits" to their candidates' accounts, as retained by the computing system, are correct. The remaining option is auditing through the computer, i.e., proving the correctness of the computer program by subjecting it to a wide variety of simulated voter-choice sets (the values that would be on ballots if there were ballots) [4] and determining if the results produced by each machine to be used are consistent with the values established on the input voter-choice sets. A check for the presence of hidden code must be also carried out.

6.1   Lack of Audit Value of a Computer-Generated Ballot

It is important to note that a hard-copy ballot, created by a programmed computer, even if the input is provided by the voter, does not automatically constitute a document-ballot that is an independent of the computing machinery. It has been noted that "the fact that the voter can see his or her choices on a display, or even receives a printout of the choices made, does not prove that those were the choices actually recorded in the machine to be summarized for generating the results of the election" [4]. A printout or hard-copy ballot received from the machine is not independently created by the voter; it is subject to the correctness or incorrectness of the computer program that created it. With electronic non-ballot voting systems, the computer program actually casts the votes. The computer may actually cast votes that differ from the voter's intent if the program was written to carry out that insidiously incorrect activity. Note, however, if each voter has the capability to review a computer-created hard-copy ballot, actually cast it following his/her own examination and approval and then have the cast ballot become the only source of vote-recording and counting, it would be considered a document-ballot. Then the voting system would not be a non-ballot system.

6.2   The Vote-Entry Section of a Precinct-Located Non-Ballot Voting Unit

A non-ballot, direct-recording electronic (DRE) voting unit located at a polling station, when engaged in an election, is used in sequence by a succession of voters. Each voter monopolizes the unit while voting. The unit may be analyzed as a machine constructed of two sections, the vote-entry section and the vote-summarizing section.

The data inputs to the vote-entry section are the selections of the voter. Its outputs are the final voter selections, i.e., the voter-choice set, established when the voter has completed the selection process, has informed the system that he/she is finished voting and is not permitted by the logic of the system to further revise or make additional selections. The outputs of the vote-entry section are the inputs to the vote-summarizing section.

The vote-entry section of the DRE voting unit performs steps similar to the vote-recording function that a voter performs when filling out a document-ballot but, as indicated above, the activity does not result in the creation of a document-ballot. The vote-entry section of the DRE machine, supposedly, has been designed to simply follow the instructions of the voter in recording his/her choices (except for the prevention of overvoting), but since the internal construction of the vote-entry section is not seen and is not known by the voter, there is no real assurance to the voter that this is the case. This situation is the auditability problem of a non-ballot voting system.

6.3   Design of the Vote-Entry Section

Design of DRE voting systems should promote voter confidence and should provide the means for effective examination by an auditor. The following design features are strongly recommended as contributing to auditability and voter-confidence:

Retention of each voter-choice set: The vote-entry section will have as output the voter-choice sets, also called electronic ballot images (EBIs) by the FEC. Each EBI will be retained, and that is required under the FEC voluntary standards [3]. Each EBI should be stored in a random memory location so that the sequence of voters cannot be matched with the sequence of EBIs. Once the EBI is stored, the memory location of it should become read-only. Then, the voter's choices, after being stored, cannot be altered.

Naming of the "All Voting Completed" Indicator: Each DRE machine will have a screen location or pushbutton for the voter to complete the voting process, once the voter believes that he/she has finished making all intended selections. This screen location or pushbutton may be identified as the "final vote," "all voting completed" or "I'm finished" indicator. It should not be named simply the "vote" location or button, as that does not sufficiently distinguish its finality from the intermediate steps of completing voting on any particular contest. Voters have been known to activate the "vote" button or location before fully completing voting, thereby denying themselves the opportunity to continue voting on subsequent contests. This error cannot be reversed if the voting system has no "second chance" feature.

Second Chance Voting: It is recommended that the logic of a DRE machine end the voting session with the first selection of the "All Voting Completed" indicator by the voter only if the voter has completely voted all contests. If the voter has not cast all the votes that he/she could cast, it is recommended that the machine provide the voter with the information that additional choices could be made ("undervote feedback") so that the voter has an additional opportunity, at the voter's option, to continue voting. The message to the voter should identify the highest-level contest not yet voted (or not completely voted if the contest allows more than one vote to be cast). This provision of feedback to the voter should improve the level of confidence held by the voter after voting that he/she has voted exactly as intended.

Implementation of Undervote Feedback: Design of the undervote feedback system would need to be different in touchscreen than in pushbutton machines, where one possible implementation is the inclusion of a separate "contest not voted" light for each contest. This light could be lit, possibly in a different color than the candidate buttons, if no candidate button were selected, and would be unlit if any candidate button were selected for that contest. For "vote for N" contests, there would need to be N "contest not voted" lights or some other method of indicating (such as an additional color) that additional votes may be cast in that contest. If the voter were to push the "All Voting Completed" button when one or more "contest not voted" lights were lit, perhaps they could be caused to flash. Then, the voter would still have the opportunity of voting additional contests, prompted by a message to that effect, or could end the session immediately by pushing the "All Voting Completed" button again.

For touchscreen systems, an extra "contest not voted" line could be added to each contest screen where that line is in bold type unless a candidate for that contest has been selected (for "vote for N" contests, the line might indicate the number of additional candidates that could be selected.) For touchscreen systems, the lit "contest not voted" lines could flash when the voter touches the "All Voting Completed" area, and a message could inform the voter of the options, allowing additional chances to vote additional contests.

6.4   Audit-value of EBIs and Undervote Feedback

Audit-value of EBIs: The retention of EBIs has specific value in enabling a recount to be accomplished provided that the EBIs represent the intended choices of the voters (given their limitation as generated by the computer program). If the vote-entry section of the DRE machine is not working properly, either accidently or maliciously, the EBIs may not correspond to the intended voters' choices. Pre-election checkout of the vote-entry section of each machine is essential. The EBIs of any machine should be stored, after close of polls, on a removable diskette that could be inserted in a separately managed and maintained machine to assure that the same summations are produced. The number of precincts to be recounted should vary with the closeness of the election.

Audit-Value of Undervote Feedback and Reporting: Undervote feedback to the voter has specific audit-value, in addition to its value in giving the voter additional chances to cast more votes. The audit-value occurs in including the "contest not voted" bit or bits ("null" vote) separately in reporting the voter's actions on each contest to the vote-summarizing section of the DRE. In a "vote for one" contest, the "contest not voted" bit would be "1" if the voter failed to vote in the contest and would be "0" otherwise. In a "vote for N" contest, where N is two or three or more, there would be N "contest not voted" bits. The number of "contest not voted" bits set to "1" would be the number of additional candidates permitted to be voted for who were not voted for in that contest. The effect of the use of the "contest not voted" bits is that the total of all "1" bits transmitted to the vote-summarizing section of the DRE for each voter is the same number, regardless of the configuration of each voter's choices. That is, if each voter is entitled to cast M votes and a particular voter actually casts M-X votes for candidates, then M-X votes are recorded as assigned to candidates in the EBI for that voter transmitted to the vote-summarization section of the DRE and X votes appear in the "contest not voted" part of the EBI for that voter. This transmittal of M bits set to "1" for each voter is a cross-check on the operation of the vote-entry section of the DRE.

6.5   The Vote-Summarizing Section of the DRE

The function of the vote-summarizing section is to sum up the individual EBIs after they are recorded and transmitted from the vote-entry section and, after the polls close, report the totals for each candidate and the "contest not voted" alternatives for each contest. With the addition of the "contest not voted" bits the sum of voters' choices for each "vote for one" contest should equal the number of voters who used the particular machine (the latter equals the change in the value of the public counter for the machine during the polling period). For each "vote for N" contest, the sum of voters' choices for that contest will equal N times the number of voters who used the machine.

6.6   Entry Point for Test Data

Each DRE machine should have an entry point for simulated voter selections in electronic form, so that the computer program within the DRE may be exercised by voter-choice data in volume. This process would not check the response shown on the screen or the pushbuttons to the voter's manual inputs. It is essential to demonstrate that each voter's choices shown to the voter on the face of the DRE are exactly what the voter selects, and are correctly transmitted to the data-summarizing section.

7.   VOTER-CONFIDENCE IN INTERNET SYSTEMS

Voting over the Internet is a type of non-ballot process. Concerns expressed and solutions proposed for non-ballot systems apply to Internet voting as well. Additionally, there are important concerns about the security and suitability of the Internet for voting that are unique to that medium and are beyond the scope of this presentation to address. Nevertheless, should Internet voting become a reality, one type of voter concern that may be more intense in Internet voting is whether the voter's choices really are added in with all other recorded choices to affect the final outcomes. This concern may be particularly strong in remote Internet voting, in which the voter is recording choices at a privately owned computer terminal located in privately owned premises, and the choices must be communicated elsewhere to be summed with all other choices. To put the question in more objective terms, the situation is that the vote-entry section of the voting unit is geographically separated from the vote-summarizing section of the voting unit and the two are only connected by through communications technology.

This type of voter's concern also occurs in central-count ballot systems, in which the voter drops the ballot into a ballot box and hopes that the ballot is safely transported to the point where, hopefully, it will be entered into a summarizing computer system. The voter's concern in remote Internet voting may be alleviated with the adoption of the concept of the "digital vote certificate" (DVC) [5]. The DVC has several functions, but one of them is to allow "each voter to verify on the Internet whether their vote was received at the servers without compromising voter privacy, vote secrecy or election integrity" [5]. That is, a voter may visit the website of the election administration after voting and verify that his/her personal DVC is listed among the DVCs received with a particular set of votes. The availability of the DVC does not imply that the actual vote values can be reviewed on the website. Review of the actual values of the votes must not be possible.

REFERENCES

[1] Fredman, L.E., *The Australian Ballot: The Story of an American Reform*, Michigan State University Press, 1968.

[2] Saltman, R. G., *Effective Use of Computing Technology in Vote-Tallying*, NBS Report NBSIR 75-687, March 1975 (reprinted as NBS SP500-30, April 1978), NIST, USA; www.vote.caltech.edu/Links/#articles

[3] Federal Election Commission, *Voting System Standards*, Volumes I-II, Washington DC, April, 2002; www.fec.gov

[4] Saltman, R. G., *Accuracy, Integrity, and Security in Computerized Vote-Tallying*, NBS Report SP500-158, August 1988, NIST, USA; www.nist.gov/itl/lab/specpubs/500-158.htm

[5] Gerck, E., "Fail-Safe Voter Privacy," *The Bell*, Vol. 1, No. 8, December 2000; pp. 6-8, 12-14; San Rafael, CA 94901; online at www.thebell.net

Chapter 9

ROBUST VERIFIABLE NON-INTERACTIVE ZERO-SHARING
A Plug-in Utility for Enhanced Voters' Privacy

Aggelos Kiayias[1] and Moti Yung[2]

[1]*Graduate Centre, City University of New York, USA*
akiayias@sci.brooklyn.cuny.edu

[2]*CertCo, New York, USA*
moti@cs.columbia.edu

Abstract: Strong ballot secrecy is a fundamental property of a voting system. Traditional elections, through voter isolation, ensure that this fundamental property is satisfied convincingly. Unfortunately, in the e-voting domain, achieving strong voter privacy proved to be a much more challenging goal. In the current state of the art e-voting schemes, voter privacy relies on honesty of a quorum of authorities, namely assumptions of the form "a certain number of authorities do not collude against the privacy of the voters." Although sufficient in some settings, these assumptions do not capture voter privacy as it is understood ideally. In this work we present a "voting utility" called Robust Verifiable Non-Interactive Zero-Sharing. Our utility can be seamlessly integrated in large scale "homomorphic encryption" based e-voting schemes, and enables a set of voters to protect the privacy of their votes, even in settings where all authorities may be dishonest and try to violate voter's privacy.

Key words: Electronic Voting, Homomorphic Encryption, Non-Interactive Zero Knowledge Proofs, Enhanced Privacy, Convertible Commitment Functional.

1. INTRODUCTION

Cryptographic design of voting schemes which started in the early 80's (see Chaum, [4]), proved to be very challenging, due to the multitude and conflicting nature of properties that such schemes need to satisfy. The desired properties required from an e-voting scheme are drawn from election theory and from the real world practice. A fundamental property of a "democratic system" is the privacy of the elections: the fact that the voter chooses to keep his choice private. In present real world systems, ballot secrecy is ensured through physical means. The "simulation" of this physical concealment of the ballot in the e-voting domain proved to be a very challenging task. This is due to the fact that ballots, if are to be concealed somehow, should nevertheless be "sufficiently" accessible for the purpose of tallying, integrity, and revealing the final results.

The standard solution that has been established in the literature (see e.g. Benaloh and Yung, [2]) in order to deal with the issue of ballot secrecy is to introduce a set of authorities, that distributedly share the capability of accessing the contents of the ballots (or linking a certain voter to his cast ballot, if the scheme is based on a cryptographic mix-net). Typically there is a threshold, that the number of conceding authorities needs to exceed in order to enable the capability to access the ballots' contents. In the case that some authorities are "corrupted" (in the sense that they wish to violate the privacy of a certain set of voters), they are capable of doing so provided that their number exceeds the threshold. Raising the threshold very high is very expensive since it induces dramatic effects in the efficiency and robustness of the protocol, two properties that can be of crucial importance, especially in the large-scale setting. While this type of voter privacy might be satisfactory in some settings, it has its shortcomings and raises serious privacy concerns (e.g. as expressed by Brands, [3]).

In this work we propose a solution for enhanced privacy for voting systems that does not depend on the underlying threshold structure employed in the election scheme. Our approach is based on the development of a voter-controlled privacy mechanism, a "grass-root privacy enhancer," that can be seamlessly integrated in any homomorphic encryption based e-voting protocol (as initiated by Cohen and Fischer, [6]). Our design is a voting utility called "Robust Verifiable Non-Interactive Zero-Sharing" that can be initiated by small subsets of the voter population that are interested in enhanced ballot secrecy. The objective of the utility is to provide (computational) ballot secrecy as it is understood in the ideal physical elections setting. Namely, consider a precinct where all voters apply the utility, then a person's choice can be revealed only if all remaining voters in a precinct (and the authorities) collude against him (we call this notion Maximal Ballot Secrecy[1]). On the other hand, we mandate that the privacy enhancing mechanism should not disrupt, or interfere in any way with the way the host protocol operates (hence the mechanism should act as a plug-in to a host e-voting scheme). For example, if one precinct in a multi-precinct

---

[1] See also [12] for more details about this notion (there it was called Perfect Ballot Secrecy)

election applies the utility while others do not, it is possible to employ the protocol without the utility in the other precincts.

Giving the power to control privacy back to the voters is an important step towards building *trust* in e-voting designs. Population-wide strong voter secrecy is beyond what we can anticipate to achieve in an efficient large scale distributed electronic voting scheme. Nevertheless, giving the option to any subset of the voters to achieve it locally, as our voting utility allows, in a way that does not encumber the overall election protocol, seems to be a significant contribution towards the establishment of trusted electronic voting mechanisms.

We provide a generic description of our Robust Verifiable Non-Interactive Zero-Sharing utility and we describe a "plug-in" implementation of our utility into the efficient scheme of Cramer, Gennaro and Schoenmakers [7]. We remark that the notion of "zero-sharing" has been used in a variety of different settings in cryptography (e.g. in proactive schemes, [13]). In its simplest form it is very easy to achieve if one assumes full pair-wise connectivity (and communications) between the participants. We emphasize that our zero-sharing mechanism, that is used to achieve Maximal Ballot Secrecy, further possesses the following crucial properties: (i) it does not require bilateral communication between the participating voters (all communication is handled by a bulletin board) and hence is *non-interactive*; (ii) all actions performed by active participants generate a *universally verifiable public audit-trail* (so there can be no disputes between active participants), and finally, (iii) it has the capability to correct faults, in an adaptive manner by employing a *corrective fault tolerance mechanism* that we introduce.

2. PRELIMINARIES

2.1 The Bulletin Board

A bulletin board, [6], is a basic primitive that will be used for all necessary communication between the participants in our protocol. The bulletin board is a public-broadcast channel with (non erasable and authenticated) memory. Any party (even third-parties) can read information from the bulletin board. Writing on the bulletin board by the active parties is done in the form of appending data in a specially designed area for each party and everyone can verify the appended information and thus the entire transcript of the protocol (the board is authenticated). Erasing from the bulletin board is not possible (the board is non-erasable). In the sequel, the phrase "party X publishes value Y" means that X appends Y to the portion of the bulletin board that is assigned to X. The bulletin board authority (server) may participate in the protocol to alleviate the computational cost of the participants and administer the protocol. Server-based ciphertext processing helps in reducing the computations of the parties, whenever trusted. All computation performed by this authority will be publicly verifiable (e.g., by repeating the computation whenever not trusted).

2.2   Proofs of Knowledge

Let $R(x,w)$ be a polynomial-time relation (i.e. there exists a polynomial-time predicate A_R with the property $A_R(x,w)=1$ iff $(x,w) \in R$). A proof of knowledge is a protocol between two "players": the prover P and the verifier V. For a certain relation R, and a given x, the prover knows some w such that $(x,w) \in R$ (the so-called witness) and wants to prove this fact to the verifier. We consider "3-round" proofs of knowledge of the form $\langle m_1,c,m_2 \rangle$, where the sequence the players move are P,V,P; see also [8,9]. The prover and the verifier are implemented by four probabilistic algorithms P_1, P_2, V_1, V_2 with output in Σ^*. $P_1(x,w)=\langle m_1,s \rangle$ is the output of P in the first round (where s is kept private), $V_1(.)=c$ is the output of V in the second round (a random value from the appropriate space), and $P_2(x,w,m_1,s,c)=m_2$ is the output of P in the third round. Finally, V "accepts" iff $V_2(x,m_1,c,m_2)=1$. See *figure 1*, for a representation of 3-round proof of knowledge.

The properties of a proof of knowledge implemented by P_1,P_2,V_1,V_2 that are of interest in the context of e-voting schemes are the following: (i) *completeness*: the (honest) verifier accepts with very high probability in the case that $(x,w) \in R$. (ii) *soundness*: if the prover P is not given a witness w s.t. $(x,w) \in R$, then for any probabilistic algorithms P_1',P_2' playing the role of the prover P, it holds that the verifier rejects with very high probability. In fact we will use a more specific notion called *special soundness*: given two different "conversations" $\langle m_1,c,m_2 \rangle$ and $\langle m_1,c',m_2' \rangle$, with the same first move, the computation of a witness w s.t. $(x,w) \in R$ can be done efficiently. (iii) special honest verifier zero knowledge: it is possible to sample the space of conversations between a honest prover (using the specified algorithms P_1,P_2) and a honest verifier (using V_1) without access to a witness w such that $(x,w) \in R$. Note that this property ensures that a honest verifier does not gain any knowledge (beyond trivial) about the witness w that is available to the prover. This is sufficient to ensure zero-knowledge in our setting, as the verifier will be simulated by a "random-oracle", see below.

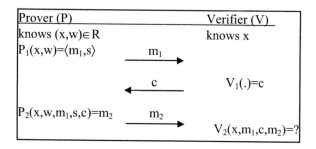

Figure 1. A 3-round Proof of Knowledge

Proofs of knowledge of this form can be made non-interactive and zero-knowledge (in the random oracle model) by employing the well-known heuristics of Fiat and Shamir [10]. Suppose that the proof of knowledge is implemented by P_1, P_2, V_1, V_2. In order to "personalize" the non-interactive version of the proof we assume additionally that the prover is identified by a publicly known identity string denoted by $I(P)$. Let H be a public hash function (thought of as a random oracle) with output in the range of V_1. In the non-interactive version the prover P computes $P_1(x,w)=\langle m_1,s\rangle$, $c=H(I(P),m_1)$, and $P_2(x,w,m_1,s,c)=m_2$ and outputs a string $PK(x)$ that equals to x concatenated by the simulated conversation $\langle m_1,c,m_2\rangle$. Any interested third party can verify the validity of the proof by checking the two equalities $c=H(I(P),m_1)$ and $V_2(x,m_1,c,m_2)=1$.

2.2.1 Proof of knowledge of Equality of Discrete-Logs

Proofs of knowledge of equality of discrete-logs over a multiplicative group G are a very useful tool in the context of e-voting schemes. The proof was introduced by Chaum and Pedersen [5], and it can be shown to be complete, sound, and special honest verifier zero-knowledge (Fig. 2). We will denote the non-interactive version of this proof of knowledge by $\mathsf{PKEQDL}(e: \gamma=\alpha^e \wedge \delta=\beta^e)$ as it ensures that the prover P knows an exponent e that satisfies the prescribed predicate, for some given values $\alpha,\beta,\gamma,\delta$ that belong in G.

2.3   E-voting Based on Homomorphic Encryption

The voting utility we present applies to a large family of voting schemes that are based on homomorphic encryption (initiated by Benaloh et al. [1,6]). The participants in the protocol are a population of voters V and a set of authorities. Each voter $V \in V$ has a unique identification string denoted by $I(V)$. Identification strings are publicly known.

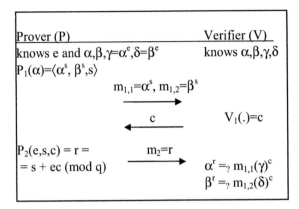

Figure 2. Proof of Knowledge of Equality of Discrete Logs

The scheme uses a homomorphic semantically secure probabilistic encryption function $E:P \to G$. The set P of plaintexts is an additive abelian group. The set of ciphertexts, G, is a multiplicative abelian group for the operation $\otimes$. Let **Choices**$\subseteq P$ denote the set of choices for a vote. The encryption function E is homomorphic in the sense that for all $a,b \in P$ it holds that the probability distribution of $E(a+b)$ is indistinguishable from the probability distribution of $E(a) \otimes E(b)$.

Ballot-casting requires from each voter V to publish his encrypted selection v_V from the set **Choices**, $B_V = E(v_V)$ to the bulletin board. Each voter, along with B_V publishes a non-interactive proof of knowledge PKB(B_V) that convinces any interested third party that the encrypted ballot B_V, is formed according to the specifications of the protocol without revealing any information about the choice v_V. In particular, among others, it has to be shown that $v_V \in$ **Choices**.

Tallying involves an operation that "pools" all encrypted ballots together using the operation $\otimes$: in particular the tallier computes $T = \prod_{V \in V} B_V$ (note that for readability we will use "$\prod$" instead of "$\otimes$" depending on the context). Due to the homomorphic property of the encryption function E, it follows that T is a valid encryption of the sum $\sum_{V \in V} v_V$. Decrypting T will reveal the result of the election. Typically a set of authorities is capable of inverting E in a distributed publicly verifiable manner.

Many e-voting schemes proposed in the literature belong to the family described above. Some well known recent examples of such schemes are Cramer et al. [7], based on the ElGamal Encryption function, and Fouque et al. [11], based on the Paillier Encryption Function.

3. ROBUST VERIFIABLE NON-INTERACTIVE ZERO-SHARING

In this section we present a high level description of our utility. The protocol will be executed by a set of voters $\{V_1,...,V_n\} \subseteq V$ from the voter population of an e-voting scheme based on homomorphic encryption. Additionally, we assume the existence of a non-trusted server (the bulletin board server) that will aid in the protocol by executing (publicly verifiable) ciphertext-processing operations. Below, we describe, in a generic way, the steps to be implemented. We remark that several disjoint subsets of voters may initiate our voting utility in an execution of the host e-voting scheme.

3.1 Generic Description

Let G be the multiplicative group of ciphertexts and P be the additive group of plaintexts for the encryption function E. Our protocol is based on the following basic notion that we introduce, called *convertible commitment functional*. A convertible commitment functional is a family $F = \{f_i : P \to G \mid i \in A\}$ with the following properties: (i) Isomorphic: for any $f_i \in F$ and all $a, b \in P$, $f(a+b) = f(a) \otimes f(b)$). (ii) One-wayness: all $f_i \in F$ are strongly one-way. (iii) Convertibility. Fix any $f \in F$. The f-transformation of $f_i \in F$ is an automorphism $g_i : G \to G$ with the property $g_i(f_i(a)) = f(a)$ for all a. We require that: (iii-a) it is easy to sample an element of F along with its f-transformation. (iii-b) given an element of F (without its f-transformation) it is computationally hard to simulate its f-transformation.

The three steps below constitute the "pre-processing" phase that is executed prior to the ballot-casting phase of the e-voting protocol.

Step 1. For a family F, a random $f \in F$ is selected. Every voter V_i samples an $f_i \in F$ along with its f-transformation g_i and publishes f_i.

Step 2. Each voter V_i selects random values $blind[i \to j] \in P$ (the blind shares) so that $\sum_{j=1..n} blind[i \to j] = 0$. Then, he publishes the values $BLIND[i \to j] = f_j(blind[i \to j])$ together with the strings $TRAIL(BLIND[i \to j])$ for $j = 1,..n$, that collectively convince any third party that the sum of $blind[i \to j]$ for $j = 1..n$ is indeed equal to 0.

Step 3. The server computes a "blind value" for each voter V_j as follows $BLIND[j] = \prod_{i=1..n} BLIND[i \to j]$. This is a publicly verifiable computation (any interested third party can verify it by repeating it). The blind values should satisfy the following two properties: (i) "cancellation property": $\prod_{j=1..n} g_j(BLIND[j]) = 1$. Indeed, this can be seen immediately from the definition, as it holds that $\prod_{j=1..n} g_j(BLIND[j]) = \prod_{j=1..n} f(\sum_{i=1..n} blind[i \to j]) = f(\sum_{i=1..n, j=1..n} blind[i \to j]) = f(0) = 1$. (ii) "randomization property": for all i=1..n, if C is a ciphertext under E, it holds that $C \otimes BLIND[i]$ is the encryption of a randomized plaintext over P.

The ballot-casting phase of the host protocol should be modified as follows: each voter V_i in the set $\{V_1,...,V_n\}$ instead of publishing their encrypted ballot B_i as described in the specifications of the protocol, they publish the "blinded" ballot $B_i' = B_i \otimes g_i(BLIND[i])$. The proof of knowledge $PKB(B_i')$ that accompanies the encrypted ballot is modified properly so that the voter proves that he indeed blinded its ballot by applying g_i over the publicly known value $BLIND[i]$.

No further modifications are needed. Indeed, when the tally $T = \prod_{v \in V} B_V$ will be computed the blinding values will be cancelled out: let $V' = V - \{V_1,...,V_n\}$, be the set of voters that do not participate in the utility. When the protocol is run together with our utility, the modified tally T', computed by the tallying authority, equals to $\prod_{v \in V'} B_V \otimes \prod_{i=1..n} B_i'$. Then, due to the cancellation property, $T' = \prod_{v \in V'} B_V \otimes \prod_{i=1..n} g_i(BLIND[i]) = T \otimes 1 = T$.

3.2   The Security Property: Maximal Ballot Secrecy

The basic security property that is satisfied by an instantiation of the voting utility we propose is *Maximal Ballot Secrecy*: the sub-tally of the votes of a subset of voters A from the set $\{V_1,...,V_n\}$ is *only* accessible to a malicious coalition of the authorities *and* the remaining voters $\{V_1,...,V_n\}$-A.

In particular this means that *only* the partial-tally of *all* the votes of $\{V_1,...,V_n\}$ will be accessible to the authorities. On the other hand, the violation of the privacy of a single voter V_i requires the collaboration of the authorities with all other voters in the set $\{V_1, V_2, ..., V_{i-1}, V_{i+1}, ... V_n\}$. We remark that our description of the security property applies to the state of knowledge prior to the announcement of the final tally. After the announcement of the final-tally the knowledge of every participant about what others voted may increase dramatically (e.g. in a yes/no voting procedure between 10 participants that ends up with 10 "yes" and 0 "no" votes there is no question after the announcement of the final tally what each individual voter voted). As a result, the security of the voters is understood to be conditioned by the uncertainty that remains after the tally announcement.

3.3   Corrective Fault Tolerance

The non-interactive zero-sharing voting utility provides high grade of security at the price of requiring more steps from the interested voters, and it is sensitive to failures (something that appears to be inevitable when maximal ballot secrecy is required). To see this consider a voter that participates in the pre-processing phase but does not participate in the ballot-casting phase. It is clear that since the shares that were issued for this voter will never be pooled together in the tally computation, the partial-tally will be inaccessible to the tallier. This means that the authorities in the host voting scheme will be forced to ignore completely the votes of the set of voters $\{V_1,...,V_n\}$ (note that there is no way for our plug-in utility to cause failure in the host protocol, since all participants' actions generate a public-audit trail; hence at any given moment any interested third party knows if the protocol progresses as specified). To prevent the rejection of the sub-tally, the active voters running our plug-in, should take some corrective steps, described in this section.

We note that the two cases we examine below are not intended to capture all possible failure possibilities. It is expected that when high grade ballot secrecy is needed, such as maximal ballot secrecy, there will be catastrophic cases where the protocol might need to restart. We remark that using generic byzantine agreement procedures, if the majority of voters is "honest", then they can prevent such restarts and deal with all fault occurrences, but this is beyond the scope of the current exposition.

3.3.1 Case (i): Some voters do not complete the pre-processing

Here we deal with the case where some of the voters that executed step 1 of the pre-processing phase, fail to publish the blind shares, i.e. fail to execute step 2 of the pre-processing phase. The remaining active voters need to cancel the shares they issued to these inactive voters.

Denote the set of voters whose shares should be cancelled by $S \subseteq \{V_1,...,V_n\}$, and the set of remaining (active) voters by S'. Each voter V_k, with $k \in S'$, publishes the value $SHARES[k \rightarrow S]=\sum_{j \in S} blind[k \rightarrow j]$. The voter also publishes a string TRAIL($SHARES[k \rightarrow S]$) to convince any third party that he publishes the correct value.

The server in step 3 of the pre-processing phase computes the blind values $BLIND[k]$ for all $k \in S'$ as follows: $BLIND[k]= f_k(SHARES[k \rightarrow S]) \otimes (\prod_{i \in S'} BLIND[i \rightarrow k])$. Now observe that the values $\{BLIND[k]\}_{k \in S'}$ satisfy the cancellation property: $\prod_{k \in S'} g_k(BLIND[k])= f(\sum_{k \in S'}(\sum_{j \in S} blind[k \rightarrow j] + \sum_{i \in S'} blind[i \rightarrow k])) = f(0) = 1$.

3.3.2 Case (ii): Some voters do not cast a ballot.

In this subsection, we deal with the case where some of the voters that participated in the pre-processing phase, fail to cast a ballot. We denote the set of voters that do not cast a ballot by U and the set of remaining voters by U'. We describe how the active voters U' engage in a corrective step and prevent the authorities from excluding their partial tally from the overall tally computation.

Every voter V_k with $k \in U'$, publishes the value $SHARES[k \to U]$ as defined in the previous subsection, together with the string $\mathsf{TRAIL}(SHARES[k \to U])$. Additionally he publishes $CANCEL[U \to k] = g_k(\prod_{i \in U}(BLIND[i \to k])$ along with the string $\mathsf{TRAIL}(CANCEL[U \to k])$ to convince any third party that he publishes the proper value. After the completion of this corrective phase, the server modifies the published ballots B_k' as follows $B_k'' = B_k' \otimes f(SHARES[k \to S]) \otimes (CANCEL[U \to k])^{-1}$, for all $k \in U'$ (a publicly verifiable computation).

Then, tallying can be done as before: let V' be the set of voters that do not participate in the zero-sharing. The tallier will compute $T = \prod_{v \in V'} B_v \otimes \prod_{k \in U'} B_k''$. To see that the tally computation is correct, observe that, $\prod_{k \in U'} B_k'' = \prod_{k \in U'} [\, B_k' \otimes f(SHARES[k \to S]) \otimes (CANCEL[U \to k])^{-1}\,] = (\prod_{k \in U'} B_k) \otimes f(\sum_{k \in U'}(\sum_{i=1..n} blind[i \to k] - \sum_{i \in U} blind[i \to k] + \sum_{j \in U} blind[k \to j])) = (\prod_{k \in U'} B_k) \otimes f(\sum_{k \in U'}(\sum_{i \in U'} blind[i \to k] + \sum_{j \in U} blind[k \to j])) = (\prod_{k \in U'} B_k) \otimes f(0) = \prod_{k \in U'} B_k$.

We note that the two corrective steps described above, are not exclusive and both can be implemented in a single execution of a protocol.

4.   AN IMPLEMENTATION OF THE UTILITY

In this section we describe how our generic construction can be instantiated in the case of the scheme of [7]. The encryption fuction is defined as follows: $E(v) = \langle G^r, H^r F^v \rangle$, where r is selected at random and G,H,F, are fixed generators of the group G of prime order q (typically a large subgroup of Z_p^* where p is a large prime) over which we assume that the Decisional Diffie Hellman Problem is hard. For more details the reader is referred to [7]. The encrypted ballot space is $G^2 = G \times G$. If $VALUE = \langle X, X' \rangle \in G^2$ we will denote X' by $VALUE_2$. The plaintext space P equals to the finite field Z_q. The set **Choices** $= \{v[1], v[2], ..., v[z]\}$ is a set of integers less than q where z corresponds to the number of candidates.

4.1   The Pre-Processing Phase

Below we show how the three steps of the pre-processing phase are instantiated. First observe that G^2 is an abelian group w.r.t. the operation $\langle X, X' \rangle \otimes \langle Y, Y' \rangle = (XY, X'Y')$. Let α be a generator of G, and let $\mathbf{F} = \{ f_i : P \to G^2 \mid f_i(x) = \langle 1, (\alpha^i)^x \rangle, i \in P - \{0\} \}$. It is easy to verify that $\mathbf{F}$ is a convertible commitment functional under the DDH assumption (see also step 1, below). Fix two functions $f, f_{ctr} \in \mathbf{F}$, with $f(x) = \langle 1, \alpha^x \rangle$ and $f_{ctr}(x) = \langle 1, \gamma^x \rangle$, so that $\log_\alpha \gamma$ is not known to any participant.

Step 1. Every voter V_i publishes a value $h_i = \alpha^{a[i]}$ where a[i] is selected at random from P. The function of F associated to voter V_i, denoted by f_i, is defined as $f_i(x) = \langle 1, (h_i)^x \rangle$. The f-transformation of f_i is defined as $g_i: G^2 \rightarrow G^2$ with $g_i(X,Y) = \langle X, Y^{b[i]} \rangle$ where $b[i] = (a[i])^{-1} \pmod q$. Observe that $g_i(f_i(x)) = f(x)$ for all $x \in P$.

Step 2. Each voter V_i selects random values $blind[i \rightarrow j] \in P$ so that $\sum_{j=1..n} blind[i \rightarrow j] = 0 \pmod q$, and publishes $BLIND[i \rightarrow j] = f_i(blind[i \rightarrow j])$ for j=1..n. Each string $\mathsf{TRAIL}(BLIND[i \rightarrow j])$ is comprised by the values $CONTROL[i \rightarrow j] = f_{ctr}(blind[i \rightarrow j])$, and $\mathsf{PKEQDL}(e: CONTROL_2[i \rightarrow j] = \gamma^e \land BLIND_2[i \rightarrow j] = (h_j)^e)$.

Step 3. The last step is executed as in the generic description. The blind values are equal to $BLIND[j] = \prod_{i=1..n} BLIND[i \rightarrow j] = \langle 1, h_j^{blind[1,j]+...+blind[n,j]} \rangle$.

Claim. At any time, after the completion of the pre-processing phase, (i) any interested third-party can verify that the blind values satisfy the cancellation property. (ii) if at least one voter follows the protocol as specified, the values $BLIND[j]$, j=1..n, satisfy the randomization property.

To see why (i) holds, consider the following: the third party checks for all i,j=1..n the proof of knowledge given in $\mathsf{TRAIL}(BLIND[i \rightarrow j])$. This ensures that each $BLIND[i \rightarrow j]$ value has the same discrete-log base h_j as the value $CONTROL[i \rightarrow j]$ base γ. Then the third party checks whether $\prod_{j=1..n} CONTROL[i \rightarrow j] = 1$, for all i=1..n. If this is the case then the blind values satisfy the cancellation property. Part (ii) of the claim is immediate since each $BLIND_2[j]$ equals $h_j^{blind[1,j]+...+blind[n,j]}$, and as a result, if at least one voter selected the blind-shares as specified, this randomizes $BLIND_2[i]$ over G.

4.2 Ballot-Casting

The ballot-casting procedure requires from each voter V_i to publish a vote $v[t] \in \mathbf{Choices}$ encrypted as $\langle A_i, B_i \rangle = \langle G^r, H^r F^{v[t]} \rangle$ where r is selected at random (ElGamal encryption). A set of authorities share in a distributed manner the value $\log_G(H)$, hence they are capable of distributedly finding the value of any of the votes (and of the final tally, based on the homomorphic properties of the ElGamal encryption).

When the set of voters $\{V_1,...,V_n\}$ runs our zero-sharing utility, each V_i publishes the modified ballot for his choice $v[t]$: $\langle A_i, B_i' \rangle = g_i(BLIND[i]) \otimes \langle G^r, H^r F^{v[t]} \rangle$. The proof of knowledge $\mathsf{PKB}(\langle A_i, B_i' \rangle)$ that shows the validity of the ballot is described in *figure 3* (note that we employ a multi-candidate variant of the scheme of [7]). Tallying is executed in the same way as in [7].

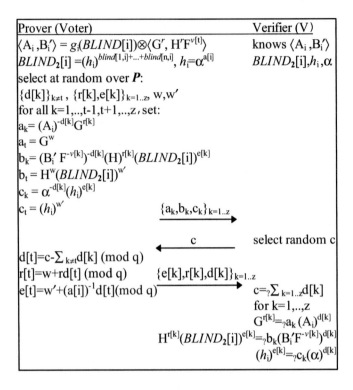

Figure 3. Proof of Ballot Validity

4.3   Corrective Fault Tolerance

The corrective fault tolerance steps are executed as described in the generic version. When voter V_k publishes the value $SHARES[k\rightarrow S]$ he should ensure that he indeed publishes the sum of the blind-shares he issued for the voters in S. In general he does this by publishing some string $TRAIL(SHARES[k\rightarrow S]))$. This is not needed in this implementation since: any third party can verify the validity of $SHARES[k\rightarrow S]$ by checking the equality: $\prod_{j\in S} CONTROL[k\rightarrow j] =_? f_{ctr}(SHARES[k\rightarrow S])$. This is because each value $CONTROL_2[k\rightarrow j]$ has the same logarithm base γ, as the blind value $BLIND_2[k\rightarrow j]$ over base h_j (by the $TRAIL(BLIND[k\rightarrow j]))$).

In the case of $TRAIL(CANCEL[U\rightarrow k])$, the voter V_k who publishes the values $CANCEL[U\rightarrow k]=g_k(\prod_{i\in U}(BLIND[i\rightarrow k])$ should ensure that he publishes the correct value. In this implementation, this can be done as follows: $TRAIL(CANCEL[U\rightarrow k])$ equals to $PKEQDL(e$: $\alpha=(h_k)^e \wedge CANCEL_2[U\rightarrow k]=(\prod_{i\in U}(BLIND_2[i\rightarrow k]))^e)$.

Note that the value $\prod_{i \in U} (BLIND_2[i \rightarrow k])$ is publicly available, and as a result the voter needs only to show that he indeed applies his private exponent $e=(a[k])^{-1}$.

REFERENCES

[1]   J. Benaloh, *Verifiable Secret-Ballot Elections*, PhD Thesis, Yale University, 1987.

[2]   J. Benaloh, M. Yung, Distributing the Power of a Government to Enhance the Privacy of Voters, *Proc. of the 5th Annual ACM Symposium on Principles of Distributed Computing*, Canada, August 1986. pp. 52-62.

[3]   S. Brands, *Rethinking Public Key Infrastructures and Digital Certificates; Building in Privacy*, The MIT Press, August 2000.

[4]   D. Chaum, Untraceable Electronic Mail, Return Addresses, and Digital Pseudonyms, *Com. of the ACM* 24(2): 84-88, 1981.

[5]   D. Chaum, T.P. Pedersen, Wallet Databases with Observers, Advances in Cryptology - CRYPTO '92, *12th Annual International Cryptology Conference*, California, USA, August 1992. LNCS 740, Springer 1993, pp. 89-105.

[6]   J.D. Cohen (Benaloh), M.J. Fischer, A Robust and Verifiable Cryptographically Secure Election Scheme, A robust and verifiable cryptographically secure election scheme (extended abstract). In *26th Annual IEEE Symposium on Foundations of Computer Science*, Oregon, USA, October 1985, pp. 372-382.

[7]   R. Cramer, R. Gennaro, B. Schoenmakers, A Secure and Optimally Efficient Multi-Authority Election Scheme, Advances in Cryptology - EUROCRYPT '97, *International Conference on the Theory and Application of Cryptographic Techniques*, Germany, May 1997, LNCS 1233, Springer 1997, pp. 103-118.

[8]   R. Cramer, I. Damgard, B. Schoenmakers, Proofs of Partial Knowledge and Simplified Design of Witness Hiding Protocols, Advances in Cryptology - CRYPTO '94, *14th Annual International Cryptology Conference*, California, USA, August 1994. LNCS 839, Springer 1994, pp.174-187.

[9]   A. De Santis, G. Di Crescenzo, G. Persiano, M. Yung, On Monotone Formula Closure of SZK, In *35th Annual IEEE Symposium on Foundations of Computer Science*, New Mexico, November 1994, pp. 454-465.

[10]   A. Fiat, A. Shamir, How to Prove Yourself: Practical Solutions to Identification and Signature Problems, *Advances in Cryptology* - CRYPTO '86, California, USA, 1986. LNCS 263, Springer 1987, pp. 186-194.

[11]   P.-A. Fouque, G. Poupard, J. Stern, Sharing Decryption in the Context of Voting or Lotteries, *4th International Conference on Financial Cryptography*, British West Indies, February 2000. LNCS 1962, Springer 2001, pp. 90-104.

[12]   A. Kiayias, M. Yung, Self-tallying Elections and Perfect Ballot Secrecy, Public Key Cryptography, *5th International Workshop on Practice and Theory in PKC*, France, February 2002. LNCS 2274, Springer 2002, pp. 141-158.

[13]   R. Ostrovsky, M. Yung, How to withstand mobile virus attacks, *Proc. of the 10th Annual ACM Symposium on Principles of Distributed Computing*, Canada, August 19-21, 1991, pp. 51-61.

Chapter 10

ISSUES, NON-ISSUES, AND CRYPTOGRAPHIC TOOLS FOR INTERNET-BASED VOTING

Rene Peralta

Dept. of Computer Science, Yale University, USA
peralta@cs.yale.edu

Abstract: Arguments for and against deploying electronic voting technology are discussed. A simple cryptographic ballot design and voting protocol is shown. We argue that a multidisciplinary effort is essential to build, deploy, and evaluate the new technology.

Key words: Electronic voting, internet-based elections, security, cryptology.

1. INTRODUCTION

I must start with a disclaimer: I am not a social scientist. Many of the issues associated with electronic voting are outside my field of expertise. Yet identifying and assessing those issues which are both important to electronic voting and within my field of expertise involves reasoning about socio-political matters. This work is as much a call for interdisciplinary co-operation as it is a presentation of issues related to electronic voting as seen through the eyes of a computer scientist.

The first legally binding online election in the US took place during March of 2000. The Democratic presidential primary in Arizona included the possibility to cast your vote using your home PC or any of a number of sites set up exclusively for this purpose. Initial accounts reported the experiment as a success (see, for example, [3]). The number of voters increased drama-tically from the previous election. The only reported technical problem was that lack of sufficient bandwidth caused response delays at peak times. Most importantly, however, the population accepted the electronic votes as valid.

In the ensuing months, however, much criticism of the experiment came to light. Some even went so far as to call it a "fiasco". Two years later, much of the public debate on this matter in the US has faded from the limelight. The issues, of course, have not gone away. Debate simmers on in academia and government. Yale University recently held a symposium on cyber-terrorism. At the closing of the event, the invited panelists were asked to name what they believed are the most important contributions academia could make to enhance cyber security. One of the panelists, a leading expert on computer security, stated that a major contribution would be to "actively oppose any attempts to [deploy] internet voting technology". This seems to be a widely held view among US security experts. I do not share this view. I believe the Internet has a valuable role to play in enhancing democratic processes. As security experts we have an important role to play in helping make this a reality.

2.   ARGUMENTS AGAINST INTERNET VOTING

There are two main arguments being made against Internet voting.[1] The first argument has to do with what is known as the "digital divide". Simply put, it is argued that important sectors of the population (the poor, the elderly, certain ethnic groups) do not have the same access to the Internet as the rest of the population. Therefore, it is argued, these groups would be further marginalized by the new technology. While the premise of this argument - that some sectors of the population have less access to the Internet than others - is an undeniable fact, the conclusion is highly suspect. It could well be that Internet voting can be used to increase voter turnout in traditionally underrepresented groups. This is a matter of proper implementation and deployment of the technology. This may not be easy to do, but it is certainly not impossible. Furthermore, we should not overlook the fact that current US electoral procedures do not make voting equally accessible to all members of the population (voting is held during a working day, people need means of transportation to get to the polling site, facilities for the handicapped are in-adequate, etc.). Thus, there is no evidence that electronic voting will worsen the problem of partly disenfranchised groups. To the contrary, there is much reason to hope the problem can be ameliorated via the new technology.[2]

---

[1]   A third argument against internet voting is that the act of going to a polling place is important in that it helps maintain a sense of community and citizenship. Voting at home will deprive us of that. There is little I can say about this issue, except that its relevance is likely to vary widely among different societies.

[2]   I am assuming here that we will have the good sense to provide convenient alternative means of voting to people who do not wish to vote via the Internet. If we do not do so,

Small-scale experiments like the Arizona Democratic primary can provide valuable information that can be used to fine-tune the technology.

A second argument against Internet voting is more clearly a true issue: the Internet is insecure. It is currently possible to severely disrupt network communication. It is even possible to bring the whole network down for a significant period of time. Network disruption can also be done on a selective basis (e.g. slow down or deny internet access to a particular sector of the population). Such an attack, particularly if it goes undetected, could subvert the electoral process. A naive implementation of Internet elections could be vulnerable to sabotage by individuals or organizations. Other factors, such as simple incompetence at any of a number of levels of supervision or design, can also compromise the integrity of an election.

3.   THE CHALLENGES

Hosting secure and fair elections or referendums over an insecure network is a many-faceted problem. Many technical challenges fall within the realm of "traditional" computer applications: we must provide an adequate interface to the voter; we must provide adequate bandwidth; we must secure both communication and data storage. This can all be done, in principle, but the financial cost may be high. Other problems are sociopolitical rather than technical: legislation must be enacted which protects the fairness and integrity of the election. In a multicultural society, we must make sure the new technologies are "multicultural" as well. Language is an obvious consideration, but there probably are other issues to consider as well. A third category of problems can be ascribed to the new technical challenges created by the particular requirements of an electoral process. It is here where modern cryptography plays a crucial role. I will focus on five basic properties:[3]

1. only eligible persons vote;
2. no person gets to vote more than once;
3. the vote is secret;
4. each (correctly cast) vote gets counted;
5. the voters trust that their vote is counted.

There is considerable confusion about what it means for the vote to be "secret". Secrecy is usually associated with having full entropy. But this clearly is not achieved in current electoral processes. A more modest goal is

---

then we will indeed partly disenfranchise sectors of the population (the elderly, for example).

[3]   The first four of these are among the 12 requirements enumerated in [8], section 2.4. The issue of voter's trust is addressed indirectly in that document as well.

for the vote of person X to have full conditional entropy given the public results at X's smallest level of aggregation. For example, if X votes at a station S, and the tally at station S is announced to be 250 votes for candidate A and 750 votes for candidate B, then we might hope for X's vote to have entropy $(0.25 \log(0.25^{-1}) + 0.75 \log(0.75^{-1})) \approx 0.81$ from the point of view of an outside observer. In practice, however, there are many predictors of X's vote which could diminish its entropy. In the digital era, a large sector of the population has already unwittingly surrendered much of what was once private: amazon.com knows what you read, your local supermarket knows what you eat, credit-card issuers know what you spend your money on, etc. All this information diminishes the entropy of the vote.

In the final analysis, it seems that what is left of the "secrecy" of votes is something akin to "plausible deniability". This means that an "adversary" cannot be absolutely certain that you voted in a particular way. Plausible deniability is not secrecy, yet it is an important component of coercion prevention. Another issue on which there is no consensus is what are the potential sources of coercion that make the secrecy of the vote necessary. In the US, much of the public, as well as an important sector of intellectuals from both left and right, believes the Government to be an important threat. To people in other countries, social entities such as the Church and the corporate sector are more important threats to electoral freedom than the Government is.

Yet other, completely different potential sources of coercion are people close to the voting individual (spouses, parents, co-workers, etc.). Spousal coercion, in particular, as been raised as a major reason not to allow "voting from home". Cryptographers can easily come up with ways that, in principle, deal with this issue. For example, voters can be issued two passwords: one to be used to cast your real vote and one to cast fake votes. Fake votes would not be counted. Thus, it has been argued, a spouse that feels coerced could always pretend to vote in one way and later vote in another. But, is this a realistic and statistically significant scenario? Spouses who are vulnerable to vote coercion yet have the sophistication to understand and use a double password system? This is highly unlikely. Worse yet, it is conceivable that the proposed solution aggravates the problem.

The last of the above properties, voter's trust, is perhaps the one we understand the least. A security expert's trust is likely to be gained by deploying sophisticated mathematical tools that constrain the power of a hypothetical, and equally sophisticated, adversary. The general population, however, will tend to distrust mechanisms it doesn't understand, think it understands mechanisms when in fact it does not, and postulate only very primitive adversaries. In US elections, the appearance of fairness and security seems to be much more important than the actual fairness and security of the process. For example, most people would think it unfair that a vote from a Wyoming resident counts more than twice (about 2.7 times, in fact) as much as the vote of a New York resident in presidential elections. The "one person - one vote" principle is a powerful image that persists in the population.

Mechanical devices and paper ballots also seem to give an important appearance of security. In the State of Connecticut, we use a large mechanical device where we set small colored levers to our desired choice of candidates and then pull on a large lever to actually cast the vote. All this makes quite a bit of noise. An adversary could easily record this noise. It is quite likely that the vote could be determined from an analysis of this recording. Furthermore, the machine keeps only a total tally of votes cast. Internal (silent) mechanical malfunctions leading to faulty counting are basically undetectable: recounts are impossible. Humorously, a local election official commented on the media that our voting devices are better than the now famous Florida paper ballots because recounts are "unnecessary". The fact that recounts are unnecessary because they are impossible, seems to have completely escaped someone who is much more knowledgeable about voting issues than the general population is.

Among researchers in the field of electronic voting, it is widely assumed that trust in the vote counting process can only be assured if each voter has the ability to verify that his/her vote was indeed counted (this is called "universal verifiability"). However, studies show that the majority of Internet users are extremely trusting of what they see on a computer screen. A message such as "your vote has been received and counted" might be enough to satisfy the voting population. Thus, universal verifiability should probably be viewed as a mechanism for legitimizing the voting procedure in the eyes of the security experts. To what extent this can be an indirect way of legitimizing the election in the eyes of the voting public is unclear. However, it is clear that universal verifiability is an important deterrent against electoral fraud (provided "verification" actually happens). Thus, it would seem that what is needed is a universally verifiable system in which the voter can delegate the power to verify to trusted intermediaries (e.g. local election officials, your ISP, your network manager, etc.). In particular, "netizen" groups might well be able to serve in this capacity. Of course, the ability to delegate verification creates new opportunities for coercion. If it is determined that coercion at a significant scale is a real possibility, then it would be necessary to limit the choices of verification intermediaries. Most stable democracies do have trusted institutions that can act in this capacity. For Civil (Latin) Law jurisdictions the Notary Public is an obvious choice for a trusted third party.[4] Unfortunately, there is no obvious such choice for Common (Anglo-Saxon) Law jurisdictions.

The first voting protocol that considers the universal verifiability property appears to be due to Cohen (now Benaloh) in her 1987 PhD thesis [4]. Other universally verifiable protocols have been proposed since then. These are discussed elsewhere in this book. The protocol presented below is universally verifiable.

Cryptographic techniques can also be used to provide what has been called "uncoercibility". In US circles, this has been defined as the voter not having the power to prove to a third party what his/her vote was [8]. It might seem that uncoercibility is mutually exclusive with universal verifiability. In fact, there are ways in which both properties can be achieved (see, for example [7,11]). However, it is my opinion that this definition of uncoercibility yields a non-issue that unnecessarily complicates protocols and distracts attention from more important issues (including more subtle and more prevalent forms of coercion).

Any election mechanism has a "statistical error", defined as the expected relative difference between the vote count (assuming no errors in the counting process) and the intentions of the voting population. What the statistical error in Internet voting will be remains to be seen. It will be affected by such components as the design of the graphic interface of the system. It is easy to design graphic interfaces that would significantly increase the statistical error of the mechanism. Below a certain threshold, it is extremely hard to lower the statistical error by enhancing the graphic interface (or any other single component of the voting mechanism).

A basic design principle for Internet voting protocols should be to avoid complicating the protocol in order to solve problems that have an expected incidence well below the statistical error. In particular, if we consider the impact on the vote count of people changing their vote because they are forced to prove to a third person what their vote was, it is very unlikely for this impact to be anywhere close to the statistical error of the system[5]. The above holds for Internet elections in stable democracies in which most forms of vote coercion are criminalized. Of course, if it is possible for, say, a large

---

[4] In both Latin Law and Common Law jurisdictions there are proposals (some of which have actually been enacted into law) to extend the role of the Notary Public to include online services. However, the role of Notary Public is much more extensive in Civil Law (see Javier Lopez's PhD thesis [10]). Interestingly, there are Civil Law enclaves in otherwise Common Law jurisdiction. Examples of these are the province of Quebec in Canada and the state of Louisiana in the US.

[5] I have no hard data to support this assertion. However, I find it hard to believe there is, in stable democracies, a significant number of people who are vulnerable to vote coercion. On the other hand there is quite a bit of literature to support the thesis that statistical error played a decisive role in the US 2000 presidential elections (see, for example [8]).

company to ask all its employees for a proof of their vote (and get away with it), then the coercion problem must be addressed.

It is important to have the above considerations in mind when discussing the manner and the extent to which a proposed technology preserves the secrecy of votes. This also means that the design and evaluation of a new voting system must be an interdisciplinary endeavor. Just as most people in the social sciences have trouble making sense of cryptographic designs, most computer scientists have a very limited understanding of issues such as the nature of people's trust, the importance of the privacy guaranteed by the voting booth, the nature and extent of spousal coercion, etc.

In the following section we present a cryptographic approach to secret and universally verifiable electronic voting.[6] There are several alternative approaches possible. It is difficult to assess the advantages of any one cryptographic design over another without a better specification of the problems to be addressed and the goals to be achieved.

4. ELECTRONIC BALLOTS

We present a ballot design based on cryptographic signatures of a special kind. The purpose of specifying a particular solution is mostly illustrative (any competent cryptographer can produce various types of solutions to this problem). The solution presented here uses "blind signatures", a technique first introduced by Chaum [6]. We also use homomorphic encryption techniques. This restricts the choice of encryption/decryption functions to those based on number theoretic techniques and assumptions (e.g. hardness of integer factorization, discrete logarithms, elliptic curve cryptosystems). There is a performance penalty for using these types of systems: they are much slower than traditional substitution/permutation ciphers such as DES.

The high level description of the voting protocol is as follows:

---

[6] The design was included as part of the supporting documentation for a US Government mandated study of internet voting (see [8]).

1. the voter constructs an "anonymous electronic ballot";
2. the voter shows adequate proof of identity to the election authority;
3. the authority "stamps" the ballot after verifying that no other ballot has been stamped for this voter;
4. the voter anonymously inserts the ballot into an electronic mail box.

Figure 1. Outline of voting protocol.

After the voting deadline passes, votes are counted and a database containing all ballots is made public. Anybody can verify that all ballots have been "stamped". Any voter can verify that his/her vote is contained in the database.

The main technical challenge is to implement untraceable electronic ballots. This can be done using public-key cryptography. Let $E(x)$ and $D(x)$ be an election authority's public encryption and decryption functions, respectively. These functions must have what is known as the "homomorphic" property. A function f has this property if $f(xy) = f(x)f(y)$ for all valid inputs x, y. Several well-known cryptographic schemes have this property. We will use RSA-1024 for expository purposes. In this scheme, an election authority produces two random 512-bit primes P and Q. The product $N = PQ$ is called the "voting modulus". The public key is the modulus N together with an odd large integer e. The encryption function E is defined by $E(x) = x^e$ modulo N. The private decryption function is defined by $D(x) = x^d$ modulo N, where $ed \equiv 1$ modulo $(P-1)(Q-1)$. The numbers P, Q, and d are kept secret by the election authority.

The next design issue is the structure of the ballot. We must make sure that:

- ballots cannot be constructed without the election authority's participation;
- ballots cannot be linked to voters' identities;
- individual voters can recognize their own ballot.

The following is a possible design:

ELECTION IDENTIFICATION		VOTER'S NONCE
VOTE	SIGNATURE OF ELECTION AUTHORITY	

Figure 2. Ballot design

The "election identification" field is a number that is the same for all ballots. It identifies the particular election being held. The "voter's nonce" field is different for each ballot. It is used by the voter to identify his/her vote in the list published after the election. Both the election identification and the voter's nonce field are "long numbers". Roughly speaking, these numbers need to be long enough so that two randomly generated numbers of that length have a negligible probability of being the same. If the number of voters is about 2^n, then the length of the voter's nonce field is at least 4n. The idea is to prevent a particular nonce to be selected by more than one voter (we call this a "collision"). For example, for about 1000 voters, a length of 40 bits for the nonce field yields a probability of under (1/2,000,000) of a collision occurring. In practice, a length of 8 bytes for the voter's nonce field yields a negligible probability of a collision unless the number of voters is in the millions. We will argue in section 6 that, for large-scale elections, there should be many aggregation centers. A side effect of this is that each aggregating center would count only a small number of votes. Thus, the chances of a collision at anyone aggregation center is negligible.

The vote field is a "short number". It only needs to be long enough to contain all the sub fields necessary for the particular election being held (in the US, voting for several public offices as well as local community issues are typically included in a ballot).

Finally, the "signature of election authority" field is a cryptographic signature of the other three fields. Let X be the concatenation of the first three fields. Then the signature on X is simply $D(X) = X^d$ modulo N. It is in the generation of this signature that the "homomorphic" property of the cryptosystem is needed. So that only eligible voters can vote, the signature must be generated at the time the voter presents his/her identification. This means that the election authority cannot be allowed to see the value X that it is about to sign. This can be achieved as follows:

1. after generating X, the voter generates an auxiliary random number R modulo N;
2. the voter constructs the number $Z = X R^e$ modulo N and presents it to the election authority;
3. the election authority issues $D(Z) = Z^d = X^d R^{ed} = X^d R$ modulo N;
4. the voter calculates $D(X) = D(Z) R^{-1}$ modulo N.

This completes the basic design, as the voter now has the last field of the ballot. Other functionalities can be added to this design using standard cryptographic and non-cryptographic techniques. In fact, an electronic ballot can, and probably should, be endowed with useful properties absent in paper ballots. But that issue is beyond the scope of this note.

5. VOTING PROCEDURES AND AGGREGATION METHODS.

The automatic tallying associated with electronic voting can be used to improve election mechanisms. The year 2000 presidential elections in the US resulted in a statistical tie (the difference in votes between the first and second majorities was below the statistical error of the process in key states). There is no second round in US presidential elections. A considerable number of people believe the candidate who was declared the winner would have lost if a second round between the two largest majorities had been held.

For a variety of reasons, modifying election procedures to include a second round is probably outside the capabilities of the US political system. However, there are a great number of alternatives (see [1] for an explanation of different systems used throughout the world). For example, we could allow voters to indicate their first and second choices in the ballot. In the tallying phase, determine the two candidates, say A and B, with the highest number of votes when counting only first choices. If neither of the two obtains over 50% of the votes, then add to A's tally (B's tally) the number of votes in which A (B) is second and B (A) is not first.

The above method is easy to implement in electronic voting, whereas it would be very difficult to implement using the current systems of paper ballots or mechanical machines. I believe this method would allow a significant percentage of the US population to express their dissatisfaction with the two dominant political parties without having to give up the right to choose between the only two viable alternatives.[7]

It is tempting to propose yet more elaborate polling methods in order to obtain more complete and accurate views of the population's choices. For example, we could implement what is called a "preferential ballot". In this type of ballot, the voter ranks all candidates. The winner is determined by a recursive application of the procedure outlined in the previous paragraph. However, as the complexity of the ballot increases, so does the statistical error of the system. That is, allowing voters to more accurately express their opinions, and ensuring that the election outcome accurately reflects the voter's wishes, may well be contradictory goals (see [12]).

---

[7] It should be noted that this tallying method is not perfect. Suppose there are three candidates (A,B,C) and five voters. Suppose the five votes are (A,B), (B,A), (C,A), (C,A), (B,A). Then the proposed method would declare B the winner. However, note that the voters would have voted 3 to 2 in favor of A over B. In fact, it can be shown that there is no perfect tallying method. It is even possible for an electorate to prefer A over B, B over C, and C over A. That is, the electorate's preferences need not be transitive. Any other method of tallying, such as asking the population to quantify the statement "I prefer A over B", will also have failure modes. This is predicted in great generality by Arrow's impossibility results [2].

On the positive side, the automation of tallying lends itself to implementation of highly sophisticated tallying methods. An election is not only supposed to determine a "winner". It is also supposed to ensure proper representation of minority views in the government. There is wide variation among democracies in this respect. The introduction of electronic voting offers a window of opportunity to enhance existing methods of power sharing should there be a societal will to do so.

6.   VOTING OVER AN INSECURE NETWORK.

The protocol described in section 4 can be used without security enhancements only within a highly benign network and social environment. Over the Internet, the voting mechanism must be resilient to a variety of failure and attack situations. In particular, it would be unwise to have an "election day". Since the Internet is vulnerable to a denial-of-service attack of significantly long duration, the voters must be able to cast their vote over a period of several days or weeks. Mechanisms would have to be put in place to discourage extensive "last minute" voting, as this would defeat the purpose of having an extended voting period.

It also a good idea for the ballots to be cast in sealed electronic envelopes (i.e. encrypted so that they cannot be selectively discarded or otherwise tampered with on the basis of who the vote is for). The envelopes should be opened only at the conclusion of the voting phase. The power to open the sealed envelopes should probably be distributed among independent agents. The cooperation of a threshold number of these agents should be necessary to open the envelopes. Standard cryptographic techniques make all this possible.

Redundancy is absolutely necessary for security. Votes should be replicated multiple times, each copy should take multiple routes to its destination, and each copy should be stored at multiple locations. This strategy can be combined with the establishment of multiple levels of aggregation. The aggregation points can be chosen to both fulfill a security need and help provide policy makers with a much richer picture of the population's views. Votes can be (simultaneously) aggregated according to age, geographical location, social status, gender, cultural identity, and many other criteria. Of course, one must tread carefully in these matters. It is for policy makers, social scientist, statisticians and other groups to define what is desirable. Cryptographers and security experts should add their expertise to define and explain what is possible.

Acknowledgements

This work was supported in part by NSF grant CCR-0081823. Discussions with and feedback from the following colleagues are gratefully acknowledged: Dana Angluin, Eduardo Engel, Michael Fischer, Ivan Jaksic, Javier Lopez, and Patricio Navia.

REFERENCES

[1]   ACE Project report. International Foundation for Election Systems, International Institute for Democracy and Electoral Assistance, and the United Nations Department of Economic and Social Affairs (http://www.aceproject.org/main/english).

[2]   Arrow G., *Social Choice and Individual Values*. John Wiley & Sons, 1951.

[3]   Baum C., *Commentary: Electronic voting likely to emerge a winner*, November 2000, http://news.com.com/2100-1023-249029.html

[4]   Benaloh, J., "Verifiable Secret-Ballot Elections". PhD Thesis, Yale University, 1987.

[5]   Benaloh J., Tuinstra D., "Receipt-Free Secret-Ballot Elections". In *26th Annual ACM Symposium on Theory of Computing*, ACM, pp. 544-553, 1994.

[6]   Chaum D., "Blind Signatures for Untraceable Payments". In *CRYPTO '82*, Plenum Press, pp. 199-203, 1982.

[7]   Hirt M., Sako K., "Efficient Receipt-Free Voting Based on Homomorphic Encryption". In *EUROCRYPT 2000*, LNCS 1807, Springer-Verlag, pp 539-556, 2000.

[8]   Internet Policy Institute. *Report of the National Workshop on Internet Voting*, March 2001, www.internetpolicy.org/research/results.html.

[9]   Herron M., Sekhon J., "Overvoting and Representation: An examination of overvoted presidential ballots in Broward and Miami-Dade counties". To appear in *Electoral Studies* (http://elections.fas.harvard.edu/election2000/HerronSekhon.pdf).

[10] Lopez J., "Design of a Notarization Infrastructure for Electronic Commerce", PhD Thesis, University of Malaga, 1999. (in Spanish)

[11] Okamoto T., "Receipt-Free Electronic Voting Schemes for Large Scale Elections". In *5th Security Protocols Workshop '97*, LNCS 1163, Springer-Verlag, pp. 125-132, 1997.

[12] Saari G., *Chaotic Elections! : A mathematician looks at voting*. AMS, 2001.

Chapter 11

PRIVATE, SECURE AND AUDITABLE INTERNET VOTING

Ed Gerck

Safevote Inc., USA
egerck@safevote.com

Abstract: Internet voting can be more than just using the Internet to vote. This paper presents the Distributed Voting System (DVS), as a safe Internet voting system using mesh networks to implement a distributed voting protocol offering, at the same time, privacy, security and auditing, with receipt-freeness and universal verifiability. A demo is available at MySafevote.com, developed using open source software. A version suitable for public elections has been developed in Java. The DVS can scale to any number of voters; it has been successfully used in Internet elections with 300,000 registered voters and 92,000 participating voters.

Key words: Internet voting, Privacy, Security, Auditing.

1. INTRODUCTION

In the context of this paper, voting is *a process that measures the choices of a group and provides a tally of these choices.* This paper presents a distributed system for voting that uses the Internet to build mesh networks affording, at the same time, privacy, security and auditing.

A voting process needs to obey a set of voting requirements, which may change according to the election (e.g., private sector vs. public sector voting), jurisdiction and legal rules (e.g., instant run-off voting vs. majority voting). The voting requirements need to be clear, decidable and, as much as possible, complete[1]. A set of high-level, technologically independent performance requirements for public elections is presented in [1].

One of the requirements in [1] is that the security of a voting process must be guaranteed from end to end, from voter registration to vote tabulation[2]. Voting system security requirements usually include voter privacy and vote secrecy. As defined in [1], voter privacy is the inability to link a voter to a vote; vote secrecy is the inability to know what the vote is[3]. In most elections voters cannot be anonymous, even though voter anonymity is often used as a misnomer for voter privacy. Most often, there is a set of conditions that must be satisfied by a voter in order to vote, which conditions, for example, dictate knowing who the voter is and where the voter lives, and also positively verifying that the voter is who the voter claims to be (e.g., by checking legal and private records, as well as other data). Thus, guaranteeing privacy in a voting process cannot usually be guarded by anonymity, which makes voter privacy even more difficult to achieve. Another important requirement is the provision of audit trails, to provide assurances that the voting process occurred as desired, creating confidence in the results.

Notwithstanding the fact that different elections may have different voting requirements, we can identify several sub-processes that are common in most elections. This is shown in Fig. 1, as a clockwise time sequence of a typical election process including eleven election sub-processes.

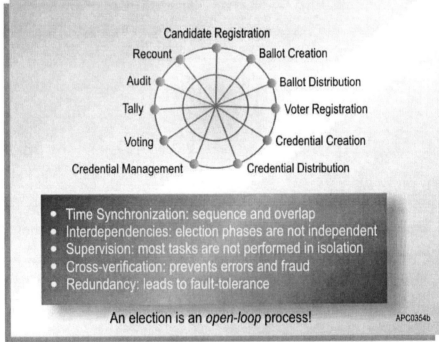

Figure 1. Clockwise time sequence of a typical election process.

Fig. 1 also shows a table with five properties that are typical of a well-designed voting process: (1) time synchronization, (2) interdependencies, (3) supervision, (4) cross-verification, and (5) redundancy. These properties help improve election integrity; for example, the number of ballots tallied must not be larger than the number of registered voters.

Voting systems comprise four main components: (i) a registration service for verifying and registering legitimate voters, (ii) voting stations where the voter makes choices on a ballot, (ii) a device called the ballot box where said ballot is collected, and (iv) a tallying service that counts the votes and announces the results. Additionally, voting systems have other components, such as an auditing service, ballot generation service, ballot management service, recounting service and storage. As discussed above, privacy, security and integrity of voting systems depend critically on these parts securely working together in combination, not just in isolation. However, these parts are not usually located in the same place and do not work together at the same time. The problem then is to guarantee that their isolated actions do correspond to a system-wide policy, at all times and in all places. This also means that Internet voting should not be considered simply as an "input" or "output" module of a conventional voting system. In short, an Internet voting system should not be built by assembling parts, even if election certified, taken from a conventional voting system.

Ballots are usually not a simple set of choices, the same for all voters. Oftentimes ballots need to be defined and controlled per voter (e.g., when ballot rotation is used, so that different voters see the same set of choices but with a different top to bottom sequence) and also per class of voters (e.g., using different ballot styles with different choices due to geo-political and regional differences). Voters may also be able to choose their ballot language, for the same set of choices.

Due to advances in computer systems and networks, including the Internet, conventional voting systems may benefit by defining some aspects of ballot usage remotely, for example by storing and tallying ballots at a server which may or may not be located at a poll site and which may serve one or more poll sites, with different ballot styles and ballot languages. The voting stations that are used to vote the ballots that are sent to the server may also be located remotely, not at the same poll site where the ballots are collected, and possibly not at a poll site at all - allowing voting from home, office or from anywhere. Driving this evolution from paper-based voting to electronic and Internet voting are economic, political and social factors. For example, considerable cost reduction can be achieved by sharing costs in a client-server system with electronic data transfer, while providing increased voter participation due to greater availability of voting places for a voter, reduced physical transportation and physical security needs for transportation of ballot boxes, and reduced time for tabulating results.

However useful as it may seem, election systems must not provide a voter receipt (i.e., a receipt allowing a voter, or any observer, to verify that the vote cast by the voter is the same vote that is tallied). An election is an *open-loop process* where a voter must not receive a receipt proving how she voted, otherwise the voter might be coerced or tempted to sell her vote. This property is often called *receipt-freeness* in the literature. Even though it is not possible to "close the loop" so that the voter's choices can be verifiable, the literature has extensively discussed the notion of a *universally verifiable election system* [1,2,3], where it should be possible for anyone (not just the voter) to verify the validity of the votes and of the tally result.

This paper describes a distributed voting system, called DVS, where distributed voting sub-processes are used to build an end-to-end security protocol for private, secure and auditable voting, with receipt-freeness and universal verifiability. The DVS also includes methods that provide for verifiability while an election is in progress (real-time auditing), which are useful to help deter fraud, minimize costs after a fraud is discovered, contain a discovered fraud, and even allow an election to proceed normally after a fraud attempt is discovered.

> *The DVS includes methods allowing for verifiability, methods that may be performed by auditors (in auditing) and also by anyone (including parties and the voters themselves), in what is called "universal verifiability."*

The DVS is based on mesh networks that can be built using the Internet, providing a cost-effective implementation, or any other network. The DVS has been tested in public and private Internet election trials, including the use of ballot rotation, ballot styles, and ballot languages, with demonstrated performance of up to 300,000 voters and practically no scalability limit to hundreds of millions of voters. Several patents have been applied for the DVS.

2.   DVS PRIVACY, SECURITY AND INTEGRITY

Central to the election privacy, security, and integrity considerations of the DVS is the ballot itself. Ballots need to be controlled from inception to end whenever and wherever they are generated, viewed, approved, controlled, distributed, voted, collected, tallied, audited, recounted and stored.

Controlling the ballot is a well-defined task for paper ballots which can be physically designed as they will appear to a voter, physically printed, physically transported, physically counted and so on. The foregoing aspects may be protected by physical tamperproof seals, and may always involve the presence of at least two authorized officials. In order to compromise a paper ballot, typically several people need to be involved and would need to collude in an entire mesh of events. However, in the DVS there is no paper to be printed or controlled. Before the vote is cast a voter may erase the choices and receive a new ballot. There are no unused ballots to be counted at the end of the election. The very definition of a "voted ballot" comes into question - what was the ballot seen and cast by the voter?

This problem is well known in conventional systems for electronic voting. Some experts contend that an electronic voting system such as the DVS can be either secure or anonymous (as in secret ballot) but not both, because an electronic voting machine can store (by means of a back channel) a different vote than that which the voter did select and no one can prove otherwise. *Of course, the same problem occurs in paper voting.* A ballot box for paper ballots can also store by means of a back channel a different vote than that which the voter did select and no one can prove otherwise. However, a factor that mitigates against an electronic voting system such as the DVS is the fact that although paper and electronic records are both vulnerable to subversion, it is a lot easier to change what is in an electronic record than it is to change what is on paper. Put most plainly, people know that ordinary voting systems can be subverted by someone who could bribe enough individuals to collude, but the physical fact of several tons of paper ballots still represents somewhat of an obstacle to an "easy subversion" in the eyes of many. In contrast, people are well aware that electronically one can modify a million records with as little as a few keystrokes. This is the "fear" that needs to be addressed in the DVS - that such a subversion can be so readily accomplished from the safety of a remote laptop that it would be unavoidable or even undetectable.

To answer these concerns, in addition to the distributed cryptographic assurances in the DVS, electronic records in the DVS are bound to multiple communication channels[4] in a manner that they are rendered demonstrably inaccessible to an attacker, both through physical access controls and through cryptographic protocols. Moreover, the DVS includes a step-by-step description of the voting process, so that when someone asks, *"What if the intruder succeeds in breaking into the system to change X?"* this can be clearly answered, for example, by (i) to change X would cause a subsequent binding failure, thus it would be detectable except with parallel access to Y and Z, which are independently inaccessible; or (ii) knowledge of an alternate (and attacker-desirable) value for X is computationally impossible to achieve during the election period, and the effort could not be leveraged to any other X.

In short, the DVS uses the concept of multiple communication channels to make it is as impossible as desired to tamper with the electronic ballot, in addition to cryptographic assurances. This includes server actions to protect each client and to protect the servers from malicious use of the clients.

Here, the question is not how many copies of paper or bits one has, but the capacity of the communication channels that the attacker needs to subvert versus the capacity of the correction channels that one has available during such an attack. The correction channels only need to be partially independent[4]. If an attacker is able to fully subvert all correction channels while attacking the other channels, then the correction channel capacity needs to be increased. The theoretical basis for such a system is Shannon's 10th theorem, which states that as long as the capacity of the correction channels exceeds the capacity of the communication channels, the error rate of a communication system can approach a value as close to zero as desired.

In the DVS, the same multi-channel design that protects casting the ballot is also used to protect presenting the ballot, in an end-to-end design. The make-up of each channel's carrier (e.g., paper, bits, electrons) or the correction channel itself (e.g., a network or a hardware channel) is irrelevant. For example, in the limiting case where the DVS is used in an isolated machine (as an off-line electronic voting system with no Internet channel, such as in Direct Recording Electronic voting machines), it is still possible to have a correction channel by adding a sufficiently redundant witness system [4] that records what the voter sees and approves as the ballot is cast by the voter, without recording who the voter is.

The witness system described in [4] can include independent witnesses controlled by every party or observer of the election. As another example, in the case where the DVS is used online with Internet channels, each voter is provided with a double-blind digital certificate (Safevote's Digital Vote Certificate[TM] [5]) that includes a nonce[5]. This feature, together with homomorphic encryption for further protecting the voting pattern from disclosing the voter's identity[6,3], allows for the introduction of witness records [4] and also for creating an effective audit trail per voter without compromising the voter's identity.

In both examples, the vote tally result can be verified with a confidence level as close to 100% as desired by auditing and tallying a fraction of the witness records[7].

3.   THE DVS PROCESS

The DVS Process is a high-level description of the distributed voting system. The main technical goal of the DVS Process is to avoid too much concentration of information and power, while allowing just enough information and power so as to make all allowed tasks possible to execute. An all-knowing, all-powerful entity would be the perfect attacker and could break any security measure. That is why we oftentimes talk about "need to know" and "separation of powers." We name these principles, respectively, *information granularity* and *power granularity.* These principles mean that information should not be provided in its entirety to a single entity and one should also avoid the scenario *The DVS avoids the scenario of a single point of control, which is recognized as a single point of failure.* where any entity is, at the same time, user, administrator and auditor. That is why election information and power should be carefully divided, for example, among local officials, the election management, the state officials and the voter. And, contrary to what is oftentimes still advocated, there should not be, and there is not, a single point of control in the DVS, which we would need to recognize as a single point of failure.

As exemplified in Fig. 2 for a public-sector voting system, the DVS Process can be conceptualized as five independent modules working in co-operation by means of a distributed protocol, building privacy, locality, and audit walls. Each module includes hardware and software.

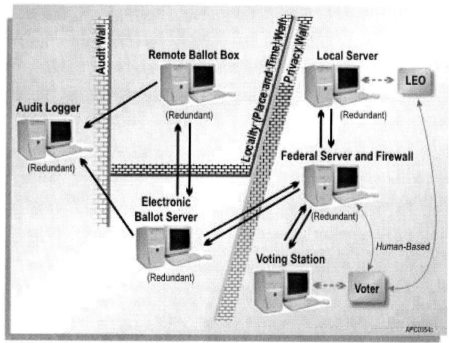

Figure 2. The DVS Process with an example of hosting and sub-system layers building "walls" for five servers. The "walls" are implemented in software and hardware.

The servers shown in Fig. 2 operate in three different layers, called the federal (or central) layer, the state (or group) layer and the local layer. In the US, where there is no direct federal role in election administration, the "federal" module shown in Fig. 2 may actually host a central state service (federating all state servers) or a federal pass-through service (e.g., authenticating access for overseas voters). The number of servers to be used in an actual implementation is a function of security, privacy, quality of service and cost requirements. The voter and the LEO (local election official) also take part in the DVS Process, as shown in Fig. 3, with well-defined human-based actions.

Voters are digitally certified, identified and authenticated in two layers - the central and the group layers. The "Federal Server and Firewall" module controls access to the central layer. The "Electronic Ballot Server" controls access to the group layer. The central layer is hierarchically above the group layer, so that group layer access first requires central layer access - thereby protecting the group layer. In the central layer, voters are known, identifiable and authenticated. In the group layer, voters are anonymous but each voter and each voter's ballot style are authenticated. In the local layer, voters are anonymous and ballots are secret. Multiple, independent auditing procedures are used in each layer, including real-time auditing.

The layers in the DVS Process provide a clear separation between voters and tallied ballots while allowing auditing, positive voter identification, anonymous voter authentication and ballot control at all times.

Authentication and authorization are used in the DVS Process to help define information and power granularity among all of its parts, including voters and election officials. However, at its most basic level, a secure voting system needs to do much more than just control authentication and authorization. No matter how much assurance is provided that each component of a secure voting system is correct, when operational factors such as collusion, internal attacks, hackers, bugs, virus, worms or errors are taken into account, the system may fail to be effective - i.e., may fail to be secure in the context of its operational use. In addition, underlying assurance problems such as insecure operating systems and reoccurring buffer over-flow vulnerabilities are not likely to improve over the coming years. Thus, the DVS Process shown in Fig. 2 brings together policy, management and implementation considerations in order to provide effectiveness assurances that the isolated actions at each component of the DVS Process do correspond to a system-wide policy, at all times and in all places, even though such actions may be remotely located to each other and done at different times.

Additional security principles such as redundancy, diversity, no single point of failure, time synchronization, process interdependencies, process supervision, process cross-verification, least privilege and trust[8] requirements were also used in designing the DVS Process. Fault tolerance is an important issue in the DVS Process due to the large number of cooperating components. The redundancy present in the DVS Process is used to enhance fault tolerance, as desired. For lack of paper trails, non-repudiation is also essential for the DVS Process. A common definition states that non-repudiation is about providing proof that a particular act was actually performed, for example as demonstrated by a trusted time-stamp. However, because a multi-party protocol can be designed to require the participation of more than two parties for an act to be performed, the concept of non-repudiation can be used in the DVS Process in a much stronger way, where non-repudiation can effectively prevent the denial of an act. The DVS Process also takes into account the "stickiness" property of electronic records that, contrary to paper records, can unwittingly leave or lead to traces that can be used by an attacker to compromise privacy and security.

4.   DVS IMPLEMENTATIONS

According to election needs, the DVS Process described in Section 3 can be used to define different DVS implementations, with different capabilities and physical distribution requirements. One solution to implement the DVS Process is the "wallet" approach used in e-commerce. In this type of solution, a communications system is defined in which a particular Object (a "control structure," for example, a Java applet or a browser plug-in - also called a "wallet" in e-commerce protocols such as SET) is installed or transferred from a server (ballot server) to a client (voting station). That control structure is a special piece of software which encapsulates both (1) data fully defining the intended server-client communications relationship, including the ballot; and (2) methods for using the data to effect that relationship, including reading and verifying a voter's digital certificate, displaying the ballot, reading the voter's choices and casting the ballot. After it is transferred to the client, the Object as a control structure runs on the client side to control communications between client and server. According to this solution, once the client computer receives such an Object, it needs only to access the Object's methods. The Object handles all communications details including cryptographic or other modules, which modules may be embedded in the Object itself or referenced by means of digital signatures to certified modules outside the Object.

The problems with the "wallet" approach are well-known in the art in e-commerce and include, for example: the need to use CDs or floppies to physically distribute the "wallet" or long downloads of hundreds of kilobytes or even some megabytes of data; unreliable behavior because the client stations may not adequately support the resources required by the "wallet" (e.g., memory, OS used, browser version); the need for frequent version changes due to bugs or discovered attacks leading to a repeated need to download ever newer versions of the "wallet" (with all the time, certification and cost penalties involved); need to rely on the user to correctly install the "wallet" without supervision; and heavy traffic load on the "wallet" server if online download is used. In fact, the shortcomings are so severe that the "wallet" approach has already been abandoned in e-commerce. Also, contrary to business applications of the "wallet" approach in e-commerce (where a certain level of fraud can be accepted as "the cost of doing business"), voting cannot be protected by insurance against fraud.

Additionally, for a public voting application there must be official verification and public trust that the "wallet" does not include malicious code or covert channels that would either bias the vote or reveal the voter's identity. Such verification and trust are time consuming to achieve and yet must be repeated for each version of the "wallet" for each operating platform. Also, Trojan horses or computer viruses at the client side may easily subvert the "wallet's" control structure and render useless all efforts to control the ballot, how it is presented and how it is voted. Again, in e-commerce this may be compensated by insurance, which is not the case in public voting. Further, although the order of candidates may be rotated and/or incremented in the ballot to prevent bias, anyone who sees the first ballot and gets access to the source code, to the downloaded binary image or to the file image of the code will be in a position to learn the assignment table between candidates and accumulators that carry the vote, in total or in part. Thus, a virus or trojan horse attack could be designed even with ballot rotation and could be used to bias the outcome of the election.

The "wallet" approach was discarded in implementing the DVS Process. Instead, a combination of modularization, encapsulation, inheritance and other software development methodologies were used by Safevote to develop a COTS (commercial off-the-shelf) solution that implements the DVS Process and can support different election needs with common browsers and with no plug-ins, Java or JavaScript required on the client side. Requiring least behavior from the client also makes it easier to include server actions to probe and protect the client against attacks (e.g., virus, Trojan horse) and to protect the servers from malicious use of clients.

The Safevote DVS implementation uses a combination of software and hardware modules, providing the functions described in Table 1.

A possible physical distribution for a DVS implemented using the modules described in Table 1 may use five machines, one for each module (in addition to the voter's machine). However, as shown in Fig. 2, it is also possible to implement the DVS with just three machines (in addition to redundant processors at each machine location):

- one central (federal) layer machine with the CPF and the AL modules;
- one group (state) layer machine with the EBS, RBB and AL modules;
- one local (county) layer machine with the LS and AL modules.

The module CPF operates under a central jurisdiction, possibly state or federal based (see "Federal Server and Firewall", Fig. 2). The modules EBS, RBB and AL operate under a group jurisdiction, possibly a state jurisdiction. The module LS operates at a local (or county) jurisdiction.

Modules	Layer	Sub-Modules	Functions
CPF (Central Processor & Firewall)	Central (Federal)	Probe	Probe and Protect Client
		DVC Verifier	Verify and Decrypt DVCs
		Reverse Proxy	Provide Pass-Through Service
		Receipt	Provide Notice of Receipt
		Interface	Interface with Client and other Modules
		Log	Postmark and Register Events
LS (Local Server)	Local (County)	DVC Issuer	Issue and Encrypt DVCs; Register Voters
		Receipt	Provide Notice of Receipt
		Interface	Interface with Client and other Modules
		Log	Postmark and Register Events
EBS (Electronic Ballot Server)	Group (State)	DVC Verifier	Verify and Decrypt DVCs
		Ballot Server	Provide Ballot Views
		Receipt	Protect Server and Client
		Interface	Provide Notice of Receipt
		Log	Interface with Client and other Modules
			Postmark and Register Events
RBB (Remote Ballot Box)	Group Local	DVC Verifier	Verify and Decrypt DVCs
		Ballot Box	Receive Return Ballots
		Receipt	Distribute Return Ballots
		Tally	Provide Notice of Receipt; Verify Voter Receipt
		Audit	Calculate Tally
		Report	Audit Inputs & Outputs
		Interface	Report Results
		Log	Interface with other Modules
			Postmark and Register Events
AL (Audit Logger)	Central, Group, Local	DVC Verifier	Verify and Decrypt DVCs
		Interface	Interface with other Modules
		Log	Postmark and Register Events

Table 1: DVS implementation table

The five software modules in the DVS are customer and election-specific, even though they contain reusable, tested code. Each module is distributed for installation only at machines performing that module's function. The software modules are developed in Java and follow the usual object-oriented design principles of localization, encapsulation, information hiding, inheritance, and object abstraction techniques. The DVS module EBS implements a state machine, which provides a verifiable and extensible platform necessary to accommodate the diversity of election procedures that need to be supported. Each state invokes different modules, controlling each function of the system. For example, casting a vote, versus accessing the database. The state machine design enables strict access control mechanisms, preventing unintended access to any part of the system.

The DVS is the only Internet voting system ever to undergo a public attack test, in November 2000 [5], 24 hours/day during 4 days. No attackers were successful, even though a public help line by email was provided to the attackers. The availability and security of the DVS does not rely on keeping its code or rules secret (which cannot be guaranteed), or in limiting access to only a few people (who may collude or commit a confidence breach voluntarily or involuntarily), or in preventing an attacker from observing any number of ballots and protocol messages (which cannot be guaranteed). The DVS also has zero-knowledge properties (e.g., observation of DVS messages do not reveal any information about the DVS). In the DVS, only keys need to be considered secret. Each DVS implementation may satisfy different election and security standards, such as the US Federal Election Commission Voting System Standards, the Controlled Access Protection (C2) level of security as defined in DoD 5200.28-STD (the Dept. of Defense Trusted Computer System Evaluation Criteria), the ITSEC Level 3 as defined in the Common Criteria for IT Security Evaluation, or the Code of Practice for Information Security Management BS 7799 (a British Standard that is the basis of the ISO/IEC 17799-1 Standard). The DVS developed by Safevote is a complete Internet voting system, including voter registration and tabulation. Voter registration is provided in terms of issuing and managing voter credentials, without any need to develop special interfaces with centralized voter registration systems. It is possible to use the DVS as a ballot delivery system, without vote tabulation. Development of the DVS started in 1997 and it has been in commercial use since 2000.

5.   OPEN SOURCE DVS: MYSAVEVOTE.COM

MySafevote.com presents a public interface for Internet voting, implementing a DVS using *open source* software. A demo is available at the site.

MySafevote.com operates with standard browsers, without plug-ins, Java or JavaScript. If available, JavaScript is used for enhanced presentation. MySafevote.com was designed to work as a Voting Portal, allowing users to manage and access different elections. The role of an election manager is similar to the role of a LEO in Fig. 2, in a public-sector voting system. The software was entirely developed by Safevote, using open source tools only (Linux, Apache, MySQL and PHP (LAMP)). Safevote chose LAMP for this service because its components have been widely used and tested and have a solid group of developers who support it. LAMP is a robust development environment with a high level of reliability that enables rapid software development. The DVS software modules used in MySafevote.com are similar to the DVS software modules developed in Java and described in Table 1.

A recent election using MySafevote.com had 267,476 voters registered online, with 91,744 voters participating over the Internet from Sweden, Spain, the United Kingdom, Belgium and Africa. MySafevote.com has also been used for elections with 1,000-12,000 voters in Brazil, Sweden, and the United States. The development of MySafevote.com was divided in two phases. Phase I ended with the development of the core technology of the Voting Portal, which was launched in 2001. Phase II will be completed by the end of Q4 2002, adding real-time management tools to the system. These tools will allow election managers to set up and manage an election without additional programming input from Safevote developers. MySafevote.com was designed to meet several stringent usability requirements as well as the legal requirements in 28+ US states that allow Internet voting in the private sector (e.g., proxy voting). Mysafevote.com has proven to be easy to use while it offers high reliability and security, protects voter privacy, and supports multiple languages. MySafevote.com includes election and security features such as ballot rotation, ballot styles, data encryption, enciphering of HTML names to prevent re-play attacks or session hijacking, voter authentication and spoof prevention. Buttons on each page can be rotated in order to prevent automated HTML attacks. The DVS state machine also controls the representation of the data, which allows for a language independent structure. The same software can present an election in English as well as Chinese, for example.

The voter authentication system is logically and physically divided into two main components: the issuer and the verifier. One server contains the issuer, which generates a Digital Vote Certificate (DVC) for every voter. The DVC is a patent pending technology. The issuer is off-line, offering maximum security and privacy for the voter. The DVCs can be delivered by email, fax or regular mail. The verifier module is part of the election server. It receives voter input during authentication, and first determines if the DVC works - where the DVC acts as a cryptographic device. If the DVC works, the verifier computes the Return Code, used to thwart spoofing, and the verifier also calculates additional voter data, such as the voter's precinct or ballot style information. In this case the DVC acts as an authorization tool. Finally, the signature of the DVC, which is unique, is used as a signature for all log activity. The multi-party election processor interfaces with a MySQL database, which contains the ballot information and the meta-ballot information (meta-ballot designates a patent pending technology), defining the sequence and rules for the races in an election. An additional feature of the software is the separation of content from presentation, which allows the look and feel of a voting site to be changed easily, and permitting the election manager to customize the voting pages. The Mysafevote.com development supports the idea that, eventually, all source code used in public elections should be publicly known and verified (open source code, open peer review), including the software in the underlying systems.

6.   CONCLUSION

Internet voting is more than just using the Internet to vote. It is an opportunity to design a cost-effective, receipt-free and universally verifiable voting system, as presented here with the Distributed Voting System (DVS). The DVS uses a multi-channel, distributed architecture to create a desired level of information and power granularity by means of hardware and software-defined layers and walls, scaling to any number of voters. Client protection is built-in. With the DVS, if we take any voter (e.g., in voter registration) we are not able to know which ballot was cast by that voter; and if we take any ballot (e.g., in tallying) we are not able to know which voter cast it. After an election, all votes and all voters are publicly known, but their connection can be both unknown and unknowable, even under best efforts and court order. However, for example as desired in the United Kingdom, a connection between a voter and a ballot can be created under court order by using DVCs that are generated with passwords linkable to each voter.

A demo is available at MySafevote.com, developed using open source software. A version suitable for public elections has been developed in Java. The DVS has been successfully used in Internet elections with 300,000 registered voters and 92,000 participating voters.

Acknowledgements

This paper includes comments from several contributors, as listed in the author's references, including Thomas Blood, Roy Saltman, Einar Stefferud, and Eva Waskell.

Notes

1. The requirements form a logical system of some complexity and thus we do not expect such a system to be both complete and consistent. See Goedel's incompleteness theorem.
2. Attacks and errors are hard to detect and prevent at the interface points.
3. To further protect voter privacy, vote secrecy may be maintained even after the tabulated results of the election are known; otherwise voters may be identified by their voting patterns, offering opportunity for vote selling and voter coercion.
4. Even if a correction channel is not 100% independent, the probability that both channels may be compromised at the same time is smaller than that of any single channel.
5. A nonce is a random number that occurs only once.
6. Suppose a fraudster gives each voter a unique, but unlikely, pattern of voted names. Ballots can then be linked to voters, effectively breaking voter privacy.
7. For example, if 10,000 ballots are cast in an election where the probability of frauds, attacks or faults leading to the loss of any ballot is at most 5% and if only 300 ballots are verified, the probability that the loss of at least one ballot will not be detected (and thus the fraud, attack or fault will not be discovered) is less than 0.1%.
8. As defined by E. Gerck in terms of a communication process, trust has nothing to do with feelings or emotions. Trust cannot be induced by self-assertions. Trust is qualified reliance on information, based on factors independent of that information. In short, trust needs multiple channels to be communicated and the channels need to be at least partially independent. More precisely, "trust is that which is essential to a communication channel, but cannot be transferred using that channel" (see E. Gerck, "Trust Points", in *Digital Certificates: Applied Internet Security*, J. Feghhi, J. Feghhi, P. Williams (Eds.), Addison-Wesley, pg. 194-195, 1998).

REFERENCES

[1]. Gerck E. Voting System Requirements. To appear in *Proc. Financial Cryptography '01*, Springer-Verlag. Preprint available at: http://www.vote.caltech.edu/wote01/pdfs/gerck.pdf. A longer version is available at http://www.thebell.net/papers/ vote-req.pdf.

[2]. Cohen J., Fischer M. A robust and verifiable cryptographically secure election scheme. In *Proc. 26th IEEE Symposium on Foundations of Computer Science* (FOCS '85), pp. 372-382. IEEE Computer Society, 1985.

[3]. Benaloh J. *Verifiable Secret-Ballot Elections*. PhD thesis, Yale University, Dept. of Computer Science, September 1987.

[4]. Gerck E. Voting With Witness Voting - Qualified Reliance on Electronic Voting. WOTE'01 Conference, California, August 2001; available at http://www.vote.caltech.edu/wote01/pdfs/gerck-witness.pdf

[5]. Gerck E. *Contra Costa Shadow Election Project 2000*, Final Report issued by Safevote Inc., 2000. Copy available upon request.

[6]. Cramer R., Franklin M, Schoenmakers B., Yung M. Multi-authority secret ballot elections with linear work. In *Advances in Cryptology* - EUROCRYPT'96, LNCS 1070, pg. 72-83, Berlin, 1996. Springer-Verlag.

Chapter 12

REMOTE VOTING VIA THE INTERNET?
The Canton of Geneva pilot project

Alexander Trechsel[1], Fernando Mendez[2], Raphaël Kies[2]

[1] *University of Geneva, Geneva, Switzerland*
alexandre.trechsel@droit.unige.ch

[2] *European University Institute, Florence, Italy*
{fernando.mendez,raphael.kies}@iue.it

Abstract: This chapter focuses on the pilot-project of introducing e-voting in the Canton of Geneva, Switzerland. The case study provides for some illuminating insights that may be applicable to other political contexts. It addresses the wider policy context, the legal framework and the most salient technical issues, as well as some of the major socio-political issues that have been raised during this key implementation phase.

Key words: Remote internet-voting; Direct democracy; e-democracy; Turnout; Deliberation; e-voting implementation.

1. INTRODUCTION

Elections are recurring events in every modern democracy. Indeed this is one of the central features of democracy with elections by and large being hold at intervals of four or five years. For most electorates democratic decision processes other than these periodic elections are, on the whole, rather rare. In this regard, however, Switzerland is somewhat of an outlier. Its institutions of direct democracy, and more precisely the referendum and initiative process can result in popular votes at the federal level of up to 4-5 times per year. Although direct democracy may complement representative democratic systems in other countries Switzerland is by far the world leader in the use of direct democratic decision-making [1]. At the sub-national level, e.g. in the cantons, direct democracy is equally as popular and over the last 30 years more than 3.000 votes have taken place [2,3]. At the communal level elections and popular votes are also held regularly.

In addition to its unique political system, offering the electorate multiple possibilities to directly participate in politics through ballot decisions, Switzerland is one of the most advanced countries in the use of Information and Communication Technology (ICT): the so called "information society" has become a reality and is developing at a very fast pace in Switzerland.

If one combines these two elements - the frequent use of ballot decisions and the high level of ICT usage - it is not surprising that Switzerland expects to be at the forefront of the development of e-democracy in general and of e-voting in particular [4]. In this contribution we would like to focus on the on-going projects in the field of e-voting that have been developed thus far and in particular on the pilot-project of the canton of Geneva.

2.   GENESIS OF THE PROJECTS ON E-VOTING IN SWITZERLAND

In the case of Switzerland e-voting is not only a trendy catchword but can be regarded as a potentially vital interface between the citizens and the public administration. It also affects all levels of ICT interaction, namely the level of information, communication and transaction [5]. The initial impulse for introducing e-voting in Switzerland has tended to follow a top-down approach. As early as 1998 the federal government decided to investigate the possibilities that ICT could offer for "strengthening the integration of the population in the democratic decision-making process" [6]. Since then the project *vote électronique* (e-voting) has become one of the two key projects - the other being the development of an e-government portal called *Guichet virtuel* - promoted by the Federal Chancellery. According to the latest official report on e-voting [7] the Swiss Government aims to not only open the political debate on e-voting but also to implement and evaluate concrete pilot -projects in the field of Internet-based voting systems. This first period of experimentation is expected to produce preliminary results by the year 2004.

As it is often the case with policy making in federal systems, such as the Swiss one, the sub-national level has been chosen as a platform for initial experiments and pilot-projects. With regard to e-voting, the cantons of Neuchâtel, Zurich and Geneva have been chosen for the first pilot-projects, enabling the federal government to learn from their implementation before attempting to do so at the federal level. At the time of writing the pilot-project of the canton of Geneva is at a particularly advanced stage. The Geneva electorate is expected to be able to cast a first binding vote over the Internet by the end of 2002, beginning of 2003. This poses the question of why Geneva? An answer to this question was provided by the Canton's Chancellor [8], who underlined the overall e-government strategy of the canton and the favourable climate for ICT-developments in Geneva. Indeed, Geneva hosts many of the headquarters of leading international organisations such as the International Telecommunication Union (ITU) and the World Intellectual Property Organization (WIPO), and is the location where the World Wide Web was developed at the European Organisation for Nuclear Research (CERN).

3.   VOTING PROCEDURES AND LEGAL ASPECTS

The canton of Geneva offers its citizens two distinct possibilities to cast their vote. First, one can physically go to the polling station on the Sunday morning of the voting weekend[1]. In Geneva, as well as in most other Swiss cantons, one has a supplementary possibility for participating in the democratic process, namely through postal voting. The latter was introduced in 1991 and extended in 1995. Whereas in 1991 the system still required the voter to make an explicit demand to the elections administration for the possibility to vote via the post since 1995 the relevant material is sent automatically to every voter. The voting material is sent out three weeks prior to the voting weekend. It contains a voting card (ID), the ballot paper as well as the voting pamphlet edited by the government. Over this three weeks period voters are able to return the envelope containing the signed voting card and the ballot card. It has to reach the elections administration by the Saturday morning of the voting weekend. If this deadline is missed only voting at the polling station is possible. Recent figures show that since its introduction, postal voting is used on average by about 95% of the voters in the canton of Geneva [9].

It is important to underline that the proposed introduction of e-voting will not replace either of these two traditional voting mechanisms but merely complement them, offering a third way to cast a vote. Therefore given that e-voting will be a complementary voting method in the canton of Geneva it will not be a potential source of inequality among the voters. This however is not the only legal requirement that e-voting procedures will have to meet. A whole body of political science literature has - over several decades - shown that voting procedures may generate fundamental effects on the outcome of elections and popular votes. Most democracies therefore codify legal rules that govern electoral procedures. In Switzerland it is not possible to simply propose a new mode of voting, e.g. via the Internet, in the absence of a specific legal basis that would formally permit the organisers of a popular vote or an election to use or experiment with a new voting method for casting votes. However, the canton of Geneva presents a unique case in the Swiss context. As a result of article 181 - the Law regulating democratic decision-making procedures - a sufficient legal basis exists for experimenting with new voting procedures. The law contains provisions that delegate to the cantonal government the power to conduct such experiments [10].

In addition, e-voting procedures will also have to respect other important democratic norms that have evolved over time. Among them, one could cite the five main constitutional principles of electoral law, which are sometimes referred to as the principles of the European electoral heritage. These include universal, equal, free, secret and direct suffrage [11,12]; for a detailed discussion of the legal requirements in the Geneva case see also [10]. In this contribution we will refrain detailing at length the legal dimension of e-voting procedures. From a comparative perspective, however, it is important to underline that most legal problems - that remote e-voting poses - seem to have been resolved in the Swiss case. Many of the legal problems currently discussed elsewhere do not exist in Switzerland for the reason that that the contentious legal issues that have been raised are already largely addressed by postal voting (for a critical discussion of legal problems related to voting from home see [13]. Postal voting is a well-established and smooth working procedure that is used by a large part of the Swiss electorate. Thus, Switzerland presents a particularly favourable context for introducing other forms of remote voting such as remote voting via the Internet.

Although the legal problems might differ from one context to another, one condition for voting procedures has to be met in all cases: it should be as secure as possible. However, neither e-voting mechanisms *nor* traditional voting mechanisms can ensure a 100% level of security [14]. If such a security threshold were required democratic decision - making processes would simply have to be abandoned everywhere in the world. Remote e-voting should, nevertheless, be as secure as possible and robust against potential inside and outside attacks, system failures, multiple voting, etc. In the case of Geneva, the first alpha and beta-versions have been tested in order to achieve these goals.

4.   ARCHITECTURE OF THE GENEVA E-VOTING SYSTEM

In the canton of Geneva, as elsewhere in Switzerland, it would only make sense to develop and offer voting via the Internet. Given that 95% of voters currently use the postal method to permit the remaining 5% of voters that physically go to the polling station to vote electronically at the booth would hardly be a worthwhile endeavour. From the beginning therefore the government of the canton of Geneva has opted for the most radical form of e-voting, namely voting from any internet-enabled computer in the world (for further distinctions of e-voting mechanisms see [15].

One of the most significant problems the promoters of the Geneva project encountered was the need to avoid multiple voting. As every voter automatically receives a voter ID card and the ballot paper in their mailbox three weeks prior to the vote providing the voter with a PIN code to vote online would not prevent the voter from using one of the other two possibilities: voting at the booth or voting via traditional mail. However, a rather innovative solution to this problem has been found. Printed on top of the voter ID card is a 12-digit PIN code that is covered by an opaque film and can be scratched off. With the PIN code and the correct answer to some supplementary questions such as place of birth, a voter is able to vote online until Saturday at noon[2]. A voter ID card where the PIN code has been uncovered is void and cannot be used for postal voting or at the ballot box. Should the voter experience any technical problem while voting online, such as a computer crash, or simply change their mind and not wish to proceed with voting via the Internet they would still have the possibility of going to the voting booth on Sunday, where the uncovered PIN code may be checked by the elections officials. If it has not been used the voter may cast his vote.

In order to cast a vote via the Internet, the voter has to access the official website of the canton of Geneva and fill in the voters ID card number, which is different from the hidden PIN code. The system then checks whether this voting card has already been used or not. If it has not been used the voter may then fill in the ballot form that is, in its form, identical to the one in paper format. Only once the voter has confirmed his ballot choice will he or she be asked to provide the PIN code and answer the supplementary questions (see above). If the authentication procedure is successful the specific operating server that is running on dedicated servers will subsequently encrypt the electronic ballot, store it and confirm to the voter that the process has been carried out successfully. Transmission relies on a Secure Socket Layer (SSL) 128 bits communication security protocol. The encryption is achieved using two different keys that are physically kept in a safe place: the safe of the security officer of the Police Department. Only the Election Commission has the necessary passwords to unlock these keys. For further details on technological aspects and security measures see [9].

It has to be noted that the technical solutions currently developed for the canton of Geneva pilot-project rely on a public-private-partnership between the Geneva administration and several private companies. While security options have been criticised by different experts, most notably the issue of the citizen's PC protection [16], another source of criticism stems from the fact that no open-source solution has been chosen, the cantonal authorities being the legal owners of the code. Criticism has been principally voiced by proponents of open-source solutions, most notably by a group of Linux-users based in the French-speaking part of Switzerland[3].

5.   DIGITAL DIVIDE, DESIRABILITY AND USER-FRIENDLINESS

In February 2001 the Research and Documentation Centre on Direct Democracy (c2d), located at the University of Geneva, was asked by the Chancellery of the Canton of Geneva to conduct a representative survey among the electorate in order to shed some light on the most salient issues related to the possible introduction of e-voting procedures.

The starting point of our survey was to address the question of the so-called digital divide among the Geneva electorate. Many studies show that the digital divide not only exists between countries with high or low levels Internet penetration [17] but also exists within countries. With regard to the canton of Geneva, our study showed that the proportion of the "online electorate" was 47.2%, in February 2001. Roughly one voter out of two uses the Internet either on a daily or on a less frequent basis [4]. It can be assumed that Internet users now form a majority among the electorate of the canton of Geneva. The study also showed the traditional gender and age cleavages appear between users and non-users of the Internet; the Internet is used more widely by the young people rather than the older, and that men tend to use the Internet more than women. Thus it has to be stressed that the introduction of e-voting in the canton of Geneva would potentially involve half of its electorate. Moreover, this group is likely to be demographically and socio-economically different to the other half of the electorate that remains unconnected to the Internet. As we shall see below this could potentially have significant political ramifications.

In a political context where the electorate can have its say via the referendum initiative process it would be imprudent to attempt to alter longstanding democratic procedures without ascertaining whether there is a certain degree of desirability among the electorate. Table 1 contains the answers to the question of whether e-voting is desired by the electorate in the canton of Geneva. Our results show that two thirds of the electorate are, either rather or strongly, in favor of the introduction of e-voting. This is not a straightforward result, the existence of a highly accessible postal voting system could well have lessened voters' desire for e-voting. The benefits may seem limited and this may have led voter to oppose its introduction. However, this appears not to be the case. 85.6% of Internet users are in favour of the introduction of e-voting. Also surprising, although to a more limited extent, even a majority (53.2%) of non-users shares their opinion!

Table 1. Desirability of e-voting in the canton of Geneva (Februrary 2001)

	n	%
Strongly in favour	278	27.8
Rather in favour	407	40.7
Rather opposed	125	12.5
Strongly opposed	85	8.5
No answer	105	10.5
Total	1000	100

Source : Kies & Trechsel (2001: 64).

In December 2001 the c2d was again asked by the cantonal Chancellery to participate in the Geneva pilot-project by conducting a test on the proposed e-voting system ("Alpha Ter" test). The latter essentially aimed at gathering valuable feedback on the prototype of the e-voting system from a random set of Internet users testing the system by casting a blank vote via the Internet[4].

With regard to the desirability of introducing e-voting procedures in the Canton of Geneva, we found that 91.6% of all Internet users were either strongly or rather in favour of introducing e-voting mechanisms (before testing the system). This figure is close to the 85.6% of Internet users in favour of e-voting that we found in the February 2001 survey. However, the "Alpha Ter" test provided us with an additional measure: the effect of having experienced e-voting by testing the prototype version on the desirability of its introduction. We tried to address the question of whether being exposed to e-voting technology increases or decreases desirability (or has no effect) among Internet users. In order to answer this question we asked the respondents the same question *before* and *after* their testing of the prototype version[5].

Table 2 contains a cross-tabulation analysis of the relationship between before- and after-testing level of desirability. The interpretation of the results contained in Table 2 contains four basic points [18]. First, respondents that were initially strongly in favour of introducing e-voting procedures remained, to a very large extent, as strongly in favour as they were before testing the prototype (94%). Second, among the respondents that were rather in favour before testing, about 51% remained rather in favour after the test, while 49% were subsequently strongly in favour. Third, no single respondent who was either strongly or rather in favour of introducing e-voting mechanisms was opposed to it after having tested the prototype system. Finally, among the very few respondents initially opposed to its introduction, about 40% become rather or strongly convinced of e-voting after having tested the system. In general, we could observe a beneficial effect of experiencing the e-voting solution developed in Geneva on the overall desirability of its introduction. There were no negative effects, which allows us to put forward the hypothesis that once introduced, e-voting mechanisms might well become the preferred voting method once electors have used it for the first time. A similar diffusion effect could be measured with regard to the introduction of postal voting: once you use it, it is highly probable that you will use it again.

Table 2. Opinion on e-voting via the internet before and after testing the prototype system

		Opinion on e-voting via the internet (before testing)				
		Strongly in favour	Rather in favour	Rather opposed	Strongly opposed	Total (n and %)
Opinion on e-voting via the Internet (after testing)	strongly in favour	94%	49%		14%	319 (74%)
	rather in favour	6%	51%	40%	29%	100 (23%)
	rather opposed			53%	29%	10 (2%)
	strongly opposed			7%	29%	3 (0.7%)
	total (n)	259	151	15	7	432 (100%)

Probability of X^2: p.<.01; gamma 0.91. 17 cases (3.8%) were excluded from the analysis for either containing no answer to the questions or for being coded as missing data [18].

Finally, the "Alpha Ter" test allowed us to test the user-friendliness of the prototype version. The survey contained several detailed questions about the voter's comprehension of the voter ID card, the quantity and the quality of the technical information of the online voting procedure, the user-friendliness of the navigation system and the filling in of the voting ballot. A final set of questions permitted us to measure the overall evaluation of the system by its users. Generally speaking, a large majority of internet users having tested the proposed e-voting technology evaluated it as being clear and containing sufficient technical information [18]. The voter ID card-related issues, such as comprehension of the authentication procedure using the PIN code etc., were also evaluated favourably, i.e. as being understandable and manageable. The same is true for the navigation facilities and the filling in of the voting ballot. On the other hand, some very technical issues, such as the certification of the official web site, were raised a smaller proportion of users. In general, it appears that the introduction of e-voting procedures is not only desired by nine out of ten voters in the survey but that the proposed system is welcomed very warmly by its users.

6.   E-VOTING AND TURNOUT

The most widely cited positive effect of introducing e-voting mechanisms is the one on turnout. Policymakers around the globe explicitly refer to
e-voting as a potential life-belt for turnout that is declining alarmingly in
many democracies both at the national and sub-national levels[6] [19]. Some
first experiences with e-voting, for example the 2000 Primary Elections of
the Democratic Party in Arizona, have shown that positive effects may well
occur [20]. With regard to the Geneva case it has to be underlined that the
effect of e-voting on turnout could only be positive or neutral, as voting via
the internet would simply constitute an alternative, complementary method
for casting one's vote. The data stemming from February 2001 survey enables us to measure this potential effect.

For this purpose we first asked the respondents whether they belonged to
the category of regular voters, occasional voters or non-voters. While the
effect of introducing e-voting mechanisms on turnout among regular voters
can be considered to be nil, we asked the occasional and non-voters (26.1%
of the overall sample) whether they believed that the possibility to use the
internet for casting their votes might incite them to participate more regularly in democratic process. Table 3 contains the results of our analysis.

Table 3: Frequency of participation to popular votes and incitation to participate more
regularly should e-voting mechanisms be introduced (in % - n's in parentheses).

		Incitation to participate more regularly				
		Yes	No	don't know	no answer	total (n & %)
Frequency of participation	Occasional	35.9 (70)	48.7 (95)	13.8 (27)	1.5 (3)	100.0 (195)
	Never	30.3 (20)	45.5 (30)	21.2 (14)	3.0 (2)	100.0 (66)
	total (n)	**34.5 (90)**	47.9 (125)	15.7 (41)	1.9 (5)	100.0 (261)

Kies and Trechsel: 54 [4].

One third (35.9%) of occasional voters and 30.3% of non-voters believe
that the introduction of e-voting procedures would incite them to participate
more regularly at the polls. This very minor difference between the two
groups is rather astounding; it shows that almost one out of three citizens
that usually refrain from participating in democratic decisions at the polls
could be encouraged to do so simply by extending the election procedures.
This proportion could be higher, given the rather important number of inde-
cisive respondents, especially among the politically abstinent (21.2% [4]).

Also, when distinguishing internet-users from non-users, the proportion
of respondents that believe e-voting will have a positive effect of e-voting on
their political mobilisation at the polls is - unsurprisingly - even higher. A
majority of internet-users (55.2%) that only occasionally or never vote belong to the category of citizens that think e-voting could change their future

political behaviour and incite them to participate more frequently in polls. Among the same category of internet-users that only occasionally or never participate and that tested the system in December 2001 this proportion was even higher, amounting to 75.6% [18].

Our survey of February 2001 showed that the overall effect on turnout of introducing e-voting mechanisms in the canton of Geneva would be a 9% increase, the latter corresponding to a total of 90 respondents, reported in Table 3, indicating that they might be encouraged to participate more frequently at the polls. The increase is not evenly distributed among the electorate, the younger segments being more enthusiastic than the elder. However, while such an increase in turnout is certainly highly significant, one has to be very careful with such figures. The calculated 9% increase of turnout is based on subjective evaluations of future political behaviour. Only through a detailed scientific analysis of voting via the Internet, once this has taken place, will it be possible to shed more light on the effects of e-voting on turnout.

7.   DELIBERATIVE ASPECTS

According to participatory democratic theory, one of the key elements of the quality of democracy is not so much how many voters participate but how they participate. In order to achieve "good" decisions voters should not only be extensively informed about the issues at stake but they should also be able to forge their opinions by deliberating amongst each other. According to the defendants of participatory democracy it is only through discussions among informed electors, in an open and free public space, that the quality of the political process can be maximised. For participatory theorists, the citizens' involvement and active participation in democracy will ultimately heighten their civic competence and therefore enhance their belief in the values of and support for the democratic system [21,22]. As we have seen, e-voting may generate positive effects on democratic decisions by heightening turnout, therefore directly increasing the quantity of participation. In addition, we argue that the introduction of e-voting mechanisms may also generate *indirect* effects on participation, and more precisely on the quality of participation.

According to Kriesi, the introduction of e-voting "provides a crucial opportunity for the reorganisation of the public sphere" in the sense that it could contribute to a partial re-homogenisation of this public sphere. While the public sphere has undergone, over time, a process of profound fragmentation (multiplication of specialised, domain-focused information channels), the official site allowing to vote via the internet may well become a political portal for gathering and exchanging election/vote-relevant information. Discussion fora, political information resources and other election/vote-related web sites exist without e-voting being introduced. However, it is reasonable to expect that an official site, where an actual transaction (the vote) can be realised, is also likely to serve as a major web portal for political information and deliberation [4].

It goes without saying that the success of a pre-voting virtual public sphere will crucially depend on its quality. The canton of Geneva pilot-project offers an opportunity for increasing the voters' - especially the ones choosing the Internet for voting - political awareness. Also, this seems to correspond to a demand among Internet users. Our study of the "Alpha Ter" test reveals that among the potential improvements desired by those testing the system more information and tools for enhancing the availability of information are strongly desired. A majority of respondents would like to have more hyperlinks to political parties (54%), the political authorities (56%) and to be able to directly contact the latter via email (67%). Also, a majority of Internet users (55%) that tested the e-voting prototype wish to see the development of discussion fora on the official web site [18]. The cantonal Chancellery took note of these demands from the electorate and is currently improving the political information and communication possibilities on the official voting web site.

8.   CONCLUSION

Although the Geneva case study has revealed certain idiosyncrasies that are specific to the Swiss political system - such as the institution of direct democracy and an accompanying high frequency of popular votes - we none-theless believe that a number of significant issues have been raised that are relevant to the ongoing debate on e-voting. Among the most salient issues identified the following are deemed to be particularly noteworthy factors influencing implementation and experimentation in the domain of e-voting:

The wider policy context: As the Geneva case study has revealed e-voting is part and parcel of a growing trend of increased use by government of ICT. As a result e-voting must be seen as an integral component of a wider pheno-menon in which ICT is increasingly interacting with our institutions of governance. As to policy implementation the Swiss have largely opted for a top-down approach, with a significant drive from the Federal level, although the testing and initial trials have been conducted in a decentralised fashion, i.e., at the cantonal level.

Legal framework: The implementation of e-voting mechanisms will have to address important legal issues. In some cases new legislation will be required while in others, such as the canton of Geneva, this may not be necessary. Geneva, in this respect presents a special, although not unique case. Another significant factor that is particularly relevant and has affected the implementation of e-voting trials are the pre-existing provisions for postal voting.

Technical issues: As discussed in the relevant section above Geneva officials have opted for a maximalist approach to e-voting in terms of the electorate's scope to vote via internet enabled computers. Not surprisingly this raises a number of crucial technical issues, such as the possibilities for multiple voting. Fortunately for the Canton of Geneva, the existing system of postal voting provided a base on which to build a relatively simple system that uses a PIN code. Other constituencies may face thornier problems in attempting to address these and other related technical issues.

Socio-political issues: A number of other important issues were identified which can be grouped under the generic label of socio-political issues. These could be considered primarily political in nature and could have important effects on the feasibility of implementing e-voting mechanisms. Questions related to the digital divide could affect politicians' propensity to consider introducing new voting mechanisms especially if they perceive themselves or their parties to be adversely affected. This is not unrelated to the expectation that e-voting is likely to increase turnout. For political scientists however, turnout is not necessarily a good indicator of democracy and many of them prefer to focus on the quality of participation. The latter must also be taken into consideration when addressing e-voting.

One of the central themes that this chapter has emphasised is that e-voting raises a whole host of thorny political, legal and technical issues - this is especially so at the implementation phase. One can be sure that achieving an appropriate policy mix between these, especially the balance between the opportunities and risks presented by e-voting, is likely to differ among countries. This will tend to be the result of different policy styles, traditions of democracy, legal frameworks and perceptions and tolerance of the risks involved to name but a few. In sum, the issues raised in the case study are some of the real, perceived and anticipated problems that officials, policy-makers and academics have had to address in the early stages of implementing a system of e-voting for the canton of Geneva.

REFERENCES

[1]   Trechsel A., Kriesi H., 1996. "Switzerland: the referendum and initiative as a center-piece of the political system" in Gallagher M., Uleri P.V. (Eds.) *The Referendum Experience in Europe*, Macmillan, pp. 185-208.

[2]   Trechsel A., Serdült U., (1999). *Kaleidoskop Volksrechte*. Die Institutionen der direkten Demokratie in den Kantonen 1970-1996, Helbing & Lichtenhahn Publ.

[3] Trechsel A., (2000). *Feuerwerk Volksrechte. Die Volksabstimmungen in den schweize-rischen Kantonen 1970-1996*, Lichtenhahn Publ.

[4] Kies R., Trechsel A. (2001). "Le contexte socio-politique", pp. 5-73. In Auer A., Trechsel A. (Eds.), *Voter par Internet?* Le projet e-voting dans le canton de Genève dans une perspective socio-politique et juridique. Geneva, Basel, Munich: Helbing & Lichtenhahn Publ.

[5] Gisler M., 2001. "Einführung in die Begriffswelt des eGovernment", pp. 13-30. In Gisler M., Spahni D. (Hrsg.), *eGovernment. eine Standortbestimmung*, Paul Haupt Publ.

[6] Federal Council, 1998. *Strategy of the Federal Council for an Information Society in Switzerland*. http://www.isps.ch/eng/stored_documents/PDF/42.pdf (May 16 2002).

[7] Federal Council, 2002. Bericht über den Vote électronique. Chancen, Risiken und Machbarkeit elektronischer *Ausübung politischer Rechte*. http://e-gov.admin.ch/vote/e-demo-dt-09.01.02.pdf (May 16 2002).

[8] Hensler R., 2002. Chances et défis du vote par Internet. Paper presented at the *3rd Worldwide Forum on e-Democracy*, Issy-les-Moulineaux (Paris), April 2002.

[9] Warynski M., 2002. "Overview of the technical problems related to the e-voting project on the canton of Geneva". Paper presented at the *Conference "E-voting and the European Parliamentary Elections"*, Florence, May 10-11 2002.

[10] Auer A., N. von Arx, 2001. "Le cadre juridique". In Auer A., Trechsel A. (Eds.), *Voter par Internet?* Le projet e-voting dans le canton de Genève dans une perspective socio-politique et juridique, Helbing & Lichtenhahn Publ.

[11] Garrone P., 2001. Le patrimoine electoral européen – Une décennie d'expérience de la Commission de Venise dans le domaine électoral. In *Revue du droit public et de la science politique en France et à l'étranger*: 1417-1454.

[12] Garrone, P., 2002. "Fundamental and political rights in electronic elections". Paper presented at the *Conference "E-voting and the European Parliamentary Elections"*, Florence, May 10-11 2002.

[13] Watt B., Birch S., 2002. "Electronic Voting: Free, Fair and Secret? - A paper on the legal constraints (and possible solutions) facing remote electronic voting". Paper presented at the *Conference "E-voting and the European Parliamentary Elections"*, Florence, May 2002.

[14] Auer A., N. von Arx, 2002. "La légitimité des procédures de vote: les défis du e-voting", pp. 491-499 in *Aktuelle Juristische Praxis*/Pratique Juridique Actuelle 5/2002.

[15] Gibson R., 2002a. "Internet Voting and the 2004 European Parliament Elections: Problems and Prospects". Paper presented at the *Conférence "E-voting and the European Parliamentary Elections"*, Florence, May 10-11 2002.

[16] Comité Sécurité, 2002. *Rapport du Comité Sécurité sur l'application du vote par Internet*. http://www.ge.ch/chancellerie/e-government/doc/rapport_securite_internet.pdf

[17] Norris P., 2001. *Digital Divide: Civic Engagement, Information Poverty and the Internet Worldwide*, Cambridge University Press.

[18] Christin T., Müller R., 2002. *Analyse quantitative du test Alpha Ter: Evaluation par questionnaire du système de vote par Internet*. c2d, University of Geneva: unpublished manuscript.

[19] IDEA, 2002. *Voter Turnout since 1945: A Global Report*, International IDEA.

[20] Gibson R., 2002b. "Elections online: Assessing Internet Voting in Light of the Arizona Democratic Primary" in *Political Science Quarterly* 116(4).

[21]   Pateman C., 1970. *Participation and Democratic Theory*, Cambridge University Press.

[22]   Barber B., 1984. *Strong Democracy*. Participatory Politics for a New Age, University of California Press.

Notes

[1]   Popular votes and elections in Switzerland always take place on a weekend.

[2]   It has to be noted that alternative authentication technologies have been evaluated. Most notably, the use of a smart card with a personal ID code validated by a Public Key Infrastructure (PKI) has been closely examined. At this stage, however, such a solution has been discarded [9].

[3]   See http://www.linux-gull.ch/

[4]   For this purpose we set up several personal computers connected to the Internet at the cantonal passport administration, a place where no online transaction is yet available. Geneva citizens still need to physically go to this office if they need a new passport or a renewal of their expired one. Therefore, we could expect to find a random sample of citizens that use the Internet and that would be willing, while waiting for their turn in the queue, to test the system in exchange for a free beverage. In 14 days the c2d team could conduct 449 interviews among Geneva voters that use the Internet and that tested the prototype system as if they were casting a real vote.

[5]   The survey question was formulated as follows: "Would you be strongly favourable, rather favourable, rather opposed or strongly opposed to the introduction of electronic voting as a complementary mean to the traditional forms of voting, námely voting at the boot or postal voting?"

[6]   To mention just one recent example, at the second round of France's General Elections on June 16, 2002, 38.4% of the electorate chose not to participate. Never before, during the 5th Republic, has turnout been as low as at 2002 Elections.

Chapter 13

E-VOTE AND PKI'S: A NEED, A BLISS OR A CURSE?

Danilo Bruschi, Giusi Poletti, Emilia Rosti

[1] *Dipartimento di Scienze dell'Informazione, Università degli Studi di Milano, Italy*
{bruschi,giusi.poletti,rose}@dsi.unimi.it

Abstract: With the increasing popularity public key infrastructures have been acquiring in recent years and the legislative support for digital signatures, electronic voting protocols are moving from a strictly research area to the commercial arena. In this paper we examine the role public key infrastructures play in electronic voting in various protocols proposed in the literature, some of which are the kernel of experimental projects and/or commercial products. Although one of the rationales to move towards electronic voting systems is cost-effectiveness, in this paper we argue that performance issues should not be overlooked, especially in case of disaster recovery, were a CA to revoke all of its certificates during an election. Based on performance evaluation studies, we show that directory service access may become the system bottleneck.

Key words: On-line voting protocols, PKI, CRL, Performance, Directory Service.

1.   INTRODUCTION

In the last two decades many researchers have focused their efforts towards the solution of the problem of on-line voting (e-voting), i.e., elections run using computers connected over the Internet. The results of such efforts is a wealth of literature [1,4,7-8,10-20,23-32]) where various protocols are defined. The main differences among the various protocols are in the cryptographic tools used to guarantee the security properties this kind of protocols should verify. Based on this observation, most e-voting protocols can be classified into three classes; the first comprises the protocols derived from Chaum's seminal paper [8], which heavily rely on asymmetric cryptography

[10-11,15-17,19-20,28,30]; the second class derives from Cohen's work [13] and it is based on the use of homomorphic functions [1,4,7,12-14,18,26-27, 31-32]; the third class combine the two approaches in order to take the best of each approach [23,25,29]. Apart from this aspect, all the e-voting protocols share a common structure. They are generally composed of two modules, one in charge of verifying the identity of all the entities involved in the protocol in order to guarantee voter eligibility and vote uniqueness, and the other one in charge of the necessary cryptographic operations on the votes in order to guarantee the security of the process (i.e., vote secrecy and voters' privacy). While protocols mainly differ for the way they implement the second module, they all adopt the same strategy to realize the first one.

Voter authentication, as well as controls of vote uniqueness, is built around the notion of digital certificates and asymmetric cryptography. This is due to the fact that most of the transactions performed during an e-voting session must be non-reputable in order to guarantee the auditability and verifiability of the system. The only tool currently known that allows satisfying such a property is the digital signature. Since all the voting protocols proposed use digital certificates and digital signatures, they all implicitly rely on Public Key Infrastructures for the management of the digital certificates.

PKI is not yet a well-known technology, although it has been around for more than a decade, because of the limited actual deployments. As a matter of fact, it is among the most controversial systems proposed in the last years by the computer security community. Even though several authors indicate PKI's as the enabling technology to offer secure services over the Internet, no significant deployment of such a technology has been seen yet. Neither experience nor theoretical studies exist that allow to evaluate the impact e-voting protocols might have on PKI's. Such an evaluation is critical as PKI's may represent a major obstacle to the deployment of e-voting protocols.

In this paper we analyze the main issues related to the deployment of an e-voting system relying on a real PKI, in order to identify the most critical aspects that need to be addressed when large scale elections are to be organized. We characterize the needs, in terms both of types of PKI services and of number of requests, of an e-voting protocol. As benchmarks for our characterization, we use one representative protocol for each of the two main classes considered before. Based on such a characterization, we identify the main functionalities an e-voting protocol requires from a PKI. This paper is organized as follows. Section 2 presents a brief overview of a PKI. Section 3 recalls the e-voting protocols considered in the paper and their use of PKI services. In Section 4 the critical issues of PKI and e-voting protocols are investigated. Section 5 discusses our contribution and concludes the paper.

2.   PUBLIC KEY INFRASTRUCTURES

An X.509 compliant Public Key Infrastructure [21-22] is composed of three main entities as illustrated in Figure 1:

- *Certification Authority*: the core of a PKI, it is a trusted system that warrants the binding between a public key and its owner by means of a certificate, which it signs with its private key and makes accessible to all users. Certificate management is completed with certificate revocation in case of accidental events, such as key compromise or loss, that force the revocation of the certificate before its natural expiration date. A CA performs the following basic operations: a) issuing end user certificates; b) issuing cross-certificates for other CAs; c) processing certificate revocation requests from end users and RAs; d) generating periodic CRL, or updates thereof.
- *Registration Authority*: an optional system component to which the CA may delegate certain functions, such as verifying users' identity or performing the *proof of possession* of the private key, with the purpose of reducing the accesses to the CA. A certificate signed by the CA guarantees its authenticity. All the communications with the CA are digitally signed. An RA performs the following operations: a) vouching for the identity of entities requesting certification of their keys; b) identity verification by requiring the entity to appear at the RA personally with a physical token or through out-of-band mechanisms; c) verification of the user's possession of the private key; d) signing an electronic certificate request and sending it to the appropriate CA; e) requesting certificate revocations for user certificates issued by CAs that have accredited it.
- *Repository or Directory Server*: a system, or a collection of distributed systems, that stores certificates and CRLs (certificate Revocation List) as distribution center for the users. It does not need to be trusted because the Certification Authority signs the objects it deals with. It usually satisfies three types of requests: a) add requests, performed by the CA to publish certificates and CRL's; b) modify requests, performed by the CA to change object attributes; c) download requests, performed by any entity wishing to verify the validity of a certificate.

In a large scale PKI there might be various CAs, RAs and Repositories. Each CA has one or more RAs that refer to it and can publish data in one or more repositories. CAs can be hierarchically organized or networked. In hierarchical models a CA delegates trust to subordinate CAs when it certifies them. Trust delegation starts at a root CA, which is trusted at every node of the infrastructure. In networked models, also known as cross certified models, trust is established between two CAs in a peer to peer relationships.

The daily activity of issuing and revoking certificates is managed by a CA in the same way in both models.

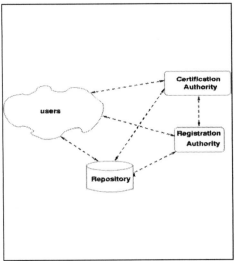

Figure 1. Standard PKI architecture (dashed lines denote communications among entities)

3.   ELECTRONIC AND ON-LINE VOTING PROTOCOLS

From the analysis of the proposed voting protocols, three main groups can be identified, namely those that build on Chaum's work focusing on asymmetric cryptography as a means to achieve secrecy and privacy, those that build on Cohen's work focusing on homomorphic functions as the key to vote secrecy and voters' privacy protection, and those that combine the two approaches in order to take advantage of the positive aspects of both. In this section we briefly recall a protocol for each of the first two groups. No protocols are described from the third group since it is a combination of the other two. The protocol selected for the Chaum family is Sensus [17] and the one for the Cohen family is Schoenmakers' protocol [14].

In the description of the protocols we focus on their interaction with the PKI. In particular, in order to evaluate the amount of work required from the PKI by an election scheme, we consider the PKI as organized in two modules, the Certification Authority, or the trusted third party that guarantees the relationship between the public keys and their owners, and the Repository, or directory service used to publicize the Certificate Revocation Lists (CRL's). Similarly, we divide the accesses to the PKI into requests for certificates to the CA and requests for CRL's to the Repository.

3.1   Sensus

Sensus [17], like most schemes of its type, is comprised of three modules, a Validator, a Tallier and the Pollster that acts on behalf of the voters.
The modules perform three consecutive phases: registration, voting and
tallying. During the registration phase:
1.   the Validator requests its digital certificate from the PKI;
2.   voters request their digital certificates from the PKI;
3.   the Tallier requests the digital certificate to the PKI.

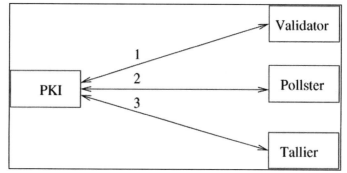

Figure 2. Interaction of Sensus modules with the PKI during the registration phase.
The numbers on the arcs refer to the description in the text.

The three interactions are depicted in Figure 2 as numbered arrows between the PKI and the corresponding entity. The total number of accesses to
the CA in this phase is $n+2$, where n is the number of eligible voters. During
the voting phase certificates are used to authenticate the modules interacting
in the application and the voter, and to guarantee confidentiality. Since votes
are sent to the Tallier anonymously, voters obtain a validated ballot from the
Validator. This will allow the Tallier to discard invalid ballots (i.e. not validated by the Validator) or ballots cast by invalid voters in the tallying phase.
   During the voting phase (Fig. 3) the following steps are executed:
1. The Pollster (on behalf of the voter) contacts the PKI in order to obtain the
   current CRL and verifies the Validator and Tallier's certificates. It then
   generates the ballot and sends it to the Validator after blinding[1] it and
   digitally signing it;
2. In order to check the voter's signature on the ballot the Validator download a CRL from the Repository of the PKI. If the voter's certificate and
   signature are valid, the Validator sends a signed ballot to the voter;

---

[1]   The term "blinding'" is used in [9] to mean the mathematical operation of combining a
   string with a set of coefficients that allow to hide the string original value so that it can be
   signed by a third party without the third party seeing the original string, the coefficients
   can then be removed to obtain the original string, which will result blindly digitally signed.

3. The Pollster verifies the Validator signature and the validity of its certificate using the information contained in the CRL previously downloaded from the PKI, it then sends the signed ballot to the Tallier anonymously;
4. When the Tallier receives the vote, it requests the CRL from the PKI in order to verify the Validator signature on the ballot. If the signature is valid, the Tallier sends the encrypted signed ballot to the voter as vote receipt;
5. The Pollster verifies the Tallier's signature on the receipt using the information of the CRL it already has.

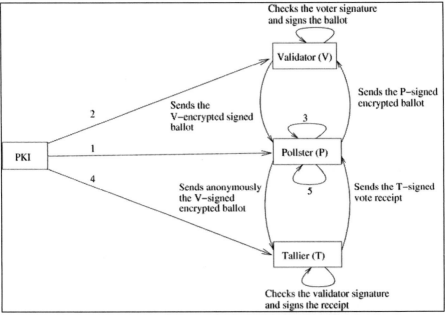

Figure 3. Interaction of Sensus with the PKI during the voting phase. The numbers on the arcs refer to the description in the text.

Supposing that a new CRL, or an update thereof, is issued every half hour, each Pollster requests only one CRL for its voting operations. On the contrary, the system modules will download as many CRL's as will be issued during their period of operation, since the same CRL can be used for several verifications, as long as it is valid.

The number of the PKI interactions can be computed as follows. With *2* modules (Tallier and Validator) and *n* voters, there are *n* CRL requests from the Pollsters and *2*k* CRL requests from the system modules, where *k* is the total number of CRL's issued over the election period of time. Assuming a CRL is issued every half hour, *k* is equal to twice the number of hours *h* an election lasts. Thus, the total number of accesses to the Repository is *n + 4h*.

In the verification phase (Fig. 4), which is executed after the election is over the following steps are performed:

1. The Tallier counts the valid ballots and publishes a signed list of the valid votes;
2. Each voter that verifies the election result requests a new CRL from the PKI since the one downloaded during the voting phase will most likely have expired.

Therefore, the total number of accesses to the PKI is:

- $n+2$ certificate requests during the registration phase;
- $4h+n$ CRL requests during the voting phase;
- up to n CRL requests during the verification phase, one for each voter that verifies the election result.

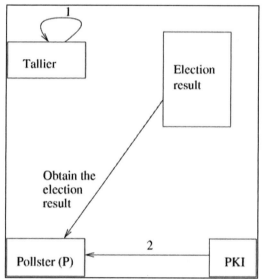

Figure 4. Interaction of Sensus modules with the PKI during the verification phase. The numbers on the arcs refer to the description in the text.

3.2 Schoenmaker's protocol

Schoenmaker's voting scheme [14, 32] is based on Cohen's work using homomorphic functions that allow hiding the vote without hiding the voter's identity, since votes are never decrypted individually. Furthermore, in order to minimize the chances for corrupted authorities, the roles of Validator and Tallier are performed by a set of l distinct sub-authorities. Each such authority has a piece of the private key necessary for vote counting according to a secret sharing scheme [33], which guarantees that corrupted authorities cannot violate the voters' privacy unless a sufficient number collude. Such a number is a parameter of the secret sharing scheme and is usually greater than $1/2 + 1$. All the communication is performed through a bulletin board implemented by a group of servers where voters post their encrypted votes.

Similarly to Sensus, the voting protocol is comprised of three phases, namely registration, voting and verification. During the registration phase (Fig. 5) the digital certificates needed to run the election are generated:

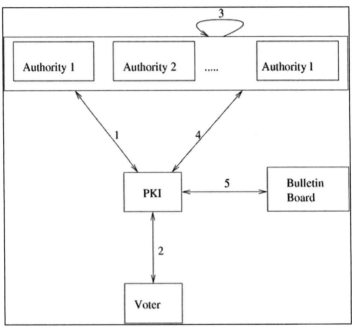

Figure 5. Schoenmaker's voting scheme interaction with the PKI during the registration phase. The numbers on the arcs refer to the description in the text.

1. the l authorities request a digital certificate to the CA;
2. each of the n voters (i.e., the application they use to vote) requests a digital certificate to the CA;
3. the authorities generate the public key;
4. the authorities download the CRL in order to verify each other's signature during the public key generation protocol. The public key used by the voters to encrypt the ballot is certified by the PKI;
5. the digital certificate for the server (or servers, r) bulletin board are requested to the CA. The bulletin board also timestamps and signs the list of authorities and of registered voters.

Thus, the total number of accesses to the PKI for the registration phase is $n+l+r+1$ for certificate requests and l for CRL downloads.

The voting phase is illustrated in Figure 6.

Figure 6. Schoenmaker's voting scheme interaction with the PKI during the voting phase. The numbers on the arcs refer to the description in the text.

The following step are performed:
1. the voter downloads the CRL from the Repository in order to verify the validity of the certificates of the software modules of the voting system; the voter prepares an encrypted ballot, signs it and posts it on the bulletin board together with a zero-knowledge proof of validity for the ballot [2];
2. the bulletin board uses the latest CRL downloaded from the Repository in order to verify the voter's signature on the received ballot and then verify the voter eligibility. At the end of the election the bulletin board timestamps and sings its content, i.e., the received valid ballots.

The number of the PKI accesses in the voting phase can be computed as follows. Given the bulletin board is comprised for r servers and there are n voters, each voter downloads a CRL, for a total of n Repository accesses, while each bulletin board server downloads a new CRL every time it is issued. Assuming, as we did in Section 3.1, that a new CRL, or an update thereof, is issued every half hour and that the election lasts h hours, the voting and registration phases requires $2hr+n$ CRL downloads. In the tallying phase each authority independently computes the sum of the valid vote and signs it. All the operations are made through the bulletin board so each message is signed. Then the authorities jointly execute the decryption protocol and the final tally is published on the bulletin board.

The tallying and verification operations are depicted in Figure 7.

The various operations are performed as follows:
1. each authority downloads the latest CRL in order to verify the other authorities' signatures on the proof of knowledge and messages produced during the decryption operations;
2. the bulletin board downloads the CRL in order to check the talliers validity during the tallying operations. When the election result is published, the bulletin board timestamps and signs all the authorities messages, the sub-tallies and the final result;
3. once the result has been published, each system module or voter may verify the result, which requires that each entity download a new CRL.
   The total number of accesses to the PKI is:
   - $n+l+r+1$ requests for certificate and l requests for CRL during the registration phase;
   - $2hr+n$ requests for CRL during the voting phase;

- $l+r$ requests for CRL during the tallying operation, and up to $n+r+l$ requests for CRL during the verification of the election result.

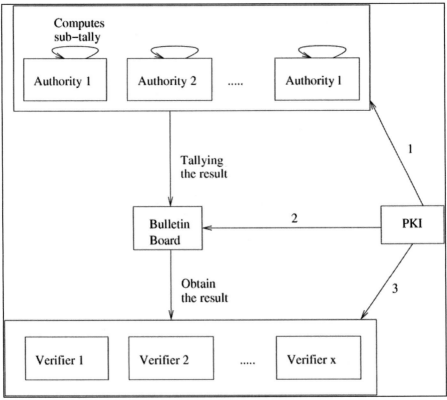

Figure 7. Schoenmaker's voting scheme interaction with the PKI during the tallying and the verification phases. The numbers on the arcs refer to the description in the text.

Like in Sensus, the number of voters plays a critical role since it is the one that can be as large as several millions, while all the other parameters are expected to be in the order of tens. Furthermore, the voting behavior as for the distribution over the election time period of the voters' operations may worsen the pure quantitative impact on the PKI if particularly skewed access patterns are observed. These will be discussed in the next section.

4. THE IMPACT OF PKI ON E-VOTING SYSTEMS

In this section we investigate the main problems that can be caused by the use of PKI's in e-voting protocol. Our considerations are based on the following assumptions. A PKI used in an e-voting system must satisfy, among others, the following properties:

- efficiency: the PKI must provide to the various modules of the e-voting protocols the information they require in a minimum amount of time;
- reliability: a misbehaving PKI component should not jeopardize the e-voting process.

The first identify the most appropriate architecture for a PKI supporting an e-voting protocol. We base our analysis on the quantitative results reported in [5] where the maximum traffic a Certification Authority can sustain with an acceptable response time, is estimated to be 3,5 requests/sec, where a request is either a new certificate request or a certificate revocation request. Furthermore, the results reported in [34] indicate that under normal operating conditions, a LDAP directory with 10000 entries has a response time of 8ms, and a maximum throughput of 140 search requests per second. This means that a PKI with a single CA can only support e-voting systems for small populations of users. Various arguments can be brought in support of such a claim, besides the facts that a centralized single CA PKI is far from satisfying any reliability constraint typical of an e-voting system and that no PKI has been implemented so far that manages huge populations of users (tens of millions). We start by considering the workload of the CA during the voting operations. As shown in Section 3, the CA is mainly involved in the registration phase, when it distributes the digital certificates required for the authentication phase during the voting sessions. During the voting session, the CA is involved in the generation of CRL's and in the generation of new certificates for voters whose original certificate has been lost or compromised. In such a case the CA revokes the old certificate and generates a new one, thus two operations are required. This means that a CA can approximately manage 10^6 voters a day, quite a smaller percentage when considering that the voter population for a medium size country like Italy is 40 million pleople, and that elections usually last a single day.

The situation is even worse if we assume that, as a consequence of some event, the CA secret key may be compromised. In this case all the voters' digital certificates would have to be revoked and new ones generated. If the CA has a sufficiently small population (i.e., the number of voters whose certificate has been signed by the CA is small), such an operation can be performed relatively quickly otherwise the entire e-voting process would have to be delayed.

Another issue to consider is the workload on the LDAP directory that is used during the voting sessions. As we have shown in Section 3, each voter accesses it at least once. The results of [34] show that in the case of small repositories, the directory can serve about 0.5M requests/sec. During the last political elections in Italy (2001), more than 20 million voters voted to polling stations between 13.00-22.00 p.m., which yields an average of 2 million voters/hour. LDAP servers should be set up in order to sustain a workload with such an arrival rate, and a possibly higher one, since the arrival process cannot be assumed to be uniform. Server replication and load balancing strategies would have to be adopted to build a system that can sustain the workload generated by an e-voting system in case of nation-wide elections. However, we wish to stress that the technology on which e-voting protocols rely is still in an evolutionary phase and is far behind the needs of the applications. The required performance goals may be satisfied, but it is unknown how the system will behave in such a context, nor is any study or simulation available of a system under similar load conditions. Furthermore, we should consider that one of the most attractive advantages of using e-voting system instead of traditional ones is the potential cost saving. If high performance hardware must be used in order to sustain the workload imposed by an election, cost reduction may no longer be an advantage.

Therefore, the only reasonable way to effectively implement e-voting protocols for domains with a large number of users (millions) is to use PKI with multiple CAs. Unfortunately, this raises one of the most serious problems of PKIs in this development phase, i.e. interoperability. In an e-voting protocol PKI interoperability issues can raise during the registration phase and during the tallying phase. During the registration phase the voter may authenticate to the CA of the election system that performs the registration using a digital certificate released by another CA. In such a case the CA of the election system must be able to accept the credential presented by the voter. In the tallying phase the ballots collected by the "local" tallier, whose certificate has been signed by a local CA, will be sent to a nation-wide CA for the final count. In this case too interoperability must be guaranteed at least between local CAs and the "general" one. However, interoperability between CA's is far to come in practice, although they all comply with the same set of standards. Many issues still need to be addressed. Some of these issues are (see [3] for a more detailed description) the use of different coding /encoding scheme for information stored in the certificates, assumptions about maximum length of names, inconsistent use of some certificate extensions, wrong use of OIDs. A reasonable approach would therefore be the adoption of the same platform for all the CA's involved in an e-voting session, which is too strong a constraint to satisfy.

A further risk to assess before starting a full deployment of PKI is related to the raising issue of security of the digital signature process. As we show in [6], a user may easily be deceived when signing a document if the system he/she uses has been infected by an appropriate malicious code. Without the user realizing it, the malware could intercept the signature request to the document selected by the user and replace it with another one, which would be signed instead (or in addition) and then distributed instead of the one meant by the user. It is clear that a virus like the one above described could create problems during an online election. Such problems range from a DoS effect due to the fact the malicious code may generate random messages that are not compliant with the protocol, to the possible subversion of the election results in case of a smart virus that selectively replaces voter generated ballots with new valid ballots with a different vote. If voting stations under the control of election officials only were used, such a problem would be solved, at the expenses of one of the major benefits of on-line voting, that is, voters' mobility. Although any polling station would be acceptable unlike in traditional election when voters may vote only from a specific one depending upon their residency, voters would have to go to a polling station possibly generating very skewed access patterns, e.g., affluence at polling stations at vacation resorts during the summer.

The last issue we consider is the organizational one. Running traditional elections on a nation-wide scale is a conspicuous organizational effort. Moving to an online solution, either as the only alternative or as a parallel system, is not, at least in the beginning, going to be a cost-effective choice. It is going to have a very high organizational cost both for voters and officials training. Data storage will also be expensive since election data must be maintained for a certain number of years. System set up and maintenance is another source of expenses since using such systems for other purposes is not advisable in order to minimize chances to compromise them and to limit the load on the system to the one generated by the election process.

5. CONCLUSIONS

In this paper we have analytically considered the main problems related to the adoption of PKI platforms in e-voting protocols. The conclusion is that the technology does not seem mature yet for such an application, since problems such as low efficiency, lack of experience with large PKIs, and interoperability can undermine the full exploitation of an e-voting protocol. In the current phase the main problem in the implementation of a large scale online voting system is not the lack of suitable cryptographic protocols but the lack of a sufficiently robust technology that can sustain the workload imposed by critical applications, such as voting, with an adequate level of reliability, as the applications require.

We also raised the issue related to the possibility of applying digital signatures to documents other than those intended by the users. Such an issue deserves further and more detailed analysis. Since one of the fundamental assumptions of all e-voting protocols is non repudiation, and the only technique we know so far to perform non-reputable transactions is the digital signature, the question is whether compromising it implies compromising the possibility of e-voting.

REFERENCES

[1]   Adler, J., Dai, W., Green, R., Neff, A. "Computational Details of the VoteHere Homomorphic Election System". November 2000; http://www.votehere.net/vh-content-v2.0/hom.pdf

[2]   Aronsson, H. "Zero Knowledge Protocols and Small Systems", Technical Report, 1995; http://saturn.tcs.hut.fi/~helger/crypto/link/zeroknowledge/

[3]   Balacheff, B., Chen, L., Plaquin, D., Proudler, G. "A trusted process to digitally sign a document", In *New Security Paradigms Workshop 2001*, ACM Press, 2001.

[4]   Benaloh, J., Tuinstra, D. "Receipt-Free Secret-Ballot Elections", In *Proc. of the 26th Annual ACM Symposium on the Theory of Computing*, ACM Press, pp. 544-553, 1994.

[5]   Bruschi, D., Curti, A., Rosti, E. *A quantitative study of Public Key Infrastructures*, Technical Report RI-DSI 268-01, Dipt. di Scienze dell'Informazione, Univ. degli Studi di Milano, 2001.

[6]   Bruschi, D., Rosti, E. "Infecting digital signatures: The new threat". In preparation, 2002.

[7]   Burmester, M., Chrissikopoulos, V., Magkos, E. "Receipt-freeness in Large-Scale Elections without Untappable Channels", 2001; http://thalis.cs.unipi.gr/~emagos

[8]   Chaum, D. "Untraceable electronic mail, return address, and digital pseudonyms", In *Com. of the ACM*, 24: 84-88, 1981.

[9]   Chaum, D. "Blind signatures for untraceable payments", In *Advances in Cryptology, CRYPTO'82*, Springer-Verlag, pp. 199-203, 1982.

[10] Chaum, D. "Security without identification: transaction systems to make big brother obsolete", In *Com. of the ACM*, 28:1030-1044, 1985.

[11] Chaum, D. "Elections with Unconditionally-Secret Ballots and Disruption Equivalent to Breaking RSA", In *Advances in Cryptology, EUROCRYPT'88*, pp.177-182, 1989.

[12] Cohen, J. "Improving Privacy in Cryptographic Elections", Technical Report YALEU/DCS/TR-454, Yale University, February 1986.

[13] Cohen, J., Fisher, M. "A Robust and Verifiable Cryptographically Secure Election Scheme", Technical Report YALEU/DCS/TR-416, Yale University, 1985.

[14] Cramer, R., Gennaro, R., Schoenmakers, B. "A Secure and Optimally Efficient Multi-Authority Election Scheme". In *Advances in Cryptology, EUROCRYPT '97*, LNCS 1233, Springer-Verlag, pp. 103-118, 1997.

[15] Cranor, L. "Electronic voting: computerized polls may save money, protect privacy", In *ACM Crossroads (electronic Journal)*, 1996.

[16] Cranor, L. "Internet Privacy: A Public Concern", 1998; www.acm.org/pubs/citations/journals/networker/1998-2-3/p13-cranor

[17] Cranor, L., Cytron, R. "Sensus: A Security-Conscious Electronic Polling System for the Internet". In *Hawaii International Conference on System Sciences*, Hawaii, 1997.

[18] DuRette, B. W. "Multiple Administrators for Electronic Voting". Bachelor's Thesis, MIT, May 1999, http://theory.lcs.mit.edu/~cis/cis-theses.html

[19] Fujioka, A., Okamoto, T., Ohta, K. "A Practical Secret Voting Scheme for Large Scale Elections". In *Advances in Cryptology, ASIACRYPT'92*, LNCS 718, Springer-Verlag, pp. 244-251, 1993.

[20] Herschberg, M. "Secure Electronic Voting Using the World Wide Web". Master's Thesis, MIT, June 1997; http://theory.lcs.mit.edu/~cis/theses/herschberg-masters.pdf

[21] Housley, R., Ford, W., Polk, W., Solo, D. "Public Key Infrastructure Certificate and CRL Profile", RFC2459, 1999.

[22] Housley, R., Polk, W. "Internet X.509 Public Key Infrastructure", RFC2528, 1999.

[23] Itoh, K., Kurosawa, K., Park, C. "Efficient Anonymous Channel and All/Nothing Election Scheme", In *Advances in Cryptology, EUROCRYPT'93*, LNCS 765, Springer-Verlag, pp. 248-259, 1993.

[24] Karro, J., Wang, J. "Towards a Practical, Secure and Very Large Scale Online Election", In *Proceedings 15th Annual Computer Security Applications Conference (ACSAC '99)*, ACM Press, 1999.

[25] Killian, J., Sako, K. "Receipt-Free Mix-Type Voting Scheme; a practical solution to the implementation of a voting booth", In *Proc. of EUROCRYPT'95*, LNCS 921, Springer-Verlag, pp. 393-403, 1995.

[26] Neff, A. "Conductiong a Universally Verifiable Electronic Election Using Homomorphic Encryption", November 2000; votehere.org/whitepapers/

[27] Neff, A. "A Verifiable Secret Shuffle and its Application to E-Voting", August 2001; www.votehere.com

[28] Nurmi, H., Salomaa, A., Santean, L. "Secret Ballot Elections in Computer Networks", *Computers & Security 36*, 10:553-560, 1991.

[29] Radwin, M. "An Untraceable, Universally Verifiable Voting Scheme", In *Seminar in Cryptology*, 1995.

[30] Salomaa, A. "Verifying and recasting secret ballots in computer networks", In *New results and new trends in computer science*, LNCS 555, Springer-Verlag, pp. 283-289, 1991.

[31] Schoenmakers, B. "Compensating for lack of transparency", In *Proc. of the 10th Conference on Computers, Freedom and Privacy*, ACM Press, pp. 231-233, April 2000.

[32] Schoenmakers, B. "Fully Auditable Electronic Secret-Ballot Elections", 2000; www.eucybervote.org/publications.html

[33] Shamir, A. "How to share a secret", In *Communication of the ACM*, 22:612-613, 1979.

[34] Wang, X., Schulzrinne, H., Kandlur, D., Verma, D. "Measurement and analysis of LDAP performance", In *ACM SIGMETRICS 2000*, ACM Press, pp. 156-165, 2000.

Chapter 14

UNTRACEABLE ELECTRONIC MAIL, RETURN ADDRESSES AND DIGITAL PSEUDONYMS[*]

David Chaum

Dept. of Electrical Engineering and Computer Sciences, Univ. of California at Berkeley, USA
david@chaum.com

Abstract   A technique based on public key cryptography is presented that allows an electronic mail system to hide who a participant communicates with as well as the content of the communication - in spite of an unsecured underlying telecommunication system. The technique does not require a universally trusted authority. One correspondent can remain anonymous to a second, while allowing the second to respond via an untraceable return address. The technique can also be used to form rosters of untraceable digital pseudonyms from selected applications. Applicants retain the exclusive ability to form digital signatures corresponding to their pseudonyms. Elections in which any interested party can verify that the ballots have been properly counted are possible if anonymously mailed ballots are signed with pseudonyms from a roster of registered voters. Another use allows an individual to correspond with a record-keeping organization under a unique pseudonym, which appears in a roster of acceptable clients.

Keywords   Electronic mail, public key cryptosystems, digital signatures, traffic analysis, security, privacy.

This work was partially supported by the National Science Foundation under Grant MCS 75-23739 and by the Air Force Office of Scientific Research under Contract F49620-9-CO173.

1. INTRODUCTION

Cryptology is the science of secret communication. Cryptographic techniques have been providing secrecy of message content for thousands of years [3]. Recently some new solutions to the "key distribution problem" (the problem of providing each communicant with a secret key) have been suggested [2,4], under the name of public key cryptography. Another crypto-graphic problem, "the traffic analysis problem" (the problem of keeping confidential who converses with whom, and when they converse), will become increasingly important with the growth of electronic mail.

This paper presents a solution to the traffic analysis problem that is based on public key cryptography. Baran has solved the traffic analysis problem for networks [1], but requires each participant to trust a common authority. In contrast, systems based on the solution advanced here can be compromis-ed only by subversion or conspiracy of all of a set of authorities. Ideally, each participant is an authority.

The following two sections introduce the notation and assumptions. Then the basic concepts are introduced for some special cases involving a series of one or more authorities. The final section covers general-purpose mail net-works.

2. NOTATION

Someone becomes a user of a public key cryptosystem (like that of Rivest, Shamir, and Adleman [5]) by creating a pair of keys K and $Inv(K)$ from a suitable randomly generated seed. The public key K is made known to the other users or anyone else who cares to know it; the private key $Inv(K)$ is never divulged. The encryption of X with key K will be denoted $K(X)$, and is just the image of X under the mapping implemented by the cryptographic algorithm using key K. The increased utility of these algorithms over con-ventional algorithms results because the two keys are inverses of each other, in the sense that $Inv(K)(K(X)) = K(Inv(K)(X)) = X$.

A message X is "sealed" with a public key K so that only the holder of the private key $Inv(K)$ can discover its content. If X is simply encrypted with K, then anyone could verify a guess that $Y=X$ by checking whether $K(Y)=K(X)$. This threat can be eliminated by attaching a large string of random bits R to X before encrypting. The sealing of X with K is then denoted $K(R,X)$. A user "signs" some material X by prepending a large constant C (all zeros, for example) and then encrypting with its private key, denoted $Inv(K)(C,X)=Y$. Anyone can verify that Y has been signed by the holder of $Inv(K)$ and deter-mine the signed matter X, by forming $K(Y)=C,X$ and checking for C.

3.   ASSUMPTIONS

The approach taken here is based on two important assumptions:
(1) No one can determine anything about the correspondences between a set of sealed items and the corresponding set of unsealed items, or create forgeries without the appropriate random string or private key.
(2) Anyone may learn the origin, destination(s), and representation of all messages in the underlying telecommunication system and anyone may inject, remove, or modify messages.

4.   MAIL SYSTEM

The users of the cryptosystem will include not only the correspondents but a computer called a "mix" that will process each item of mail before it is delivered. A participant prepares a message M for delivery to a participant at address A by sealing it with the addressee's public key K_a, appending the address A, and then sealing the result with the mix's public key K_1. The left-hand side of the following expression denotes this item which is input to the mix: $K_1(R_1,Ka(R_0,M),A) \dashrightarrow K_a(R_0,M),A$.

The $\dashrightarrow$ denotes the transformation of the input by the mix into the output shown on the right-hand side. The mix decrypts its input with its private key, throws away the random string R_1, and outputs the remainder. One might imagine a mechanism that forwards the sealed messages $K_a(R_0,M)$ of the output to the addressees who then decrypt them with their own private keys.

The purpose of a mix is to hide the correspondences between the items in its input and those in its output. The order of arrival is hidden by outputting the uniformly sized items in lexicographically ordered batches. By assumption (1) above, there need be no concern about a cryptanalytic attack yielding the correspondence between the sealed items of a mix's input and its unsealed output - if items are not repeated. However, if just one item is repeated in the input and allowed to be repeated in the output, then the correspondence is revealed for that item.

Thus, an important function of a mix is to ensure that no item is processed more than once. This function can be readily achieved by a mix for a particular batch by removing redundant copies before outputting the batch. If a single mix is used for multiple batches, then one way that repeats across batches can be detected is for the mix to maintain a record of items used in previous batches. (Records can be discarded once a mix changes its public key by, for example, announcing the new key in a statement signed with its old private key). A mix need not retain previous batches if part of each random string R_1 contains something - such as a time-stamp - that is only valid for a particular batch.

If a participant gets signed receipts for messages it submits to a mix, then the participant can provide substantial evidence that the mix failed to output an item properly. Only a wronged participant can supply the receipt Y (= $Inv(K_1)(C,K_1(R_1,K_a(R_0,M),A)))$, the missing output X (= $K_a(R_0,M),A)$, and the retained string R_1, such that $K_1(Y)=C,K_1(R_1,X)$. Because a mix will sign each output batch as a whole, the absence of an item X from a batch can be substantiated by a copy of the signed batch.

The use of a "cascade", or series of mixes, offers the advantage that any single constituent mix is able to provide the secrecy of the correspondence between the inputs and the outputs of the entire cascade. Incrimination of a particular mix of a cascade that failed to properly process an item is accomplished as with a single mix, but only requires a receipt from the first mix of the cascade, since a mix can use the signed output of its predecessor to show the absence of an item from its own input. An item is prepared for a cascade of n mixes the same as for a single mix. It is then successively sealed for each succeeding mix: $K_n(R_n,K_{<n-1>}(R_{<n-1>},...,K_2(R_2,K_1(R_1, K_a(R_0,M),A))...))$ -->.

The fist mix yields a lexicographically ordered batch of items, each of the form $K_{<n-1>}(R_{<n-1>},... ,K_2(R_2,K_1(R_1,K_a(R_0,M),A))...)$ -->.

The items in the final output batch of a cascade are of the form $K_a(R_0,M),A$, the same as those of a single mix.

5.   RETURN ADDRESSES

The techniques just described allow participant x to send anonymous messages to participant y. What is needed now is a way for y to respond to x while still keeping the identity of x secret from y. A solution is for x to form an untraceable return address $K_1(R_1,A_x),K_x$, where A_x is its own real address, K_x is a public key chosen for the occasion, and R_1 is a key that will also act as a random string for purposes of sealing. Then, x can send this return address to y as part of a message sent by the techniques already described. (In general, two participants can exchange return addresses through a chain of other participants, where at least one member of each adjacent pair knows the identity of the other member of the pair). The following indicates how y uses this untraceable return address to form a response to x, via a new kind of mix: $K_1(R_1,A_x),K_x(R_0,M)$--> $A_x,R_1(K_x(R_0,M))$.

This mix uses the string of bits R_1 that it finds after decrypting the address part $K_1(R_1,A_x)$ as a key to re-encrypt the message part $K_x(R_0,M)$. Only the addressee x can decrypt the resulting output because x created both

R_1 and K_x. The mix must not allow address parts to be repeated - for the same reason that items of regular mail must not be repeated. This means that x must supply y with a return address for each item of mail x wishes to receive. Also notice that conventional as opposed to public key cryptography could be used for both encryptions of M.

With a cascade of mixes, the message part is prepared the same as for a single mix, and the address part is as show in the following input: $K_1(R_1,K_2(R_2,...,K_{<n-1>}(R_{<n-1>},K_n(R_n,A_x))...)),K_x(R_0,M)$ -->.

The result of the first mix is $K_2(R_2,...,K_{<n-1>}(R_{<n-1>},K_n(R_n,A_x))...)$, $R_1(K_x(R_0,M))$ -->, and the final result of the remaining n-1 mixes is A_x, $R_n(R_{<n-1>}...R_2(R_1(K_x(R_0,M)))...)$.

Untraceable return addresses allow the possibility of "certified" mail: They can provide the sender of an anonymous letter with a receipt attesting to the fact that the letter appeared intact in the final output batch. The address A that is incorporated into a certified letter is expanded to include not only the usual address of the recipient, but also an untraceable return address for the sender.

When this return address appears in the output batch of the final mix, it is used to mail the sender a signed receipt, which includes the message as well as the address to which it was delivered. The receipt might be signed by each mix.

6.   DIGITAL PSEUDONYMS

A digital "pseudonym" is a public key used to verify signatures made by the anonymous holder of the corresponding private key. A "roster", or list of pseudonyms, is created by an authority that decides which applications for pseudonyms to accept, but is unable to trace the pseudonyms in the completed roster. The applications may be sent to the authority anonymously, by untraceable mail, for example, or they may be provided in some other way.

Each application received by the authority contains all the information required for the acceptance decision and a special unaddressed digital letter (whose messages is the public key K, the applicant's proposed pseudonym). In the case of a single mix, these letters are of the form $K_1(R_1,K)$. For a cascade of n mixes, they are of the form $K_n(R_n,...,K_2(R_2,K_1(R_1,K))...)$. The authority will form an input batch containing only those unaddressed letters from the applications it accepts. This input batch will be supplied to a special cascade whose final output batch will be publicly available. Since each entry in the final output batch of the cascade is a public key K from an accepted applicant, the signed output of the final mix is a roster of digital pseudonyms.

Notification of applicants can be accomplished by also forming a roster for unaccepted applications and then using the technique of certified mail to return a single batch of receipts to both sets of applicants. Of course, repeats must not be allowed within or across batches.

If only registered voters are accepted for a particular roster, then it can be used to carry out an election. For a single mix, each voter submits a ballot of the form $K_1(R_1,K,Inv(K)(C,V))$, where K is the voter's pseudonym and V is the actual vote. For a cascade of mixes, ballots are of the form $K_n(R_n,...,K_2 (R_2,K_1(R_1,K,Inv(K)(C,V)))...)$. The ballots must be processed as a single batch, as were the letters used to form rosters. Items in the final lexicographically ordered output batch are of the form $K,Inv(K)(C,V)$. Since the roster of registered voters is also ordered on, it is easy for anyone to count the votes by making a single pass through both batches at once. Each ballot is counted only after checking that the pseudonym which forms its prefix, is also contained in the roster and that the pseudonym properly decrypts the signed vote V.

An individual might be known to an organization only by a pseudonym that appears in a roster of acceptable clients. Clients can correspond with the organization via untraceable mail and the organization can correspond with the clients using untraceable return addresses. If applicants identify themselves in their applications, or if they sign applications with pseudonyms that appear in a roster issued by an authority that requires identification, then the organization is assured that the same client cannot come to it under different pseudonyms. Under special circumstances, such as default of payment, a particular pseudonym could be shown to correspond to a particular application (without revealing any other correspondences) if each mix in turn supplied the appropriate R_n.

7.   GENERAL PURPOSE MAIL SYSTEMS

One way to construct a general purpose, untraceable mail system is to require that every message pass through a cascade. Of course, mixes can operate continuously or periodically, and long messages will be encrypted first and then split into multiple items. In order to hide the number of messages sent, each participant supplies the same number of messages to each batch (some of which might be randomly addressed dummies). In order to hide the number of messages received, each participant privately searches the entire output for messages directed to it.

Such a system may prove too costly for some participants. One way to reduce the cost is to allow mail to be addressed to subsets of participants, such as a local net. Participants that take advantage of such arrangements need search only the mail addressed to a particular subset. Another way to economize is for a participant to send for each batch only the number of dummy messages suggested by a random value (chosen from some suitable distribution), as opposed to always sending the maximal number of messages. This can substantially reduce message traffic and consequently, the size of output batches. While these techniques may open the door to some kinds of statistical attack, the system size that necessitated them may reduce the effectiveness of such attacks.

In a large, general-purpose mail system with many mixes, it may be impractical for every message to pass through every mix. In such a case, a sequence of mixes will be selected for each message, perhaps on the basis of network topology or trust. Notice that if a participant can choose mixes it trusts with its traffic volume data as early members of its sequences, then these mixes can discard dummies they receive from the participant and deliver small, fixed-sized batches (padded with dummies) directly to the participant.

A new kind of mix will be presented here that allows a sequence of mixes to be selected for each message. It also:

(a) hides the number and identity of the mixes a message must pass through,

(b) allows incrimination of a mix that does not properly forward items, and

(c) makes no distinction between regular mail and mail sent by untraceable return address. It is based on the idea that every item of mail is composed of the same number of fixed-sized blocks.

The operations performed by this new kind of mix are always the same. First it removes the first block and adds a random block J of junk to the end, to maintain the item's length of l blocks. Then, using its private key, the mix decrypts the block removed during the first step. This yields a key R, which the mix uses to encrypt each of the l blocks of the item (using either public-key or conventional cryptography). It also yields the address A (either of a recipient or of another mix) to which the item will be forwarded.

The left-hand side of the following shows how an item is prepared to pass through a single mix:

$$K_2(R_2,...,K_{<n-1>}(R_{<n-1>},K_n(R_n,A_x))...),R_1(K_x(R_0,M)) \to ,$$

$A_1:[K<A_1>(R<A_1>,A)],[Inv(R<A_1>)(M_1)],[Inv(R<A_1>)(M_2)],...[Inv(R<A_1>)(M_{<l-1>})] \to A:[M_1],...[M_{<l-1>}],[R<A_1>(J<A_1>)]$, where square brackets show the extent of each block, and the sealed message $K_a(R_0,M)$ is divided into pieces M_i, such that $K_a(R_0,M) = M_1,M_2,...,M_{<l-n>}$. The A_1: indicates that the left-hand side is delivered to mix A_1, while the A: means that the right-hand side is delivered to address A. Items with the same first block should be regarded as repeats.

A message prepared to be passed through mixes A_1 through A_n has the form:

A_1:$K<A_1>(R<A_1>,A_2)]$,$[Inv(R<A_1>)(K<A_2>(R<A_2>,A_3))]$,....,$[Inv(R<A)$ $(Inv(R<A_2>)...Inv(R<A_{<n-1>}>)(K<A_n>(R<A_n,A))...)]$,$Inv(R<A_1>)$ $(Inv(R<A_2>)...Inv(R<A_n>)(M_1)...)]$,....,$[Inv(R<A_1>)(Inv(R<A_2>)...Inv(R<A_n>$ $)(M_{<l-n>})...)]$ -->.

The result leaving A_1 is:

A_2:$[K<A_2>(R<A_2,A_3)]$,$[Inv(R<A_2>)(K<A_3>(R<A_3>,A_4))]$,....,$[Inv(R<A_2>)(In$ $v(R<A_3>)...Inv(R<A_{<n-1>}>)(K<A_n>(R<A_n,A))...)]$,$[Inv(R<A_2>)$ $(Inv(R<A_3>)...Inv(R<A_n>)(M_1)...)]$,....,$[Inv(R<A_2>)(Inv(R<A_3>)...Inv(R<A_n>$ $)(M_{<l-n>})...)]$,$[R<A_1>(J<A_1>)]$ -->,

and the final result leaving An is:

A:$[M_1]$,$[M_2]$,....,$[M_{<l-n>}]$,$[R<A_n>(R<A<n-1>>...R<A_1>(J<A_1>)...)]$,...., $[R<A_n>(J<A_n>)]$.

An intermediate mix always knows which mix it received its input from - by assumption (2) - but if a mix broadcasts copies of its fixed-size output batches, then only individual recipient mixes need be able to recognize their own input in a broadcast batch.

The untraceable return address x sends to y contains the key K_x that y uses to encrypt the message part. It also includes, in the case of a single mix, what y will use as the first block of the item it submits to the mix:

A_1: $[K<A_1>(R<A_1>,A_x)]$,$[M_1]$,....,$[M_{<l-1>}]$ --> A_x: $[R<A_1>(M_1)]$,....,$[R<A_1>(M_{<l-1>})]$,$[R<A_1>(J<A_1>)]$,

where $K_x(R_0,M) = M_1,M_2,...,M_{<l-n>}$.

Only $_x$ can decrypt the item it receives since it created $_{R<A1>}$ and $_{Kx}$. When a message is to pass through n mixes, the untraceable return address contains the first n blocks:

A_1: $[K<A_1>(R<A_1>,A_2)]$,$[Inv(R<A_1>)(K<A_2>(R<A_2>,A_3))]$, ..., $[Inv(R<A_1>)(Inv(R<A_2>)...Inv(R<A<n-1>>)(K<A_n>(R<A_n>,A_x))...)]$, $[M_1]$,$[M_2]$,....,$[M_{<l-n>}]$ -->.

After being operated on by mix A_1 it will have the form:

A_2: $[K<A_2>(R<A_2>,A_3)]$, ..., $[Inv(R<A_2>)(Inv(R<A_3>)...Inv(R<A<n-1>>)(K<A_n>(R<A_n>,A_x))...)]$, $[R<A_1>(M_1)]$,$[R<A_1>(M_2)]$,....,$[R<A_1>(M_{<l-n>})]$,$[R<A_1>(J<A_1>)]$ -->,

and the final result leaving A_n is:

A_x: $[R<A_n>(R<A_{<n-1>}>...R<A_1>(M_1)...)]$,..., $[R<A_n>(R<A<n-1>>...R<A_1>(M_{<l-n>})...)]$, $[R<A_n>(R<A<n-1>>...R<A_1>(J<A_1>)...)]$,....,$[R<A_n>(J<A_n>)]$.

8.   SUMMARY AND CONCLUSION

A solution to the traffic analysis problem has been presented that allows any single intermediary to provide security for those messages passing through it.

In addition, the solution allows messages to be sent or received pseudonymously. Through the notion of a roster of pseudonyms, it also provides some new and interesting kinds of limited anonymity.

Acknowledgements

I owe a great deal to R. Fabry's outstanding and multifaceted support. Special thanks are due C. Sequin, who has read my work with great care and provided many stimulating discussions. I would also like to thank D. Gusfield, B. Mont-Reynaud, A. Moose, and S. Wecker for their comments and encouragement. The referees have been very helpful.

References

[1].   Baran P., *On distributed communications: IX security secrecy and tamper-free considerations,* Memo RM-3765-PR, Rand Corp., Santa Monica CA, August 1964.

[2].   Diffie W., Hellman M., New directions in cryptography, *IEEE Transactions on Information Theory*, IT-22, 6, pg. 644-654, November 1976.

[3].   Kahn D., *The Code Breakers: The Story of Secret Writing*, Macmillan, New York 1967.

[4].   Merkle R., Secure communications over insecure channels, *Com. of the ACM*, Vol. 21, no. 4, pg. 294-299, April 1978.

[5].   Rivest R., Shamir, A., Adleman, L., A method for obtaining digital signatures and public-key cryptosystems, *Com. of the ACM*, Vol. 21, no. 2, pg. 120-126, February 1977.

INDEX